Accounting Rev
for Leaving Cert
Higher Level

Michael McLoughlin

Fourth Edition

Gill & Macmillan

Gill & Macmillan Ltd
Hume Avenue
Park West
Dublin 12
with associated companies throughout the world
www.gillmacmillan.ie

978 0 7171 4134 0

Print Origination by Replika Press Pvt Ltd, India

The paper used in this book is made from the wood pulp of managed forests. For every tree felled, at least one tree is planted, thereby renewing natural resources.

Contents

Chapter **1**

Company Final Accounts

Question 1

Question 1 is always a set of final accounts. This question carries 120 marks, which is 30 per cent of the total.

The question involves a set of company, sole trader, manufacturing or departmental final accounts, each including a lot of adjustments. It is essential to practise these questions thoroughly.

The fastest method is to lay out the questions in blank form. Enter the figures as they appear in the question beside the correct space in the blank form. Enter the figures in the first column and adjust them as required. The adjustments are included in the solutions to the questions. Sample marking schemes are included to some questions.

The basic rule is practise, practise, practise.

Remember, if you are not going to answer question 1, then you must answer two questions from numbers 2, 3 and 4. Each of these questions carries 60 marks.

Question 1.1

Ballindine Ltd has an authorised share capital of €960,000 divided into 560,000 ordinary shares of €1 each and 400,000 11 per cent preference shares of €1 each. The following trial balance was extracted from its books at 31 December 2007.

Entry	Debit (€)	Credit (€)
Issued Capital: Ordinary Shares		450,000
Preference Shares		200,000
Profit and Loss		18,000
Stocks (including heating oil €1,500)	48,500	
Debtors and Creditors	55,400	63,200
Buildings at Cost	495,000	
Delivery Vans (cost €160,000)	105,000	
12% Debentures		125,000
Provision for Bad Debts		2,000
Bank		34,000
Light and Heat	5,000	
Purchases and Sales	590,000	830,000
9% Investments (1/1/2007)	150,000	
Salaries and General Expenditure	86,700	
Audit Fees	14,000	

Question 1.1 Table *continued*

Entry	Debit (€)	Credit (€)
Insurance of Vans (including suspense)	5,800	
Advertising (incorporating 4 months' investment income)	18,000	
Interim Dividends for 6 Months	28,000	
Debenture Interest Paid for First 4 Months	5,500	
Directors' Fees	35,300	
Goodwill	80,000	
	1,722,200	1,722,200

You are also given the following information.

1. Stock at 31 December 2007 was valued at €52,300. This includes heating oil of €900 and stocks that cost €4,000 and have a net realisable value of €2,500.
2. The suspense figure arises because an incorrect figure was entered for debenture interest (although the correct figure has been entered in the bank account) and purchases returns of €800 were entered only in the creditors account.
3. Goods sent to a customer on approval on 31 December 2007 had been entered in error as a credit sale. The selling price of these goods was €4,500, which represents cost plus 50 per cent mark-up.
4. Repairs to delivery vans costing €3,000 were carried out by the firm's own workforce. €500 of this represented parts taken from the firm's own stocks, and the remainder represented salary paid.
5. Provide for depreciation at the rate of 20 per cent of cost per annum from date of purchase to date of sale. On 31 July 2007 a van that had cost €15,000 on 1 April 2004 was traded against a new van costing €20,000. An allowance of €6,000 was received for the old van. The cheque for the net amount was treated in error as a purchase of trading stock, and this was the only entry made in the books.
6. The directors recommend:
   (a) The preference dividend due be paid.
   (b) A final dividend of 10 per cent be paid on the ordinary shares.
   (c) Provision be made for debenture interest due.
   (d) A bad debt of €400 be written off and the provision for bad debts be adjusted to 4 per cent of the remaining debtors.

You are required to prepare the:
(a) Trading and profit and loss accounts for the year ended 31 December 2007.
(b) Balance sheet at 31 December 2007.

Solution to Q 1.1

Ballindine Ltd
Trading and Profit and Loss Accounts for the Year Ended 31 December 2007

	Workings	(€)	(€)	(€)
Sales			825,500	
Less Costs				
Opening Stock		47,000		
Purchases		574,700		
		621,700		
Closing Stock		52,900		
			568,800	
Gross Profit			256,700	
Investment Income	W5		13,500	
Profit on Disposal			1,000	
				271,200
Less Expenses				
Establishment and Administration				
Light and Heat	W2	5,600		
Salaries and General		84,200		
Directors' Fees		35,300		
			125,100	
Financial				
Audit Fees		14,000		
Bad Debt		400		
Increase in Provision		20		
			14,420	
Selling and Distribution				
Van Insurance	W3	7,100		
Delivery Van Repairs		3,000		
Depreciation for Year		32,417		
Advertising	W4	22,500	65,017	204,537
Operating Profit				66,633
Less interest	W6			15,000
Net Profit				51,633
Less Appropriations				
Ordinary Dividend		Paid	17,000	
		Proposed	45,000	(62,000)
Preference Dividend		Paid	11,000	
		Proposed	11,000	(22,000)
				(32,337)
Add P & L Balance 1/1/2007				18,000
P & L Balance 31/12/2007				(14,337)

Balance Sheet at 31 December 2007

	Workings	Cost (€)	Depreciation (€)	Net Book Value (€)
Fixed Assets				
Buildings		495,000		495,000
Vans	W1	165,000	77,417	87,583
		660,000	77,417	582,583
9% Investment				150,000
Goodwill				80,000
				812,583
Current Assets				
Stock			52,900	
Debtors		50,500		
Less Provision for Bad Debts		(2,020)	48,480	
Stock of Heating Oil	W2		900	
Investment Income Due	W5		9,000	
			111,280	
Current Liabilities				
Creditors		63,200		
Bank		34,000		
Debenture Interest Due	W6	10,000		
Ordinary Dividend Due		45,000		
Preference Dividend Due		11,000		
Working Capital/Net Current Assets			163,200	(51,920)
				760,663
Financed by		**Authorised**	**Issued**	
OSC		560,000	450,000	
11% Preference Shares		400,000	200,000	
		960,000		650,000
Reserves				
Profit and Loss				(14,337)
Long-Term Liabilities				
12% Debentures				125,000
				760,663

4

Workings

W1

	Cost (€)	Depreciation (€)	Net Book Value (€)
Vans	160,000	(55,000)	105,000
	(15,000)	10,000	(5,000)
	20,000		

Depreciation on Old Van	
2004 $15,000 \times 20\% \times \frac{3}{4} =$	2,250
2005–2006 $15,000 \times 20\% \times 2 =$	6,000
2007 $15,000 \times 20\% \times \frac{7}{12} =$	1,750
	10,000
Depreciation for Year	
$145,000 \times 20\% =$	29,000
$15,000 \times 20\% \times \frac{7}{12} =$	1,750
$20,000 \times 20\% \times \frac{5}{12} =$	1,667
	32,417

W2

Light and Heat

(€)		(€)
1,500	Profit & Loss	5,600
5,000	Balance	900
6,500		6,500
Balance 900		

W4

Advertising

	(€)		(€)
	18,000	Profit & Loss	22,500
Investment	4,500		
	22,500		22,500

W3

Van Insurance (including suspense)

(€)		(€)
5,800	Profit & Loss	7,100
500		
800		
7,100		7,100

W5

Investment Income

	(€)		(€)
Profit & Loss	13,500	Advertising	4,500
		Balance	9,000
	13,500		13,500
Balance	9,000		

> NOTE: In this book, the solutions shown follow the official marking scheme for accounting in the Leaving Certificate Examinations.
>
> The solutions are printed and the marks allocated to each line/figure are highlighted and shown in a circle like this ➏ alongside. These marks are then totalled for each section/page and shown in a square like this **40**.

From 2005 exam, Question 1, page 185.
Solution to Q 1.1 **35**

Manufacturing Account of James Ltd for the Year Ended 31/12/2007

		€	€
Opening Stock of Raw Materials			48,000 ➊
Purchases of Raw Materials	W 1		432,280 ➌
Carriage In			5,510 ➋
			485,790
Less Closing Stock of Raw Materials			51,000 ➊
Cost of Raw Materials Consumed			434,790
Direct Costs:			
Factory Wages	W 2	158,220 ➍	
Hire of Special Equipment		12,000 ➋	170,220
Prime Costs		**605,010**	
Factory Overheads:			
General Factory Overheads		50,300 ➋	
Depreciation on Plant and Machinery	W 3	49,800 ➌	
Depreciation on Buildings		10,160 ➌	
Loss on Sale of Machine	W 4	1,500 ➍	
Factory Cost			111,760
			716,770
Work in Progress 1/1/2007			24,150 ➋
			740,920
Less Work in Progress 31/12/2007			(28,550) ➋
			712,370
Less Sale of Scrap Materials	W 5		(3,700) ➍
Cost of Manufacture			708,670 ➊
Gross Profit on Manufacturer			91,330
Goods Transferred from Factory at CMV			800,000 ➊

Trading and Profit and Loss Account for Year Ended 31/12/2007   **40**

		€	€
Sales	**W 6**		925,400 **⑤**
Opening Stock of Finished Goods		85,500 **②**	
Goods Transferred @ CMV		800,000 **②**	
		885,500	
Less Closing Stock of Finished Goods	**W 7**	97,500 **⑥**	
Cost of Goods Sold		788,000	(788,000)
Gross Profit on Trading			137,400
Gross Profit on Manufacture			91,330
			228,730
Less Expenses:			
Administration Expenses			
Administration Expenses	**W 8**	22,900 **⑥**	
Selling and Distribution Expenses:			
Selling Expenses		68,420 **②**	(91,320)
			137,410
Discount (Net)	**W 9**		3,000 **③**
Operating Profit			140,410
Less Debenture Interest	**W 10**		(8,325) **④**
Net Profit before Taxation			132,085
Less Taxation			(10,000) **②**
Profit after Tax			122,085
Less Preference Dividend Paid		8,000 **①**	
Preference Dividend Due		8,000 **①**	
Ordinary Dividend Paid		9,000 **①**	
Ordinary Dividend Due		18,000 **①**	
			(43,000)
Retained Profit			79,085
Profit and Loss Balance 1/1/2007			82,300 **②**
Profit and Loss Balance 31/12/2007			161,385 **②**

Balance Sheet of James Ltd as at 31/12/2007   **45**

		Cost €	Accumulated Depreciation €	Net €	€
Intangible Assets					€
Patents					70,000 **②**
Tangible Assets:					
Factory Buildings	**W 11**	508,000 **②**	55,160 **②**	452,840	
Plant and Machinery	**W 3,12**	238,000 **②**	135,100 **③**	102,900	
		746,000	190,260	555,740	555,740
					625,740

Current Assets:

Stocks Raw Materials	51,000 ②		
Work in Progress	28,550 ②		
Finished Goods	97,500 ②	177,050	
Debtors W 13		84,800 ⑤	
		261,850	

Creditors: Amounts Falling Due within One Year:

Trade Creditors	57,700 ②		
Bank	11,450 ②		
VAT	12,730 ②		
Dividends Due	26,000 ④		
Taxation	10,000 ②		
Debenture Interest Due	8,325 ③		126,205
Net Current Assets			135,645
			761,385

Financed By:
Creditors: Amounts Falling Due after More than One Year

9% Debentures		100,000 ②

Capital and Reserves:	**Authorised**	**Issued**
Ordinary Shares at €1 Each	550,000 ①	300,000 ②
8% Preference Shares at €1 Each	250,000 ①	200,000 ②
	800,000	500,000
Profit and Loss Balance 31/12/2007		161,385
		661,385
		761,385

Question 1.1 Workings

1	Purchases of Raw Materials	450,280 – 18,000	=	432,280
2	Factory Wages	198,220 – 40,000	=	158,220
3	Depreciation on Plant and Machinery	26,000 + 23,800	=	49,800
		47,600 + 2,200	=	49,800
	Accumulated Depreciation on Plant	104,000 – 18,700 + 49,800	=	135,100
4	Loss on Disposal of Machine	22,000 – 18,700 – 1,800	=	(1,500)
5	Sale of Scrap Materials	5,500 – 1,800	=	3,700
6	Sales	935,000 – 9,600	=	925,400
7	Closing Stock of Finished Goods	92,000 – 2,500 + 8,000	=	97,500
8	Administration Expenses	23,900 – 1,000	=	22,900
9	Discount	4,000 – 1,000	=	3,000
10	Debenture Interest	6,300 + 2,025	=	8,325
	Debenture Interest	1,575 + 6,750	=	8,325
11	Cost of Factory Buildings	450,000 + 18,000 + 40,000	=	508,000
12	Cost of Plant and Machinery	260,000 – 22,000	=	238,000
13	Debtors	94,400 – 9,600	=	84,800

Question 1.2

Carey Ltd has an authorised capital of €990,000, divided into 690,000 ordinary shares at €1 each and 300,000 7 per cent preference shares at €1 each. The following trial balance was extracted from its books on 31/12/2009.

	€	€
Land and buildings at cost	780,000	
Accumulated depreciation – land and buildings		39,000
Patents (incorporating 2 months' investment income received)	58,200	
6% investments 1/5/2009	180,000	
Delivery vans at cost	172,000	
Accumulated depreciation – delivery vans		78,000
Stocks 1/1/2009	76,600	
Purchases and sales	620,000	990,000
Directors' fees	80,000	
Salaries and general expenses	176,000	
Debenture interest paid	4,500	
Profit and loss balance 1/1/2009		67,600
Debtors and creditors	73,900	81,000
Provision for bad debts		3,600
Interim dividends for first 6 months	40,000	
9% debentures (including €80,000 9% debentures issued at par on 31/3/2009)		230,000
VAT		16,500
Bank		5,500
Issued capital		
550,000 ordinry shares at €1 each		550,000
200,000 7% preference shares €1 each		200,000
	2,261,200	2,261,200

The following information and instructions are to be taken into account:

1. Stock at 31/12/2009 at cost was €85,000 – this figure includes old stock which cost €8,000 but has a net realisable value of 60 per cent of cost.

2. Patents which incorporated two months' investment income are to be written off over a five-year period commencing in 2009.

3. Provide for depreciation on delivery vans at the annual rate of 20 per cent of cost from the date of purchase to the date of sale.
   NOTE: On 31/9/2009 a delivery van which had cost €60,000 on 1/6/2007 was traded in against a new van which cost €84,000. An allowance of €22,000 was given on the old van. The cheque for the net amount of this transaction was incorrectly treated as a purchase of trading stock. This was the only entry made in the books in respect of this transaction.

4. Buildings are to be depreciated at the rate of 2 per cent of cost per annum (land at cost was €130,000). At the end of 2009 the company revalued the land and buildings at €880,000.

5. The figure for bank in the trial balance has been taken from the firm's bank account. However, a bank statement dated 31/12/2009 has arrived showing a credit balance of

9

€4,040. A comparison of the bank account and the bank statement has revealed the following discrepancies:

(i) Investment income €2,700 had been paid direct to the firm's bank account.

(ii) A cheque for €780, issued to a supplier, had been entered in the books (cash book and ledger) as €870.

(iii) A credit transfer of €750 had been paid direct to the firm's bank account on behalf of a debtor who has recently been declared bankrupt. This represents a first and final payment of 30c in the €1.

(iv) A cheque for fees €6,000 issued to a director had not yet been presented for payment.

6. The directors recommend that:

(i) The preference dividend due be paid.

(ii) A final dividend on ordinary shares be provided, bringing the total dividend up to 9c per share.

(iii) Provision be made for both investment income and debenture interest due.

(iv) Provision for bad debts be adjusted to 4 per cent of debtors.

You are required to prepare a:

(a) Trading and profit and loss account for the year ended 31/12/2009. **(75)**

(b) Balance sheet as at 31/12/2009. **(45)**

(120 marks)

Solution to Q. 1.2

(a) Trading, Profit and Loss Account for the Year Ended 31/12/2007 75

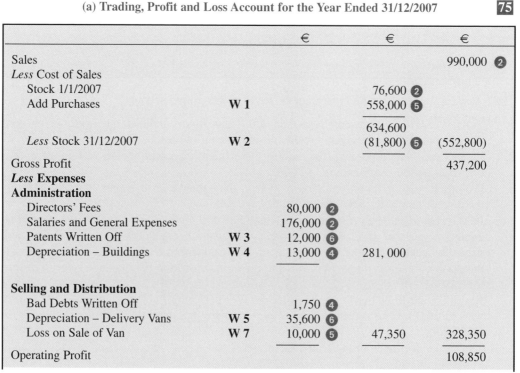

	€	€	€
Sales			990,000 ②
Less Cost of Sales			
Stock 1/1/2007		76,600 ②	
Add Purchases **W 1**		558,000 ⑤	
		634,600	
Less Stock 31/12/2007 **W 2**		(81,800) ⑤	(552,800)
Gross Profit			437,200
Less **Expenses**			
Administration			
Directors' Fees	80,000 ②		
Salaries and General Expenses	176,000 ②		
Patents Written Off **W 3**	12,000 ⑥		
Depreciation – Buildings **W 4**	13,000 ④	281, 000	
Selling and Distribution			
Bad Debts Written Off	1,750 ④		
Depreciation – Delivery Vans **W 5**	35,600 ⑥		
Loss on Sale of Van **W 7**	10,000 ⑤	47,350	328,350
Operating Profit			108,850

Decrease in Provision for Bad Debts	W 6	744 ⑤	
Investment Income	W 8	7,200 ④	7,944
			116,794
Debenture Interest			(18,900) ⑤
Net Profit for Year before Taxation			97,894
Less Appropriation			
Preference Dividend Paid		7,000 ②	
Ordinary Dividend Paid		33,000 ③	
Preference Dividend Proposed		7,000 ②	
Ordinary Dividend Proposed		16,500 ③	(63,500)
Retained Profit			34,394
Profit and Loss Balance 1/1/2007			67,600 ②
Profit and Loss Balance 31/12/2007			101,994 ⑥

(b) Balance Sheet at 31 December 2007　　　　　**45**

		Cost €	Accumulated Depreciation €	Net €	Total €
Intangible Fixed Assets					
Patents (60,000 – 12,000)					48,000 ③
Tangible Fixed Assets					
Land and Buildings	W 9	880,000 ①		880,000	
Delivery Vans	W 10	196,000 ②	85,600 ③	110,400	
		1,076,000	85,600	990,400	990,400
Financial Assets					
8% Investments					180,000 ②
					1,218,400
Current Assets					
Stock				81,800 ②	
Investment Income Due				2,700 ③	
Debtors	W 11		71,400 ③		
Less Provision			2,856 ①	68,544	
				153,044	
Creditors: Amounts Falling Due within One Year					
Creditors	W 12		81,090 ③		
Preference Dividend Due			7,000 ②		
Ordinary Dividend Due			16,500 ③		
Debenture Interest Due			14,400 ③		
VAT			16,500 ②		
Bank	W 13		1,960 ⑤	(137,450)	
					15,594
					1,233,994

Financed by
Creditors: Amounts Falling Due after More than One Year

8% Debentures			230,000 ❷

Capital and Reserves	Authorised	Issued	
Ordinary Shares at €1 Each	690,000	550,000 ❶	
6% Preference Shares at €1 Each	300,000	200,000 ❶	
	990,000	750,000	
Revaluation Reserve **W 14**		152,000 ❸	
Profit and Loss Balance		101,994	
Shareholders' Funds			1,003,994
Capital Employed			1,233,994

Workings

1. **Purchases**	620,000 – 62,000	= 558,000
2. **Closing Stock**	85,000 – 3,200	= 81,800
3. **Patents Written Off**	(€58,200 + €1,800) × 20%	= 12,000
4. **Depreciation – Buildings**	2% of (780,000 – 130,000)	= 13,000
5. **Depreciation – Delivery Vans**	25,800 + 9,800	= 35,600
	34,400 + 1,200	= 35,600
	22,400 + 9,000 + 4,200	= 35,600
6. **Decrease in Provision for Bad Debts**	3,600 – 2,856	= 744
7. **Loss on Sale of Van**	60,000 – 22,000 – 28,000	= 10,000
8. **Investment Income**	1,800 + 2,700 + 2,700	= 7,200
9. **Land and Buildings at Cost**	780,000 + 100,000	= 880,000
10. **Delivery Vans at Cost**	172,000 + 84,000 – 60,000	= 196,000
Accumulated Depreciation D. Vans	78,000 + 35,600 – 28,000	= 85,600
11. **Debtors**	73,900 – 750 – 1,750	= 71,400
12. **Creditors**	81,000 + 90	= 81,090
13. **Bank Overdraft as per Trial Balance**	5,500	
Less Investment Income	(2,700)	
Less Credit Transfer Received	(750)	
Less Bank under Credited	(90)	= (1,960)
Alternative	(4,040 – 6,000)	= (1,960)
14. **Revaluation Reserve**	100,000 + 39,000 + 13,000	= 152,000

Question 1.3

The following trial balance was extracted from the books of M. O'Brien on 31/12/2006.

	€	€
9% Investments 1/6/2006	200,000	
Buildings (cost €980,000)	933,000	
Delivery Vans (cost €150,000)	80,500	
5% Fixed Mortgage (including increase of €200,000 5% mortgage received on 1/4/2006)		500,000
Patents (incorporating 3 months' investment income)	55,500	
Debtors and Creditors	77,600	86,500
Purchases and Sales	668,000	982,000
Stocks 1/1/2006	67,700	
Commission	24,000	
Provision for Bad Debts		3,800
Salaries and General Expenses	194,100	
Discount (Net)		4,600
Rent		15,000
Mortgage Interest Paid for First 3 Months	4,000	
Insurance (incorporating suspense)	8,700	
VAT		5,500
PRSI		2,300
Bank		70,900
Drawings	37,500	
Capital		680,000
	2,350,600	2,350,600

The following information and instructions are to be taken into account:
1. Stock at 31/12/2006 at cost was €74,500. This figure includes damaged stock which cost €6,600 but which now has a net realisable value of €1,900.
2. Provide for depreciation on vans at the annual rate of 15 per cent of cost from the date of purchae to the date of sale.
   NOTE: On 31/3/2006 a delivery van which had cost €42,000 on 31/5/2003 was traded against a new van which cost €48,000. An allowance of €20,000 was made on the old van. The cheque for the net amount of this transaction was entered in the bank account but was incorrectly treated as a purchase of trading stock. These were the only entries made in the books in respect of this transaction.
3. Patents, which incorporate three months' investment income, are to be written off over a five-year period commencing in 2006.
4. The suspense figure arises as a result of the posting of an inccorrect figure for mortgage interest to the mortgage interest account and discount received €700 entered only in the creditors account. The correct interest was entered in the bank account.
5. Provision to be made for mortgage interest due.
6. A new warehouse was purchased during the year for €240,000 plus VAT of 12.5 per cent. The amount paid to the vendor was entered in the buildings account. No entry was made in the VAT account.
7. Provide for depreciation on buildings at the rate of 2 per cent of cost per annum. It was decided to revalue the buildings at €1,100,000 on 31/12/2006.
8. Provision for bad debts to be adjusted to 4% of debtors.

You are required to prepare a:
(a)   Trading and profit and loss account for the year ended 31/12/2006.   **(75)**
(b)   Balance sheet as at 31/12/2006.   **(45)**

(120 marks)

Solution to Q 1.3

(a) Trading, Profit and Loss Account for the Year Ended 31/12/2006

		€	€	€
Sales				982,000 ❷
Less Cost of Sales				
Stock 1/1/2006			67,700 ❷	
Add Purchases	**W 1**		640,000 ❻	
			707,700	
Less Stock 31/12/2006	**W 2**		(69,800) ❻	(637,900)
Gross Profit				344,100
***Less* Expenses**				
Administration				
Salaries and General Expenses		194,100 ❷		
Patents Written Off	**W 3**	12,000 ❻		
Insurance	**W 4**	9,650 ❽		
Depreciation – Buildings	**W 5**	19,000 ❸	234,750	
Selling and Distribution				
Loss on Sale of Delivery Van	**W 7**	4,150 ❻		
Commission		24,000 ❷		
Depreciation – Delivery Vans	**W 6**	23,175 ❺	51,325	(286,075)
				58,025
Add Operating Income				
Reduction in Provision for Bad Debts	**W 8**			696 ❹
Rent				15,000 ❷
Discount	**W 9**			5,300 ❺
Operating Profit				79,021
Investment Income				10,500 ❸
				89,521
Mortgage Interest	**W 10**			(22,500) ❻
Net Profit for Year				**67,021** ❼

(b) Balance Sheet as at 31 December 2006

		Cost €	Accumulated Depreciation €	Net €	Total €
Intangible Fixed Assets					
Patents (€60,000 – €12,000)					48,400 ❹
Tangible Fixed Assets					
Buildings	W 11	1,100,000 ❷		1,100,000	
Delivery Vans		156,000 ❷	74,825 ❸	81,175	
		1,256,000	74,825	1,181,175	1,181,175
Financial Assets					
Investments					200,000 ❷
					1,429,175
Current Assets					
Stock				69,800 ❷	
VAT	W 12			24,500 ❺	
Investment Income Due				6,000 ❸	
Debtors			77,600 ❷		
Less Provision			3,104 ❶	74,496	
				174,796	
Creditors: Amounts Falling Due within One Year					
Creditors			86,500 ❷		
Mortgage Interest Due			18,750 ❸		
PRSI			2,300 ❷		
Bank			70,900 ❷	(178,450)	(3,654)
					1,425,521
Financed by:					
Creditors: Amounts Falling Due after More than One Year					
9% Fixed Mortgage					500,000 ❷
Capital and Reserves					
Capital 1/1/2006				680,000 ❶	
Add Net Profit				67,021 ❶	
				747,021	
Less Drawings				37,500 ❷	
				709,521	
Revaluation Reserve	W 13			216,000 ❹	925,521
Capital Employed					1,425,521

Question 1.3 – *Workings*

1.	**Purchases**	668,000	
	Less Payment for Van	(28,000)	640,000
2.	**Closing Stock**	74,500	
	Less Valueless Stock	(4,700)	69,800
3.	**Patents**		
	(€55,500 + €4,500) ÷ 5		12,000
4.	**Insurance**	8,700	
	Add Mortgage Interest	250	
	Add Discount Received	700	9,650
5.	**Depreciation – Buildings**		
	2% of €950,000		19,000
6.	**Depreciation – Delivery Vans**		
	(€22,500 + €675) or (€5,625 + €17,550) or (€16,200 + €1,575 + €5,400)		23,175
7.	**Loss on Sale of Van**		
	(€42,000 – €17,850 – €20,000)		4,150 loss
	Provision for Depreciaton – Vans		
	(€69,500 – €17,850 + €23,175)		74,825
8.	**Provision for Bad Debts**		
	(€3,800 – €3,104)		696 CR
9.	**Discount**	4,600	
	Add Unrecorded Discount	700	5,300
10.	**Mortgage Interest**	4,000	
	Less Suspense	(250)	
	Add Interest Due	18,750	22,500
11.	**Buildings**	98,000	
	Less VAT	(30,000)	
	Add Revaluation	150,000	1,100,000
12.	**Vat Account**	5,500	
	Less VAT on Buildings	(30,000)	24,500
13.	**Revaluation Reserve**		
	Land and Buildings	150,000	
	Provision for Depreciation (47,000 + 19,000)	66,000	216,000

Chapter 2
Ratios and Analysis

Ratios

It is essential that all the ratios are known. Even more important is the ability to comment on the significance of the ratios.

1. Gross Profit Percentage/Margin
2. Mark-Up Percentage
3. Rate of Stock Turnover
4. Net Profit Percentage/Margin
5. Length of Credit Given to Debtors
6. Length of Credit Received from Creditors
7. Interest Cover
8. Working Capital Ratio
9. Liquid Asset Ratio
10. Capital Gearing Ratio
11. Return on Capital Employed
12. Return to Equity Shareholders
13. Earnings per Share
14. Price Earnings Ratio
15. Dividend per Share
16. Dividend Cover
17. Dividend Yield

Practise writing out the ratios until you are absolutely sure that you know them all.

Indicators of Bankruptcy

The indicators of bankruptcy have been developed in the US and are called 'Z scores'. The higher the score, the less likelihood of insolvency. The results show that almost every company that failed in a particular year showed warning signs in the previous year's results.

Five ratios are used:

1. $\dfrac{\text{Working Capital}}{\text{Total Assets}}$

2. $\dfrac{\text{Retained Earnings}}{\text{Total Assets}}$

3. $\dfrac{\text{Profit before Interest and Tax}}{\text{Total Assets}}$

4. $\dfrac{\text{Market Value}}{\text{Total Debt}}$

5. $\dfrac{\text{Sales}}{\text{Total Assets}}$

When you are asked for a particular ratio, do not just write down the answer. Write down the formula in words. Then write down the first line of the formula in figures. Finally, show all your calculations to the last line. For example,

Issued Ordinary Share @ €1 €500,000
10% Preference Shares @ €1 €300,000
Net Profit €150,000
(ignore tax)

You are asked for the earnings per share.

$$\text{Earnings per share} = \frac{\text{Net Profit} - \text{Preference Dividend} - \text{Tax}}{\text{Number of Ordinary Shares}}$$

$$= \frac{150,000 - 30,000}{500,000}$$

$$= \frac{120,000}{500,000} = 24 \text{ cent}$$

(Note: The cent designation is essential.)

When asked to comment on the performance of the company, i.e. whether the company is a good investment either on the part of a prospective shareholder or a lending institution, it is vital that you are able to comment properly and make proper comparisons.

The following are the key areas.

1 Profitability

Profitability – return on capital employed and return to equity shareholder and compare to present return on risk-free investment. Compare with previous year if possible.

2 Liquidity

Current ratio 1.5 to 2 : 1.
Quick ratio 1 : 1.

3 Gearing

A lowly geared company cannot get into financial difficulty. High gearing **may** be acceptable if the company is highly profitable.

4 Trends

If you are given figures for only one year, it is very difficult to do anything other than look at the reserve figures. If you are given results for more than one year, there are a lot of comparisons that can be made, and it is a matter of emphasising the most important.

5 Company Sector

Comment and compare to industry norm if given.

6 Company Name

Look at company title to see if it is a plc or a private company.

7 Fixed Assets

Look for full breakdown, giving composition and depreciation policy.

8 Debentures

Rate of interest and amount of interest and interest cover. Refer back to gearing, look at redemption date and effect on future liquidity.

9 Dividends

Dividend cover and yield are important to ensure that dividends are not paid out of reserves. Look at the market price of the shares. If the company is not a plc, note that there is not a ready market for the shares.

10 Purchase of Shares

If being asked to buy shares in the company, see if the number of shares being bought would give control of the company. Look at the cost of borrowing and the present dividend policy.

11 Loan

If being asked to lend to the company, state that you must know for what purpose the finance is required and how the future interest cover, capital gearing ratio and liquid asset ratio will be affected.

12 Investments

If the company has investments, compare cost and market value to see if selling these might help alleviate any liquidity problem the company might have.

13 Earnings

Look at earnings per share and price earnings ratio, and consider the industry norm if one is given.

14 Audit

State that in order to comment fully on a particular company, you would require a full set of unqualified audited accounts for a number of years.

If the company has liquidity/profitability and you are asked to suggest some type of corrective action, you might suggest some of the following: sale and leaseback, factoring of debtors, sale of investment, issue of shares (if possible), capital reduction scheme or even closedown.

Question 2.1

The following figures have been taken from the final account of Down 'n' Out Ltd at 31 December 2007. This is a business involved in the manufacture of furniture. The authorised share capital is €960,000 made up of 500,000 €1 ordinary shares and 230,000 €2, 9 per cent preference shares.

	€
Sales	780,000
Cost of Sales	600,000
Total Expenses	150,000
Profit and Loss (1/1/2007)	90,000
Profit and Loss (31/12/2007)	30,000
Proposed Dividends	48,000
Fixed Assets	700,000
Current Assets (including stock €90,000)	140,000
Trade Creditors	60,000
General Reserve (1/1/2007)	40,000
10% Debentures 2008 Secured	120,000
Issued Ordinary Shares 300,000 @ €1 each	
Issued Preference Shares 100,000 @ €2 each	

(a) Calculate the following:
   (1) Opening stock if the rate of stock turnover is ten times.
   (2) Price earnings ratio if the market price of one ordinary share is 80 cent.
   (3) Interest cover.
   (4) Dividend yield on one ordinary share.
   (5) Gearing ratio and its effect on the distribution of profits.
(b) Down 'n' Out Ltd has applied to your bank for a loan of €180,000. You are the assistant lending officer. Write a report to your manager outlining your reasons for giving/not giving the loan.

Solution to Q 2.1(a)

Down 'n' Out Ltd Trading and Profit and Loss Accounts		
	(€'000)	(€'000)
Sales		780
Less Cost		600
Gross Profit		180
Less Expenses		150
Net Profit		30
+ Balance		90
		120
– Proposed Dividends		
Preference	18	
Ordinary	30	48
		72
Balance (31/2/2007)		30
To General Reserves		42
General Reserve (1/1/2007)		40
General (31/12/2007)		82

Balance Sheet at 31 December 2007			
	(€'000)	(€'000)	(€'000)
Fixed Assets			700
Current Assets			
Stock	90		
Drs, etc.	50	140	
Current Liabilities			
Creditors	60		
Dividends	48	108	
NCA			32
			732
Financed by			
Ordinary Shares		300	
9% Preference		200	
		500	
Reserves			
General Reserve	82		
Profit and Loss	30	112	
10% Debentures		120	
			732

(1)   Rate of Stock Turnover $= \dfrac{\text{Cost of Sales}}{\text{Average Stock}} = 10$

$$= \frac{600}{x} = 10$$

Therefore
$$x = 60$$
and if
$$\text{closing stock} = 90$$
then
$$\text{opening stock} = 30$$
(note a 300 per cent increase)

(2)   Price Earnings Ratio $= \dfrac{\text{Market Price}}{\text{Earnings per Share}}$

Earnings per Share $= \dfrac{\text{Net Profit} - \text{Preference Dividend}}{\text{Number of Ordinary Shares}}$

$$= \frac{30 - 18}{300} = 4 \text{ cent}$$

Price Earnings Ratio $= \dfrac{80}{4} = 20 \text{ times}$

(3)   Interest Cover $= \dfrac{\text{Net Profit} + \text{Interest}}{\text{Interest}}$

$$= \dfrac{30 + 12}{12} = 3.5 \text{ times}$$

(4)   Dividend Yield $= \dfrac{\text{Dividend per Share}}{\text{Market Price}} \times \dfrac{100}{1}$

Dividend per Share $= \dfrac{\text{Ordinary Dividends}}{\text{Number of Ordinary Shares}} = \dfrac{30}{300} = 10 \text{ cent}$

Dividend Yield $= \dfrac{10}{80} \times \dfrac{100}{1} = 12.5\%$

(5)   Gearing Ratio and Debt/Equity Ratio

Preferences Shares + Debentures : Ordinary Shares
200 + 120 : 300
320 : 300
1.07 : 1

The company is highly geared, and this burden must be met before there is anything available for the equity holders.

Solution to Q 2.1(b)
To:
From:
Date:
Re: Loan to Down 'n' Out of €180,000
Down 'n' Out are well named, and I would not advance the loan for the following reasons.

(i)   The return on capital employed is only 5.74 per cent. Even in times of low interest rates, this is not acceptable and is less than the return achievable on risk-free investments.
(ii) The company has a liquidity problem. The current ratio is 1.3 : 1, which is well below the norm of 2 : 1. The liquid asset ratio is only 0.46 : 1, which is well below the desired figure of 1 : 1.
(iii) The company is in the furniture-manufacturing business, which is extremely competitive and cyclical. The stock during the year has increased by 300 per cent, indicating a high build-up of slow-moving stock.
(iv) Dividends are being maintained but are being paid out of reserves, while the company is trying to borrow money to solve its liquidity problems.
(v)   The debentures are due for repayment within the next twelve months and there are no liquid assets for this purpose; this is probably, in part, why the loan is being requested.
(vi) The interest cover at present is only 3.5 times. Further borrowing will only reduce this at least in the short term.
(vii) The actual value of any fixed assets offered as security must be doubtful, and the debenture holders at present have a prior security.
(viii) The firm's Z scores (predictors of bankruptcy) are generally poor.

$$\dfrac{\text{Working Capital}}{\text{Total Assets}} = \dfrac{32}{840}$$

$$\frac{\text{Retained Earnings}}{\text{Total Assets}} = \frac{112}{840}$$

$$\frac{\text{Operating Profit}}{\text{Total Assets}} = \frac{42}{840}$$

$$\frac{\text{Market Value}}{\text{Total Debt}} = \frac{240}{320}$$

$$\frac{\text{Sales}}{\text{Total Assets}} = \frac{780}{840}$$

Note: The actual value of the fixed assets and the stock must be questioned.

(ix) The company is not a plc, and this makes it less attractive as a lending proposition.

(x) The company is already highly geared, and further borrowing will, in the short term at least, only increase this high gearing and place an even bigger burden on the firm.

(xi) To even consider lending to this company in future, a clear explanation of why the finance is required would have to be given, together with three to five years of unqualified audited accounts. Even then, it is doubtful if this company would be a good lending proposition.

Question 2.2

The following are the summarised final accounts of two manufacturing companies, Soda Ltd and Tonic Ltd, for the year ended 31 December 2007.

Summarised Profit and Loss Accounts for the Year Ended
31 December 2007

	Soda Ltd		Tonic Ltd	
	(€)	(€)	(€)	(€)
Sales		700		540
Cost of Goods Sold		310		230
Gross Profit		390		310
Debenture Interest	40		20	
Other Expenses	190	230	140	160
Net Profit		160		150

Balance Sheet at 31 December 2007

	(€)	(€)	(€)	(€)
Fixed Assets at Cost		820		370
Accumulated Depreciation		360		80
		460		290
Current Assets				
Trade Debtors	115		60	
Stocks	80		40	
Bank	10			
	205		100	
Current Liabilities				
Trade Creditors	80		55	
Net Current Assets		125		45
		585		335
Financed by				
Shareholders' Funds		345		220
Debentures		240		115
		585		335

The following information is also available:

1. Approximately 90 per cent of each company's sales are made on credit.
2. Each company's stock level remains approximately constant throughout the year.

Requirement: Write a report to the managing director of Soda Ltd comparing the performance of her company with that of Tonic Ltd. Your report should include reference to appropriate ratios and any other information that you consider relevant.

Solution to Q 2.2

Your answer should be put into report format with comments on the following.

	Soda Ltd	Tonic Ltd
Gross Profit (%)	55.71	57.41
Net Profit (%)	22.86	27.78
Return on Capital Employed	34.19	50.75
Expenses/Sales (%)	32.86	29.63
Interest Cover	5	8.5
Working Capital Ratio	2.56 : 1	1.82 : 1
Liquid Asset Ratio	1.56 : 1	1.09 : 1
Credit to Debtors (days)	66	45
Credit from Creditors (days)	94	87
Stock Turnover	3.88	5.75
Working Capital/Total Assets	0.19	0.12
Debt/Equity	0.7 : 1	0.52 : 1

Question 2.3

The following figures have been taken from the final accounts of Gill plc, a wholesaler in home computers and games software, whose authorised capital is €1,000,000, made up of 800,000 ordinary shares at €1 each and 100,000 8 per cent preference shares at €2 each. The firm has already issued 500,000 ordinary shares and 50,000 preference shares.

	(€)
Fixed Assets (cost €500,000)	490,000
Investments (market value €80,000)	160,000
Current Assets (stock €200,000, debtors €69,000)	269,000
Current Liabilities (bank €2,000, trade creditors €90,000)	92,000
General Reserve (1/1/2008)	25,000
9% Debentures 2010 secured	90,000
Sales	920,000
Opening Stock	58,000
Cost of Sales	730,000
Total Expenses for the Year	96,000
Profit and Loss Balance (1/1/2008)	18,000 CR
Profit and Loss Balance (31/12/2008)	12,000 CR
Proposed Dividends	32,000

(a) Calculate the following:
  (i)   Dividend per ordinary share.
  (ii) Interest cover.
  (iii) Market value of one ordinary share whose dividend yield is 5 per cent.
  (iv) Cash sales if the average period of credit is 1.2 months.
  (v)   Price earnings ratio.
(b) Would the shareholders be satisfied with the policies, performance and state of affairs of the above company? Use relevant ratios and information to support your answer.
(c) Comment on the liquidity of Gill plc and suggest appropriate action.

Solution to Q 2.3(a)

(i) Dividend per ordinary share

$$\frac{\text{Ordinary Dividend}}{\text{Number of Ordinary Shares}} = \frac{24,000}{500,000} = 4.8 \text{ cent}$$

(ii) Interest cover

$$\frac{\text{Net Profit} + \text{Interest}}{\text{Interest}} = \frac{94,000 + 8,100}{8,100} = 12.6 \text{ times}$$

(iii) Market value of one ordinary share

$$\frac{\text{Dividend per Share} \times 100}{\text{Market Price}} = \frac{4.8 \times 100}{5 \times \text{Market Price}} = 96 \text{ cent}$$

(iv) Cash sales

$$\frac{69,000 \times 12}{\text{Credit Sales}} = 1.2$$

Credit Sales = 690,000
Total Sales = 920,000
Cash Sales = 920,000 – 690,000 = €230,000

(v) **Price earnings ratio**

$$\frac{\text{Market Price}}{\text{Earnings per Share}} = \frac{96}{18.8} = 5.1 : 1$$

Solution to Q 2.3(b)

Trends: Gill plc has increased its reserves from €43,000 at the beginning of the year to €105,000 at the end of the year. This has more than doubled its reserves even after providing for dividends amounting to €32,000. This would seem to suggest an improved performance over recent years.

Profitability: The firm's profitability is satisfactory. The return on capital employed and the return to equity shareholders of 12.8 and 15.9 per cent, respectively, are better than the return available at present from risk-free investments. The earnings per share is 18.8 cent, and it would take 5.6 years for a share to recoup its market price.

Dividend policies: The dividends are covered 2.9 times. Therefore the shareholders are receiving 34 per cent of available profits. The policy of paying out dividends is creating cash flow problems for the company. The dividend per share is 4.8 cent and the dividend yield is 5 per cent, whereas the preference shareholders receive 8 per cent.

Investment policy: The investments have dropped 50 per cent in value, from €160,000 to €80,000. This places a question mark over its investment policy.

Debentures: The debentures are due for repayment in 2009. This will put a great strain on the firm's liquidity. As the debentures are secured on the fixed assets, the repayments could place the future of Gill plc in jeopardy, as the 2 per cent depreciation indicates that these assets are buildings or they are totally under-depreciated, and therefore the depreciation policy must be questioned.

Sector: Gill plc is involved in the home computer and games software business. This is a very competitive sector.

Closing stock: The shareholders would be very concerned that the firm's huge closing stock is more than four times its opening stock.

Interest cover: The interest cover is 12.6 times. This is a very favourable situation and indicates that borrowings are being put to good use.

Gearing: The firm is low geared as the fixed interest capital is 24 per cent of total capital employed.

The shareholders would not be satisfied with the policies and state of affairs but would be satisfied with the performance of Gill plc.

Solution to Q 2.3(c)

The working capital ratio and acid test ratio are 2.2 to 1 and 0.6 to 1, respectively. The working capital ratio is above the accepted norm of 2 : 1. This shows that working capital is sufficient to meet the day-to-day costs of running the firm. The firm should not let this go too high above 2 : 1, as this would indicate a build-up of stock or a poor use of resources.

The acid test ratio is below the accepted norm of 1 : 1. This shows more accurately the ability of the firm to pay its short-term debts. Gill plc would have difficulty paying its immediate debts:

1. Sell investments. Any surplus cash not required for working capital should be reinvested more profitably. Income from this would improve profitability.
2. Sell stock at an auction and raise at least €55,000.
3. Make a right issue of about 60,000 shares.
4. Sell some of the fixed assets and lease back.
5. Delay the payments of dividends.

Question 2.4
The balance sheets of J. Giles are as follows.

	31 March 2007		31 March 2008	
	(€)	(€)	(€)	(€)
Fixed Assets		260,000		205,000
Current Assets				
Stocks	86,000		84,000	
Debtors	94,000		58,000	
	180,000		142,000	
Current Liabilities	(174,000)	6,000	(59,000)	83,000
		266,000		288,000
Capital				
Opening Balance	262,900			266,000
Add Net Profit	15,600			36,000
Less Drawings	(12,500)			(14,000)
Closing Balance	266,000			288,000

The following information was extracted from the trading accounts for the years ended 31 March 2007 and 2008, respectively.

	2007 (€)	2008 (€)
Sales	505,000	385,000
Gross Profit	152,900	172,750
Opening Stock	82,000	86,000

Required: Calculate the following ratios for each year and comment on the position shown for the second year as compared with the first.

1. Gross profit ratio.
2. Stock turnover.
3. Working capital ratio.
4. Acid test ratio.
5. Period of credit given.

Solution to Q 2.4

1. Gross Profit Ratio
= (Gross Profit × 100)/Sales
Year Ended 31 March 2007: €152,900 × 100/€505,000 = 30.3%
Year Ended 31 March 2008: €172,750 × 100/€385,000 = 44.9%

The ratios have increased from 30.3 to 44.9 per cent. Possible explanations are:

(i) Changes in the types of goods sold, where some lines carry different rates of gross profit than others.
(ii) Increase in the selling price of goods without a proportionate increase in the cost price.
(iii) Elimination of inefficiencies and factors such as theft which would reduce the profit margin.

2. Stock Turnover
= Cost of Sales/Average Stock
where Cost of Sales = Sales Gross Profit.
Year Ended 31 March 2007: €352,100/€84,000 = 4.2 times
Year Ended 31 March 2008: €212,250/€85,000 = 2.5 times

In the first year the average stock was turned over 4.2 times. This has deteriorated to 2.5 times in the second year. This has happened because although sales and purchases have fallen considerably, stock levels have remained relatively constant. It may well be possible to reduce stock levels if this reduction is likely to be permanent.

3. Working Capital Ratio
= Current Assets : Current Liabilities
As at 31 March 2007: €180,000 : €174,000 = 1.04 : 1
As at 31 March 2008: €142,000 : €59,000 = 2.41 : 1

Current assets were roughly equal to current liabilities at 31 March 2007. However, Mr Giles might have difficulty paying his liabilities on time, depending on how quickly his current assets could be turned into cash. His position at 31 March 2008 appears comfortable, with current assets equal to 2.41 times current liabilities.

4. Acid Test Ratio
= Current Assets – Stock : Current Liabilities
As at 31 March 2007: €94,000 : €174,000 = 0.54 : 1
As at 31 March 2008: €58,000 : €59,000 = 0.98 : 1

At 31 March 2007, quick assets (those readily convertible into cash) amounted to only 54 per cent of current liabilities. If the current liabilities are required to be paid promptly, Mr Giles would not be able to meet these in full. At 31 March 2008, quick assets approximately equalled current liabilities, and he should then have been in a position to meet the total liabilities.

5. Period of Credit Given
= (Debtors × 365)/Sales
Year Ended 31 March 2007: (€94,000 × 365)/€505,000 = 68 days
Year Ended 31 March 2008: (€58,000 × 365)/€385,000 = 55 days

The average period of credit given to customers has decreased from 68 days to 55 days. This ratio reflects the time taken by customers to pay and should approximate the credit terms allowed by the business. The situation has improved, and viewed in conjunction with the fall in sales, this would suggest that Mr Giles has been more selective in deciding to whom he sells goods on credit.

Question 2.5
The following figures have been extracted from the final accounts of O'Gara Plc, a manufacturer in the healthcare industry, for the year ended 31 December 2008.

Trading and Profit and Loss Account for Year Ended 31/12/2008

	€
Sales	980,000
Cost of Goods Sold	(620,000)
Total Operating Expenses for Year	(207,000)
Interest for Year	(10,000)
Net Profit for Year	143,000
Proposed Dividends	(68,000)
Retained Profit for Year	75,000

Ratios and Figures for Year Ended 31/12/2007

Earnings per Ordinary Share	18c
Dividend per Ordinary Share	6.5c
Quick Ratio	0.75 to 1
Market Price of Ordinary Share	€1.90
Return on Capital Employed	14%
Return on Equity Funds	7.6%
Interest Cover	9 times
Gearing	35%

Balance Sheet as at 31/12/2008

Intangible Assets	160,000	
Tangible Assets	790,000	
		950,000
Current Assets (including stock €66,000, debtors €74,000)		160,000
Trade Creditors		(73,000)
Dividends		(68,000)
		969,000
10% Debentures 2008/2009		100,000
Issued Capital		
650,000 Ordinary Shares @ €1 Each		650,000
100,000 13% Preference Shares @ €1 Each		100,000
Profit and Loss Balance		119,000
		969,000

You are required to:

(a) Calculate the following for 2008:
   (i) Cash sales if the average period of credit to debtors is one month.
   (ii) Earnings per share.
   (iii) The market price of one ordinary share if the price earnings ratio is 11.
   (iv) The ordinary dividend cover.
   (v) The dividend yield. (50)

(b) A friend of yours has been given the opportunity to buy ordinary shares in O'Gara Plc but before doing so asks your opinion. What advice would you give? Use ratios, percentages and other information from the above to support your conclusions.   (50)

(100 marks)

Solution to Q 2.5

(a)   50

Cash Sales

$$\frac{\text{Debtors} \times 12}{\text{Credit Sales}} \qquad = 1 \qquad\qquad \text{Credit Sales} = \frac{74,000 \times 12}{1}$$

Credit Sales   = 888,000

Cash Sales   = 980,000 – 888,000   = **€92,000** ⑫

Earnings per Share

$$\frac{\text{Net Profit} - \text{Pref Div} \times 100}{\text{Number of Ordinary Shares}} = \frac{130,000 \times 100}{650,000} = \textbf{20c} \enspace ⑩$$

Market Price

$$\frac{\text{Market Price}}{\text{Earnings per Share}} \quad = 11$$

$$\frac{x}{20} \qquad = 11 \qquad\qquad = \textbf{220c} \enspace ⑧$$

Dividend Cover

$$\frac{\text{Net Profit after Pref Div}}{\text{Ordinary Dividend}} = \frac{130,000}{55,000} = \textbf{2.4 times} \enspace ⑩$$

Dividend Yield

$$\frac{\text{Dividend per Share} \times 100}{\text{Market Price}} = \frac{8.46c \times 100}{220c} = \textbf{3.85\%} \enspace ⑩$$

(b)   50

I would advise my friend to buy shares in O'Gara Plc Ltd for the following reasons:

Gearing ⑩
Gearing is 20.6 per cent or 0.26 to 1. The company is low geared at 20.6 per cent and interest cover is 15.3 times. Therefore there is little risk from outside investors. Last year's gearing and interest cover were 35 per cent and 9 times, respectively. These figures indicate improved situations and that the company is less at risk and is better able to pay interest in 2008 than in 2007. The prospects of being able to pay dividends are good.

Dividends ⑩
Dividend per share is 8.46c. The divdend per share has increased from 6.5c since 2007. The company's dividend cover is 2.4 times and dividend yield is 3.85 per cent. The dividend policy is such that a shareholder can expect a decent amount of profits will be

paid out each year, while at the same time the long-term prospects of capital gain are good. The real return to ordinary shareholders would be 9.1 per cent based on available profits.

Profitability ⑩

O'Gara Plc is a profitable firm because its return on capital employed of 15.8 per cent and on equity funds of 6.9 per cent indicate that the firm is earning much more (three times) than the return from risk-free investments of about 4 per cent to 6 per cent. These are big increases from 14 per cent and 7.6 per cent, respectively, in 2007. The earnings per share has increased by 2c from 18c in 2007 to 20c in 2008.

Liquidity ⑩

O'Gara Plc has a liquidity problem. It would have difficulty paying its immediate debts. This difficulty has worsened since 2007 and the company is less able to pay its immediate debts in 2008, as indicated by the acid test ratio. This ratio has worsened from 0.75 in 2007 to 0.67 in 2008. This ratio indicates that O'Gara Plc has only 67c available to pay each €1 owed immediately. The company had 75c available in 2007.

Reserves ❺

The firm is retaining profits and building up reserves, which augers well in the long term and should bring about an increase in the market price of the share. Reserves have risen by €75,000 to €119,000 since 2007.

Market Price ❺

The share value has gone up by 30c to €2.20 since 2007 and is likely to continue in its upward movemet based on current year performance.

Real value of fixed assets/security

The real value of fixed assets and intangible assets should be questioned. There are no write-offs. Although there are intangible assets valued at €160,000 there is little risk to the company, as this is only 20 per cent of the tangible fixed assets and this ensures that there is adequate security for the loan.

Sector

The healthcare industry is a growth area and the sector has good prospects.

Price earnings ratio

The price earnings ratio is 11. This means that at the present rate of earnings it would take 11 years to earn back the price of a share.

Interest cover

Interest cover is 15.3 times and has improved from 9 times in 2007. There should be more profits availabe to the shareholders.

Question 2.6

The following figures have been extracted from the final accounts of Coulter Ltd, a service provider in the leisure industry, whose authorised capital is €900,000, made up of 650,000 ordinary shares at €1 each and 250,000 10 per cent preference shares.

Trading and Profit and Loss Accounts for Year Ended 31/12/2009

	€	
Sales	1,100,000	
Costs of Goods Sold		
Stock 1/1/2009	63,000	
Purchases	751,000	
Stock 31/12/2009	(74,000)	(740,000)
Total Operating Expenses for the Year		(208,000)
Interest for Year		(15,000)
Net Profit for Year		137,000
Proposed Dividends		(66,000)
Retained Profits for Year		71,000

Ratios and Figures for Year Ended 31/12/2008

Earnings per Ordinary Share	22c
Dividend per Ordinary Share	2.9c
Quick Ratio	0.9 to 1
Market Value of Ordinary Share	€1.75
Return on Capital Employed	14%
Return on Equity Funds	19%
Interest Cover	9 times
Gearing	40%

Balance Sheet as at 31/12/2009

Intangible Assets	140,000	
Fixed Assets	760,000	900,000
Current Assets	170,000	
Current Liabilities		
Trade Creditors	(35,000)	
Proposed Dividends	(66,000)	69,000
		969,000
9% Debentures 2014/2015		160,000
Issued Capital		
500,000 Ordinary Shares @ €1 Each	500,000	
200,000 10% Preference Shares @ €1 Each	200,000	
Profit and Loss Balance	109,000	809,000
		969,000

You are required to answer the following:

(a) (i) Cash purchases if the average period of credit received from creditors is 1.5 months.

(ii) Earnings per share.

(iii) How long it would take one ordinary share to recoup (recover) its 2008 market price based on present dividend payout rate.

(iv) The dividend yield for 2008.

(v) The market value of one ordinary share in 2009 if the price earnings ratio is 9. **(50)**

(b) Assume that the company wishes to raise further finance by issuing the remaining shares at €2 per share. Would you as a shareholder be prepared to purchase these shares? Outline your reasons for purchasing/not purchasing some shares. Your answer should include all relevant information included in the above figures and references to any other information that you consider necessary. **(50)**

(100 marks)

Solution to Q 2.6

(a) 50

Cash Purchases

$$\frac{\text{Creditors} \times 12}{\text{Credit Purchases}} = 1.5 \quad \text{Credit Purchases} = \frac{35,000 \times 12}{1.5}$$

Credit Purchases   = 280,000

Cash Purchases   = 751,000 – 280,000   =   €471,000 ⑫

Earnings per Share

$$\frac{\text{Net Profit after Div} \times 100}{\text{Number of Ordinary Shares}} = \frac{117,000 \times 100}{500,000} = 23.4c \ ⑩$$

Period to Recover Price

$$\frac{\text{Market Price}}{\text{Dividend per Share}} = \frac{175}{9.2} = 19 \text{ years} \ ⑫$$

Dividend Yield

$$\frac{\text{Dividend per Ordinary Share} \times 100}{\text{Market Price}} = \frac{2.9 \times 100}{1.75} = 1.66\% \ ⑧$$

Price Earnings Ratio

$$\frac{\text{Market Price}}{\text{Earnings per Share}} = 9 = \frac{\text{Market Price}}{23.4} = 9 \ 210.6c \ ⑧$$

(b) 50

Dividends ⑩

	2009	2008
Dividend per Share	92c	2.9c
Dividend Yield	4.37%	1.66%
Dividend Cover in 2008	2.5 times	7.6 times
Real Return – Div Yield × Div Cover	10.9%	12.6%

The dividend policy of the company has eased over the two years as the percentage of profits paid out has increased from 13.15% to 40%.

The real return of 10.9 per cent and 12.6 per cent are well above the return from risk-free investments of less than 5 per cent.

Market value of shares ⑧
The market value of each share increased from €1.75 in 2008 to €2.11 in 2009. The shares are now being offered at €2.00. This is 11c above the 2009 value. The price earnings ratio in 2009 is 9 and 8 in 2008.

Profitability ⑧
The return on shareholders' equity increased from 19 per cent in 2008 to 19.2 per cent in 2009. The return on capital employed increase from 14 per cent in 2008 to 15.7 per cent in 2009. This indicates a healthy trend and the value of shares would further increase if this trend continues.
The return is better than the return from risk-free investments of less than 5 per cent.

Proportion of shares owned ⑥
The remaining 150,000 shares would give the purchaser 23 per cent ownership of the company. This amount added to shares already owned would bring the owner's shareholding close to the point of having to bid for the remainder of the shares.

Liquidity ⑥
The acid test ratio improved from 0.9 to 0.95. This is a satisfactory position as the company now has 95c available to pay each €1 owed in the short term. The company does not have a liquidity problem.

Gearing ⑥
The firm is low geared. The gearing has improved from 40 per cent in 2008 to 37 per cent of total capital in 2009. Interest cover in 2008 was 9 times and this cover has increased to 10 times in 2009. This indicates that there is little risk from creditors and a better prospect of higher dividends.

Sector ⑥
The leisure industry is a growth industry. People are prepared to spend more of their disposable income on leisure.

Chapter **3**

Incomplete Records

When dealing with what are known as Type A questions, i.e. cash/bank payment-type questions, it is a good idea to treat them as an exercise in basic bookkeeping.

First, enter the opening balances in general journal format to find the missing goodwill figure. Next enter all the figures in T accounts as opening balances. Then open a cash account and credit all the payments. Complete the double entry by debiting these accounts.

Do the same with the bank account, i.e. credit all the payments and then debit the other. The main problem areas in these questions arise with loans and interest calculations and with drawings. If the amount of the loan is funded, i.e. of an endowment type, then the total of the loan in the balance sheet will always be the original amount borrowed. If the loan is being repaid, then the amount of repayments made reduce the loan balance. Loan repayments do not go into the profit and loss account.

When allocating the figure for drawings for interest, light and heat, insurance, etc., you will be clearly instructed as to which way to calculate it – amount paid, amount used, amount payable, etc. By using the T account format and reading the instructions carefully, you will get the correct answer.

In Type B questions, you have the same difficulties as in Type A regarding loans and drawings, but you go through the question in a different manner. First, enter the opening figures in the general journal in order to find goodwill. Then enter the appropriate opening figures in the year end balance sheet/statement of affairs. Find the closing figures for stock, debtors, creditors, etc. and enter them in the balance sheet. Keep the number of accounts to a minimum, opening accounts only for expenses and drawings. Do not open a bank account. Finally, the missing balance sheet figure will be the net profit which you will use in the profit and loss account to work back to the sales figure.

Question 3.1 (*Type A*)
On 1 January 2007 Eddie Dunphy purchased the business of Charlton & Co. for €125,000 consisting of the following tangible assets and liabilities: premises €99,000; stock €22,000; creditors €16,800; debtors €14,900; electricity due €540; and three months' insurance prepaid €1,500.

During 2007 Dunphy did not keep a full set of accounts but was able to supply you with the following information.

Cash payments: Purchases €43,400; general expenses €28,300; lodgements €53,000; light and heat €4,600.

Bank payments: Annual insurance premium €6,300; creditors €35,000; delivery van
                 €18,000; interest €1,800; household furniture €5,600.
Bank lodgements: Lotto win €25,000; cash €53,000; debtors €27,500.

During the year Dunphy took from stock goods to the value of €250 per month and cash of
€600 per month.

On 1 September 2007 Dunphy borrowed €80,000, part of which was used to purchase an
adjoining premises for €72,000. The rate of interest was 9 per cent per annum, payable
monthly on the last day of each month. The capital sum was to be repaid in one lump sum in
the year 2021, and to provide for this the bank was to pay €360 per month on the last day of
each month into an investment account.

Dunphy estimated that one-third of light and heat used, insurance paid and interest payable
should be attributed to the private section of the premises.

Included in the assets and liabilities of the business on 31 December 2007 were: creditors
€16,400; stock €23,000; debtors €15,400; cash €680, electricity due €500, stock of heating
oil €360; €25 interest earned by the fund to date.

Prepare trading and profit and loss accounts for the year ended 31 December 2007 and a
balance sheet at 31 December 2007.

Solution to Q 3.1

E. Dunphy
Opening Entries
Method – Showing All Accounts

	Dr (€)	Cr (€)
Capital		125,000
Premises	99,000	
Stock	22,000	
Creditors		16,800
Debtors	14,900	
Electricity		540
Insurance	1,500	
Goodwill	4,940	
	142,340	142,340

Capital Account (1)

	(€)		(€)
		Opening Balance	125,000
		Bank	25,000

Premises Account (2)

	(€)		(€)
Opening Balance	99,000		
Loan	72,000		

Opening Stock (3)

	(€)		(€)
Opening Balance	22,000		

Total Creditors (4)

	(€)		(€)
Bank	35,000	Opening Balance	16,800
Balance	16,400	Credit Purchases	34,600
	51,400		51,400

Total Debtors (5)

	(€)		(€)
Opening Balance	14,900	Bank	27,500
Credit Sales	28,000	Balance	15,400
	42,900		42,900

Light and Heat Account (6)

	(€)		(€)
Cash	4,600	Opening Balance	540
Balance	500	Drawings	1,400
		Profit and Loss	2,800
		Balance	360
	5,100		5,100

Insurance Account (7)

	(€)		(€)
Opening Balance	1,500	Drawings	2,100
Bank	6,300	Profit and Loss	4,650
		Balance	1,050

Goodwill Account (8)

	(€)		(€)
Opening Balance	4,940		

Cash Account (9)

	(€)		(€)
Cash Sales	137,180	Purchases	43,400
		General Expenses	28,300
		Bank	53,000
		Light and Heat	4,600
		Drawings	7,200
		Balance	680
	137,180		137,180

Purchases Account (10)

	(€)		(€)
Cash	43,400	Drawings	3,000
Credit	34,600	Trading Account	75,000
	78,000		78,000

General Expenses (11)

	(€)		(€)
Cash	28,300		

Bank Account (12)

	(€)		(€)
Capital	25,000	Insurance	6,300
Cash	53,000	Creditors	35,000
Debtors	27,500	Delivery Vans	18,000
Loan	8,000	Interest	1,800
		Drawings	5,600
		Investment Fund	1,440
		Balance C/D	45,360
	113,500		113,500

Delivery Vans (13)

	(€)		(€)
Bank	18,000		

Interest (14)

	(€)		(€)
Bank	1,800	Drawings	800
Balance C/D	600	Profit and Loss	1,600
	2,400		2,400

Drawings (15)

	(€)		(€)
Bank	5,600		
Purchases	3,000		
Cash	7,200		
Light and Heat	1,400		
Interest	800		
Insurance	2,100		
	20,100		

Loan Account (16)

	(€)		(€)
		Premises	72,000
		Bank	8,000

Investment Fund Account (17)

	(€)		(€)
Bank	1,440		
Income	25		

Sales Account (18)

	(€)		(€)
Trading Account	165,180	Credit	28,000
		Cash	137,180
	165,180		165,180

Investment Income (19)

	(€)		(€)
		Fund	25

Eddie Dunphy
Trading and Profit and Loss Account for the Year Ended 31 December 2007

	(€)	(€)
Sales		165,180
Less Cost of Sales		
Opening Stock	22,000	
Purchases	75,000	
	97,000	
Less Closing Stock	23,000	
Cost of Sales		74,000
Gross Profit		91,180

Eddie Dunphy *(Continued)*

	(€)	(€)
Less Expenses		
Insurance	4,650	
General Expenses	28,300	
Light and Heat	2,800	
Interest	1,600	37,350
		53,830
Investment Income		25
Net Profit		53,855

Balance Sheet at 31 December 2007

	(€)	(€)	(€)
Fixed Assets			
Premises	171,000		
Delivery Vans	18,000		
Goodwill	4,940		
Investment Fund	1,465	195,405	
Current Assets			
Stock	23,000		
Debtors	15,400		
Bank	45,360		
Stock of Heating Oil	360		
Insurance Prepaid	1,050		
Cash	680		
		85,850	
Less Current Liabilities			
Creditors	16,400		
Interest	600		
Electricity Bill	500		
		17,500	68,350
Net Current Assets			263,755
Financed by			
Capital		150,000	
Plus Net Profit		53,855	
		203,855	
Less Drawings		20,100	
		183,755	
Loan		80,000	263,755

Question 3.2 (*Type B*)

On 1 January 2007 D. Swindler purchased a business for €110,000 consisting of the following tangible assets and liabilities: premises €86,000; stock €13,000; debtors €11,000; equipment €14,000; creditors €14,000; wages due €2,500; insurance prepaid €600.

During 2007 Swindler did not keep a full set of books but was able to supply you with the following information on 31 December 2007.

1. On 1 June 2007 Swindler borrowed €60,000 from International Finance Plc, some of which was used to purchase an adjoining premises for €56,000. It was agreed that Swindler would pay interest on the last day of each month at the rate of 11 per cent per annum. The capital sum was to be repaid in one lump sum on 30 May 2022, and to provide for this, the bank was to transfer €350 on the last day of each month into an investment account, commencing immediately.
2. Each week Swindler withdrew the following for personal use: stock €70 and cash €90.
3. During the year the following payments were made: insurance €2,400; wages €18,900; interest €3,300; motor vehicles €18,000; light and heat €4,450; sundry expenses €22,000. A €10,000 legacy was lodged to the business bank account.
4. Swindler estimated that one-third of the light and heat used, interest payable and insurance paid should be attributed to the private section of the premises. Two-thirds of the value of the motor vehicles were for private use.
5. Included in the assets and liabilities of the firm on 31 December 2007 were: stock €15,000; debtors €12,500; creditors €14,500; bank €17,000; electricity due €470; €40 interest earned by the fund to date.
6. Swindler's gross profit was 30 per cent of sales.

Prepare in as much detail as possible:

(a) Statement/balance sheet showing Swindler's profit/loss for the year.
(b) Trading and profit and loss accounts for the year.
(c) Advise Swindler.

Note: Do not omit section (c) even when revising this topic. This is omitted by many students in examination.

Solution to Q 3.2

General Journal

	DR (€)	CR (€)
Capital		110,000
Stock	13,000	
Premises	86,000	
Debtors	11,000	
Equipment	14,000	
Creditors		14,000
Wages Due		2,500
Insurance Prepaid	600	
Goodwill	1,900	
	126,500	126,500

Drawings

Purchases	3,640		
Cash	4,680		
Interest	1,283		
Motor Vehicles	12,000		
Insurance	800		
Light and Heat	1,640		
	24,043		

Wages Account

Bank	18,900	Balance	2,500
		Profit and Loss	16,400

Insurance Account*

Balance	600	Drawings	800
Bank	2,400	Profit and Loss	2,200
	3,000		3,000

*Should there be a balance on account at year end?

Interest Account

Bank	3,300	Drawings	1,283
Balance	550	Profit and Loss	2,567
	3,850		3,850

Light & Heat

Bank	4,450	Drawings	1,640
Balance	470	Profit and Loss	3,280
	4,920		4,920

Loan $60,000 \times 11\% \times 7/12 = 3,850$

Balance Sheet at 31 December 2007

	(€)	(€)	(€)
Fixed Assets			
Premises (86,000 + 56,000)			142,000
Equipment			14,000
Motor Vehicles			6,000
Investment Fund (7 × 350) + 40			2,490
Goodwill			1,900
			166,390
Current Assets			
Stock		15,000	
Debtors		12,500	
Bank		17,000	
		44,500	
Less Current Liabilities			
Creditors	14,500		
ESB Bill	470		
Interest	550		
	15,520	28,980	
Net Current Assets			195,370
Financed by			
Capital (110,000 + 10,000)		120,000	
Plus Net Profit		39,413	
Less Drawings		(24,043)	
Term Loan		60,000	195,370

Trading and Profit and Loss Accounts for the Year Ended 31 December 2007

	(€)	(€)
Sales		286,067
Less Cost of Sales		
Opening Stock	13,000	
Purchases (205,887 − 3,640)	202,247	
	215,247	
Less Closing Stock	15,000	
Cost of Sales		200,247
Gross Profit		85,820
Less Expenses		
Wages	16,400	
Insurance	2,200	
Insurance	2,567	
Light and Heat	3,280	
Sundry Expenses	22,000	46,447
		39,373
Plus Fund Income		40
Net Profit		39,413

Question 3.3

On 1/1/2007 R. Roberts purchased a business for €210,000 consisting of the following tangible assets and liabilities: premises €180,000, stock €16,400, debtors €14,000, three months premises insurance prepaid €900, trade creditors €20,400 and wages due €2,400.

During 2007 Roberts did not keep a full set of accounts but was able to supply the following information on 31/12/2007.

Cash payments:	Lodgements €104,000, general expenses €32,300, purchases €86,200.
Bank payments:	Delivery vans €33,200, creditors €42,200, light and heat €6,400, interest €2,475, annual premises insurance premium €4,800, covenant for charitable organisation €2,000, furniture €16,000.
Bank lodgements:	Debtors €35,000, cash €104,000, dividends €4,500.

Roberts took from stock goods to the value of €90 and cash €100 per week for household use during the year. Roberts borrowed €90,000 on 1/9/2007, part of which was used to purchase an adjoining premises costing €75,000. It was agreed that Roberts would pay interest on the last day of each month at the rate of 11 per cent per annum. The capital sum was to be repaid in a lump sum in the year 2017 and to provide for this the bank was to transfer €600 on the last day of each month from Roberts' bank account into an investment fund. Roberts estimated that 25 per cent of furniture and light and heat used as well as 20 per cent of interest payable for the year should be attributed to the private section of the premises.

Included in the assets and liabilities of the firm on 31/12/2007 were stock €18,300, debtors €22,500, trade creditors €34,800, cash €600, electricity due €560, and €66 interest earned by the fund to date.

You are required to show, with workings, the:

(a)	Trading, profit and loss account for the year ended 31/12/2007.	**(60)**
(b)	Balance sheet as at 31/12/2007.	**(40)**
		(100 marks)

Solution to Q 3.3

(a) Trading and Profit and Loss Account for Year Ended 31 December 2007

		€	€	€
Sales	**W 1**			271,800 ❿
Less cost of sales				
Stock at 1 January 2007			16,400 ❸	
Add purchases	**W 2**		138,120 ❽	
			154,520	
Less stock 31 December 2007			18,300 ❸	136,220
Gross profit				135,580
Less expenses				
General expenses	**W 3**		29,900 ❺	
Covenant			2,000 ❶	
Insurance	**W 4**		4,500 ❼	
Interest	**W 5**		2,640 ❼	
Light and heat	**W 6**		5,220 ❼	44,260
				91,320
Add income from investment fund				66 ❷
Net profit				91,386 ❼

(b) Balance Sheet as at 31 December 1999

		€		€		€	
Intangible fixed assets							
Goodwill				21,500	➋		
Tangible fixed assets							
Buildings				255,000	➊		
Delivery vans				33,200	➊		
Furniture				12,000	➊	321,700	
Investments						2,466	➎
						324,166	
Current assets							
Stock at 31 December 2007		18,300	➊				
Trade debtors		22,500	➊				
Bank	**W 7**	49,025	➏				
Cash		600	➊				
Prepayment (insurance)		1,200	➌	91,625			
Less creditors: amounts falling due within one year							
Creditors		34,800	➊				
Interest due		825	➋				
Electricity due		560	➊	36,185		55,440	
						379,606	➌
Financed by							
Creditors: amounts falling due after more than one year							
Loan						90,000	➊
Capital – Balance at 1/1/2007		210,000	➊				
Add capital introduced		4,500	➋				
Add net profit		91,386		305,886			
Less drawings	**W 8**			16,280	➑	289,606	
Capital employed						379,606	

Workings

1 **Sales**			
Payments by debtors		35,000	
Amount owed by debtors 31/12/2007		22,500	
		57,500	
Less amount owed on 1/1/2007		14,000	
Credit sales		43,500	
Cash sales (104,000 + 32,300 + 86,200 + 600 + 5,200)		228,300	271,800
2 **Purchases**			
Payments to creditors		42,200	
Creditors at 31/12/2007		34,800	

	77,000	
Less creditors at 1/1/2007	20,400	
Credit purchases	56,600	
Cash purchases	86,200	
Total purchases	142,800	
Less drawings – goods	4,680	138,120

3 General expenses

Amount paid	32,300	
Less wages due 1/1/2007	(2,400)	29,900

4 Insurance

Amount paid	2,450	
Add insurance prepaid 1/1/2007	900	
Less insurance prepaid 31/12/2007	(1,200)	4,500

5 Interest for year (4/12 × €9,900)

Interest paid	2,475	
Interest due 31/12/2007	825	
	3,300	
Less drawings (1/5)	660	2,640

6 Light and heat

Amount paid	6,400	
Add electricity due 31/12/2007	560	
Less drawings (1/3)	(1,740)	5,220

7 Bank

Receipts

Lodgements	104,000	
Debtors	35,000	
Capital/dividends	4,500	
Loan	90,000	233,500

Less payments

Creditors	42,200	
Insurance	4,800	
Light and heat	6,400	
Furniture	16,000	
Vans	33,200	
Covenant	2,000	
Interest	2,475	
Investment (4 × 600)	2,400	
Buildings	75,000	184,475
Balance		49,025

8 Drawings

Furniture	4,000
Drawings of cash	4,680
Drawing of goods	5,200
Interest	660
Light and heat	1,740
Total	16,280

9 Goodwill		Goodwill Account				
Assets	Premises	180,000	**Liabilities**	Creditors	20,400
	Stock	16,400		Wages due	2,400
	Debtors	14,000		Capital	210,000
	Insurance prepaid	900			
		211,300			
	Missing figure – goodwill	21,500			
		232,800			232,800

Question 3.4

J. O'Higgins lodged €350,000 to a business bank account on 1/1/2008 and on the same day purchased a business for €320,000, including the following assets and liabilities: buildings €290,000, stock €16,700, three months' rates prepaid €2,400, debtors €32,500, wages due €3,600 and trade creditors €58,000.

O'Higgins did not keep a full set of books during 2008 but estimates that the gross profit was 40 per cent of sales and he was able to supply the following additional information on 31/12/2008.

1. Each week O'Higgins took from stock goods to the value of €100 and cash €150 for household expenses.
2. On 1/10/2008 O'Higgins borrowed €300,000, part of which was used to purchase an adjoining premises costing €250,000. It was agreed that O'Higgins would pay interest on the last day of the month at the rate of 6 per cent per annum. The capital sum was to be repaid in one lump sum in the year 2016 and, to provide for this, the bank was instructed to transfer €2,500 on the last day of every month from O'Higgins's business account into an investment fund.
3. During the year, O'Higgins lodged dividends €2,500 to the business bank and made the following payments: light and heat €7,200, interest €3,000, wages and general expenses €98,000, equipment €16,000, rates for twelve months €10,800 and college fees €4,500.
4. O'Higgins estimated that 25 per cent of the equipment, light and heat *used* and interest *payable* should be attributed to the private section of the premises. O'Higgins further estimates that 70 per cent of college fees should be attributed to a family member and the remainder to an employee.
5. Included in the assets and liabilities of the firm on 31/12/2008 were stock €17,200, debtors €34,300, trade creditors €29,900, cash at bank €68,462, electricity due €560 and €75 interest earned by the investment fund to date.

You are required to prepare, with workings, a:

(a) Statement/balance sheet showing O'Higgins's profit or loss for the year ended 31/12/2008.   **(50)**
(b) Trading, profit and loss account, in as much detail as possible, for the year ended 31/12/2008.   **(40)**
(c) Summary of the advice you would give to O'Higgins in relation to the information given above.   **(10)**

(100 marks)

Solution to Q 3.4

(a)   **50**

Balance Sheet as at 31 December 2008

	€	€
Intangible Assets		
Goodwill		40,000 ❸
Fixed Assets		
Buildings (290,000 + 250,000)	54,000 ❸	
Equipment	12,000 ❸	552,000
Financial Assets		
Investments		7,575 ❹
		599,575
Current Assets		
Stock at 31 December 2008	17,200 ❶	
Trade Debtors	34,300 ❶	
Bank	68,462 ❶	
Rates Prepaid	2,700 ❹	122,662
Less Creditors: Amounts Falling Due within One Year		
Creditors	29,900 ❶	
Interest Due	1,500 ❸	
Electricity Due	560 ❷	(31,960)
Working Capital		90,702
		690,277
Financed by		
Creditors: Amounts Falling Due after More Than One Year		
Loan		300,000 ❷
Capital – Balance at 1/1/2008	350,000 ❷	
Add Capital Introduced	2,500 ❸	
Less Drawings **W 10**	(23,215) ❿	329,285
		629,285
Add Net Profit **W 1**		60,992
Capital Employed		690,277 ❼

(b) 40

Trading and Profit and Loss Account for Year Ended 31 December 2008

		€	€
Sales	W 3		440,905 ❷
Less Cost of Goods Sold			
Stock at 1 January 2008		16,700 ❷	
Add Purchases (270,243 – 5,200)	W 5	265,043 ❷	
		281,743	
Less Stock 31 December 2008		(17,200) ❷	
Cost of Sales	W 4		264,543 ❷
Gross Profit	W 2		176,362 ❷
Add Investment Income			75 ❸
			176,437
Less Expenses			
Wages and General Expenses	W 6	95,750 ❻	
Light and Heat	W 7	5,820 ❻	
Rates	W 8	10,500 ❻	
Interest	W 9	3,375 ❻	115,445
Net Profit	W 1		60,992 ❶

(c) 10

O'Higgins should keep a detailed cash book and general ledger supported by appropriate subsidiary day books. This would enable O'Higgins to prepare an accurate trading and profit and loss account and therefore would avoid reliance on estimates.

Workings

1 **Net Profit for Year (Balancing Figure in Balance Sheet)** € €
Total Net Assets 690,277
Less Loan (300,000)
Less Capital after Drawings and before Profit (329,285) 60,992

2 **Gross Profit**
Net Profit + Expenses – Gains = (60,987 + 115,450 – 75) 175,362

3 **Sales**
Gross Profit = 40% of sales = $176,362 \times 2.5$ 440,905

4 **Cost of Sales**
Sales Less Gross Profit = 440,905 – 176,362 264,543

5 **Purchases**
Cost of Sales + Closing Stock – Opening Stock 264,543 + 17,200 – 16,700 265,043

6 **Wages and General Expenses** – Amount Paid 98,000
Add College Fees 30% of €4,500 1,350
Less Wages Due at 1/1/2008 (3,600) 95,750

7 **Light and Heat** – Amount Paid | 7,200 |
Add Electricity Due 31/12/2008 | 560 |
Less Drawings | (1,940) |

Profit and Loss Account | | 5,820

8 **Rates – Amount Paid** | 10,800 |
Add Rates Prepaid 1/1/2008 | 2,400 |
Less Rates Prepaid 31/12/2008 | (2,700) |

Profit and Loss Account | | 10,500

9 **Interest** – Amount Paid | 3,000 |
Add Interest Due | 1,500 |
Less Drawings | (1,125) |

Profit and Loss Account | | 3,375

10 **Drawings**
College Fees – Family Member | 3,150 |
Equipment | 4,000 |
Drawings of Stock | 5,200 |
Cash | 7,800 |
Light and Heat | 1,940 |
Interest | 1,125 | 23,215

Chapter **4**
Club Accounts

Remember:

Accumulated Fund = Capital

Excess of Income over Expenditure = Profit

Excess of Expenditure over Income = Loss

Life Membership = Reserve

Levy Reserve Fund = Reserve

In doing the questions in this chapter, follow these steps.

1. Enter the accumulated fund figures in a general journal format but do not add them, as they are usually not complete.
2. Lay out a blank bar trading account and fill in the figures as you find them. Remember that:

   Sales = Receipts – Opening Debtors + Closing Debtors.

   Stock figures are as given.

   Purchases = Payments to Creditors – Opening Creditors + Closing Creditors.

3. Lay out the income and expenditure account on a separate page.

   Subscriptions = Receipts + Prepaid at Beginning of Year + Due at End of Year – Due at Beginning of Year (last year's) – Prepaid at End of Year (next year's).

   Set off linked items to show a profit/loss for the item, e.g. catering receipts – catering expenses to show a catering profit/loss. In calculating loan interest, only allocate to the income and expenditure that portion paid or payable for the year. The previous interest was a liability at the beginning of the year and goes back into the accumulated fund calculation.

4. In the balance sheet, do not omit items such as depreciation, investments, subscriptions due/prepaid. Again, remember that life membership and levy reserve are actually reserves.
5. Do not omit section (d) where you are asked to advise the club on its financial policy. You are only asked for a brief answer, but a large number of students omit it altogether.

Question 4.1

Included in the assets and liabilities of the Love All Tennis Club on 1 January 2007 were the following: clubhouse and land €190,000; equipment at cost €7,500; bar stock €8,000; subscriptions in advance €500; bar debtors €350; bar creditors €3,200; affiliation fees due €300.

The club treasurer has supplied the following account of the club's activities for the year ended 31 December 2007.

Receipts	(€)	Payments	(€)
Bank Current Account	10,000	Sundry Expenses	14,500
Bar Receipts	78,000	Bar Purchases	57,000
Subscriptions	43,500	Affiliation Fees	900
Disposal of Equipment (cost €2,000)	800	Competition Prizes	1,100
Interest from 6% Government		Catering Costs	3,100
Investment of €15,000	1,350	Purchase of 7% Government	
Catering Receipts	4,600	Bonds on 31 August 2007	12,000
Competition Receipts	600	Transfer to Deposit Account	
		on 31 December 2007	10,000
		Purchase of Prize Bonds	200
		Repayment of €14,000 Loan	
		on 30 June 2007 with	
		1.5 years' interest	16,520
		Balance	23,530
	138,850		13,850

You are given the following additional information:

1. Bar Stock on 31 December 2007 is €8,800.
2. Subscriptions include three life memberships of €800 each, and there are subscriptions due of €500.
3. Equipment at 31 December 2007 is to be depreciated at the rate of 20 per cent per annum.
4. Bar debtors and creditors are €360 and €3,400, respectively.
5. Life membership is to be credited to income over a five-year period beginning in 2007.

Prepare the following:

(a) A statement of accumulated fund at 1 January 2007.
(b) An income and expenditure account for the year ended 31 December 2007.
(c) A balance sheet at 31 December 2007.
(d) A report to the members on the advisability of purchasing a piece of land adjoining their property that has come on the market at €200,000.

Solution to Q 4.1(a)

The Love All Tennis Club
Accumulated Fund on 1 January 2007

	Dr (€)	Cr (€)
Clubhouse and Land	190,000	
Equipment	7,500	
Bar Stock	8,000	
Subscriptions in Advance		500
Bar Debtors	350	
Bar Creditors		3,200
Affiliation Fees Due		300
Bank	10,000	
6% Government Investment	15,000	
6% Investment Income Due	450	
Loan		14,000
Interest Due		1,680
Accumulated Fund		211,620
	231,300	231,300

Solution to Q 4.1(b)

Income and Expenditure Account for the Year Ended 31 December 2007

	Workings*		(€)
Income			
Bar Profit	W1	21,610	
Subscriptions	W2	42,100	
Catering Profit (4,600 – 3,100)		1,500	
6% Investment Income		900	
7% Investment Income		280	
Life Membership		480	66,870
Expenditure			
Sundry Expenses		14,500	
Affiliation Fees (900 – 300)		600	
Loss on Competitions (1,100 – 600)		500	
Interest		840	
Loss on Disposal of Equipment		1,200	
Depreciation of Equipment		1,100	18,740
Excess of Income			48,130

Workings

W1 Bar Trading Account

	(€)
Sales (78,000 – 350 + 360)	78,010
Less Cost of Opening Stock	8,000
Add Purchases (57,000 – 3,200 + 3,400)	57,200
	65,200
Less Closing Stock	8,800
Cost	56,400
Gross Profit	21,610

W2 Subscriptions 43,500 + 500 – 2,400 + 500 = 42,100

	(€)
Life Membership	2,400
Income	480
Reserves	1,920

Solution to Q 4.1(c)

Balance Sheet at 31 December 2007

	Cost (€)	Accumulated Depreciation (€)	Net (€)
Fixed Assets			
Clubhouse and Land	190,000		190,000
Equipment	5,500	1,100	4,400
	195,500	1,100	194,400
6% Government Stock			15,000
Prize Bonds			200
7% Government Bonds			12,000
			221,600
Current Assets			
Bank	23,530		
Closing Stock	8,800		
Bar Debtors	360		
Deposit Account	10,000		
Subscriptions Due	500		
Income Due on 7% Bond	280		
	43,470		
Less Current Liabilities/Creditors	3,400		40,070
			261,670
Financed by			
Accumulated Fund	211,620		
Excess of Income	48,130		
Life Membership	1,920		
			261,670

Solution to Q 4.1(d)

Points in favour of purchase:

The club has liquid assets of government investments €27,000; deposit account €10,000; current account €23,530. In addition:

- It has repaid its loan.
- It could levy its members.
- It could offer reduced life membership (which might reduce its future income).
- It could apply for lottery funding.
- It could finance some borrowing.

Points against purchase:

- The land might not be suitable for development.
- There may be planning permission problems.
- Development costs may be very high.
- The club may have a burden of interest/loan repayments in the future.

Question 4.2

Included in the assets and liabilities of the Below Par Golf Club at 1 January 2008 were the following: clubhouse and land €180,000; life membership €18,000; equipment at book value €17,000; bar debtors €250; bar creditors €5,600; levy reserve fund €40,000, bar stock €6,600.

The club treasurer has supplied the following information regarding the club's activities during the year ended 31 December 2008.

Receipts	(€)	Payments	(€)
Bank Current Account	12,000	Catering Expenses	3,400
Interest from 7% Government		Sundry Expenses	24,000
Investments 2007	2,100	Greenkeepers' Wages	15,900
Interest from 7% Government		Bar Purchases	56,750
Investments 2008	2,100	Repayment of €30,000 Loan	
Catering Receipts	5,800	on 30 September 02 with	
Bar Receipts	84,600	2.5 Years' Interest	38,000
Subscriptions	96,300	Equipment	9,000
		Transfer to Deposit Account	
		on 31 December 08	20,000
		Balance	35,850
	202,900		202,900

You are given the following additional information.

1. Bar stock is €6,900.
2. Equipment owned at 31 December 2008 is valued at €23,500.
3. Subscriptions include the following: two life memberships, which brings the total to fourteen, a levy for the year of €50 on 400 members and a levy of €50 on ten members which has been pending since last year.
4. Debtors and creditors are €300 and €5,500, respectively.
5. Greenkeepers' wages due are €1,400.

Prepare the following:

(a) A statement of accumulated fund at 1 January 2008.
(b) An income and expenditure account for the year ended 31 December 2008.
(c) A balance sheet at 31 December 2008.
(d) A report to the members on funding a €100,000 extension.

Solution to Q 4.2(a)

Below Par Golf Club
Accumulated Fund on 1 January 2008

	Workings	Dr (€)	Cr (€)
Clubhouse and Land		180,000	
Life Membership			18,000
Equipment (net)		1,700	
Bar Debtors		250	
Bar Creditors			5,600
Levy Reserve Fund			40,000
Bar Stock		6,600	
Bank		12,000	
7% Investments		30,000	
Investment Income Due		2,100	
Levy Fund Due		500	
Loan	W3		30,000
Interest Due	W3		5,600
Accumulated Fund			149,250
		248,450	248,450

Solution to Q 4.2(b)

Income and Expenditure Account for the Year Ended 31 December 2008

	Workings*	(€)	(€)
Income			
Bar Profit	W1	28,300	
7% Investment Income		2,100	
Catering Profit (5,800 – 3,400)		2,400	
Subscriptions	W2	72,800	105,600
Expenditure			
Sundry Expenses		24,000	
Greenkeepers' Wages (15,900 + 1,400)		17,300	
Loan Interest	W3	2,400	
Depreciation – Equipment		2,500	46,200
Excess of Income			59,400

*Workings

W1. Bar Trading Account

	(€)	(€)
Sales (84,600 − 250 + 300)		84,650
Less Cost		
Opening Stock	6,600	
Add Purchases (56,750 − 5,600 + 5,500)	56,650	
	63,250	
Less Closing Stock	6,900	
Cost of Sales		56,350
Profit		28,300

W2. Subscriptions

	(€)
Subscriptions	96,300
Life	(3,000)
Levy	(20,000)
Levy	(500)
	72,800

W3. Loan

	(€)
Repaid	38,000
Loan	30,000
Total Interest	8,000
0.5 Year's Interest	1,600
1 Year's Interest	3,200
9 Months' Interest	2,400
Interest Due	5,600

Solution to Q 4.2(c)

Balance Sheet at 31 December 2008

	Cost (€)	Account Depreciation (€)	Net (€)
Fixed Assets			
Clubhouse and Land	180,000		180,000
Equipment	26,000	2,500	23,500
	206,000	2,500	203,500
7% Investments (or C/A)			30,000
Current Assets			
Stock	6,900		
Debtors	300		
Bank	35,850		
Deposit Account	20,000		
		63,050	
Less Current Liabilities			
Creditors	5,500		
Greenkeepers' Wages	1,400	6,900	56,150
			289,650
Enhanced by			
Accumulated Fund			149,250
Excess of Income			59,400
Levy Reserve Fund			60,000
Life Membership			21,000
			289,650

Solution to Q 4.2(d)
Don't wait two years
Why
35,850 in current account
20,000 in deposit account
30,000 in investment fund
Loan paid off
Lottery funding?

Question 4.3

Included in the assets and liabilities of the Nokemdown Indoor and Outdoor Bowling Club on 1 January 2007 were the following: clubhouse and land €285,000; equipment €28,000; bar stock €16,000; life membership €30,000; bar debtors €130; bar creditors €4,300; levy reserve fund €16,000; 6 per cent investment income due €300; wages due €200.

The club treasurer has supplied the following information for the year ended 31 December 2007.

Receipts	(€)	Payments	(€)
Catering Receipts	7,600	Bar Current Account	4,560
Annual Grant	5,500	Equipment	9,000
Subscriptions	53,200	Catering Costs	8,300
Interest from 6% Investments	1,800	Wages	15,200
Bar Receipts	72,600	General Expenses	24,000
Sale of Equipment	1,600	Bar Purchases	61,000
		Repayment of €16,000 Loan on 30 September 2007 with 2.25 Years' Interest	19,600
		Balance	540
	142,200		142,200

You are also given the following information.

1. Bar stock on 31 December 2007 is €16,500.
2. Subscriptions include the following:
    (i)   Three life memberships, bringing the total to sixty-three.
    (ii) Levy for 2007 is 400 members at €40.
    (iii) Levy from five members for 2006.
    (iv) Subscriptions due €400.
3. Bar debtors and creditors are €150 and €4,800, respectively.
4. Book value of equipment €31,000.

Prepare the following:

(a) A statement of accumulated fund at 1 January 2007.
(b) An income and expenditure account for the year ended 31 December 2007.
(c) A balance sheet at 31 December 2007.
(d) A report to the club on their financial position.

Solution to Q 4.3(a)

Nokemdown Indoor and Outdoor Bowling Club Accumulated Fund 1 January 2007

	Dr (€)	Cr (€)
Clubhouse and Land	285,000	
Equipment	28,000	
Bar Stock	16,000	
Life Membership		30,000
Bar Debtors	130	
Bar Creditors		4,300
Levy Reserve Fund		16,000
Investment Income Due	300	
Wages Due		200
Bank		4,560
6% Investments	25,000	
Levy Fund Due	200	
Loan		16,000
Interest Due		2,400
Accumulated Fund		281,170
	354,630	354,630

*Workings

W1. Subscriptions

	(€)
Subscriptions	53,200
Life Membership	(1,500)
Levy 2007	(16,000)
Levy 2006	(200)
Due	400
	35,900

W2. Bar Trading Account

		(€)
Sales (72,600 – 130 + 150)		72,620
Less Cost Opening Stock	16,000	
Purchases		
(61,000 – 4,300 + 4,800)	61,500	
	77,500	
Less Closing Stock	16,500	
Cost of Sales		61,000
Profit		11,620

Solution to Q 4.3(b)

Income and Expenditure Account for the Year Ended 31 December 2007

	Workings*	(€)	(€)
Income			
Annual Grant		5,500	
Subscriptions	W1	35,900	
Investment Income		1,500	
Bar Profit	W2	11,620	54,520
Expenditure			
Catering Loss (8,300 – 7,500)		800	
Wages (15,200 – 200)		15,000	
General Expenses		24,000	
Loan Interest		1,200	
Depreciation – Equipment	W 3	4,400	45,400
Excess of Income			9,120

W3. Equipment Depreciation

$$\text{Equipment } (28{,}000 - 1{,}600 + 900) = 35{,}400$$
$$\text{Value 31 December 2007} = 31{,}000$$
$$\text{Depreciation} = 4{,}400$$

Solution Q 4.3(c)

Balance Sheet at 31 December 2007

	Cost (€)	Accumulated Depreciation (€)	Net (€)
Fixed Assets			
Clubhouse and Land	285,000		285,000
Equipment	35,400	4,400	31,000
	320,400	4,400	316,000
Current Assets			
Bar Stock	16,500		
Bar Debtors	150		
Bank	540		
6% Investments	2,500		
Subs Due	400		
	42,590		
Less Current Liabilities			
Creditors	4,800		
Net Current Assets			37,790
			353,790
Financed by			
Accumulated Fund	281,170		
Excess of Income	9,120		
Levy Reserve Fund	32,000		
Life Membership	31,500		
			353,790

Solution to Q 4.3(d) Advice to Club (3 or 4 points)

Question 4.4

Included among the assets and liabilities of the Green Glen Golf Club on 1/1/2009 were the following: clubhouse and course €740,000, bar stock €3,800, equipment (at cost) €28,600, life membership €36,000, bar debtors €155, bar creditors €2,450, subscriptions received in advance €1,800, 6% government investments €40,000, investment income due €150, levy reserve fund €60,000 and wages due €2,400.

The club treasurer has supplied the following account of the club's activities during the year ended 31/12/2009:

Receipts	€	Payments	€
Bank Current Account	4,440	Bar Purchases	80,500
Investment Income	1,450	Sundry Expenses	185,600
Entrance Fees	17,000	Catering Costs	4,460
Catering Receipts	6,650	Equipment	44,500
Annual Sponsorship	33,000	Coaching Lessons	4,650
Subscriptions	254,200	Repayment of €30,000 Loan on 31/12/2009	
Bar Receipts	112,660	together with 1.25 Years' Interest	34,500
		Transfer to Building Society 31/12/2009	70,000
		Balance	5,190
	€429,400		€429,400

You are given the following additional information and instructions:

1. Bar stock on 31/12/2009 was €4,300.
2. Equipment owned on 31/12/2009 is to be depreciated at the rate of 20 per cent of cost.
3. Clubhouse and course to be depreciated by 2 per cent of cost.
4. Bar debtors and bar creditors on 31/12/2009 were €110 and €2,770, respectively.
5. Subscriptions include:
   (i)   Two life memberships of €6,000 each.
   (ii) Subscriptions for 2010 amounting to €2,400.
   (iii) Levy for 2009 of €200 on 300 members.
   (iv) Levy of €200 on eight members for 2008.
6. Life membership was to be written off over a twelve-year period commencing in 2009.

You are required to:

(a) Show the club's accumulated fund (capital) on 1/1/2009. **(30)**
(b) Show the income and expenditure account for the year ended 31/12/2009. **(35)**
(c) Show the club's balance sheet on 31/12/2009. **(20)**
(d) Indicate the points you, as treasurer, might make if the members at the AGM of the club proposed to reduce the annual subscription by 20 per cent. **(15)**

(100 marks)

Solution to Q 4.4

(a) 30

Accumulated Fund at 1 January 2009

Assets		€		€
Clubhouse and Course		740,000	❶	
Bar Stock		3,800	❶	
Equipment		28,600	❶	
Bar Debtors		155	❶	
6% Government Investments		40,000	❷	
Interest on Investments		150	❷	
Levy Due		1,600	❸	
Bank Current Account		4,440	❸	818,745
Less Liabilities				
Life Membership		36,000	❷	
Creditors		2,450	❶	
Subscriptions Prepaid		1,800	❷	
Levy Reserve Fund		60,000	❷	
Wages Due		2,400	❶	
Loan		30,000	❷	
Loan Interest Due		900	❸	133,550
Accumulated Fund/Capital at 1 January 2009 ❶				685,195 ❷

(b) 35

Income and Expenditure Account for the Year Ended 31 December 2009

Income			€		€
Bar Profit	W 1		32,295	❻	
Investment Income	W 2		2,400	❸	
Subscriptions	W 3		180,000	❻	
Life Membership	W 4		4,000	❸	
Entrance Fees			17,000	❶	
Annual Sponsorship			33,000	❶	
Profit from Catering			2,190	❷	270,885
Less Expenditure					
Sundry Expenses (185,600 – 2,400)			183,200	❸	
Loan Interest			3,600	❷	
Depreciation – Equipment			14,620	❷	
Depreciation – Clubhouse and Courts			14,800	❷	
Coaching Lessons			4,650	❶	220,870
Surplus of Income over Expenditure for Year					50,015 ❸

(c) `20`

Balance Sheet as at 31/12/2009

	Cost €	Dep to date €	NBV €
Fixed Assets			
Clubhouse and Courts	740,000 ❶	14,800 ❶	725,200
Equipment	73,100 ❷	14,620 ❶	58,480
	813,100	29,420	783,680
Investments			
6% Government Investments		40,000 ❶	
Building Society		70,000 ❶	110,000
			893,680
Current Assets			
Bar Stock		4,300 ❶	
Bar Debtors		110 ❶	
Investment Income Due		1,100 ❸	
Bank		5,190 ❶	
		10,700	
Less Creditors: Amounts Falling Due within One Year			
Subscriptions Prepaid	2,400 ❶		
Bar Creditors	2,770 ❶	5,170	
Working Capital			5,530
Total Net Assets			899,210
Financed by			
Creditors: Amounts Falling Due after More than One Year			
Life Membership			44,000 ❷
Levy Reserve Fund			120,000 ❷
Accumulated Fund			
Balance at 1 January 2009		685,195 ❶	
Add Excess of Income for Year		50,015	735,210
Capital Employed			899,210

(d) `15`

A reduction in subscriptions of 20 per cent for 2010 would involve a reduction in club income of €36,000. ❻

Although the club is financially sound as it has €5,190 in the bank, €70,000 in the building society, investments worth €40,000 and has paid off a loan of €30,000, these funds are set aside for future capital expenditure. ❸

The club's surplus of income for the year 2009 of €50,015 would seem to indicate that the club is capable of bearing a reduction of 20 per cent. However, almost all of this surplus is provided by entrance fees of €17,000 and sponsorship of €33,000 and this income cannot be guaranted in future years. ❸

It can be argued that a reduction in membership fees could attract more members and thus bring in entrance fees as well as increased bar profit. However, it would *not* be prudent to reduce subscription fees at present and instead it would be advisable to retain the present level of fees and use these fees to provide improved facilities for the members and thus attract more members. ❸

Workings

1   Bar Profit – Bar Trading Account for Year Ended 31/12/2009

	€	€
Sales (112,660 – 155 + 110)		112,615
Less Cost of Goods Sold		
Stock at 1 January 2009	3,800	
Add Purchases (80,500 + 2,770 – 2,450)	80,820	
Less Stock 31 December 2009	(4,300)	80,320
Bar Profit		32,295

2   Investment Income

	€	
Income Received	1,450	
Less Income Due 1/1/2009	(150)	
Add Income Due 31/12/2009	1,100	
Income and Expenditure Account		2,400

3   Subscriptions

	€	
Subscriptions Received	254,200	
Add Subscriptions Prepaid at 1/1/2009	1,800	
Less Subscriptions Prepaid at 31/12/2009	(2,400)	
Less Levy for 2009	(60,000)	
Less Levy for 2008	(1,600)	
Less Two Life Memberships	(12,000)	
Income and Expenditure Account		180,000

4   Life Membership 1/1/2009

Life Membership 1/1/2009	36,000	
Add Membership Received	12,000	
Less Amount Transferred to I & E Account	(4,000)	
Balance 31/12/2009		44,000

5   Profit on Catering – Catering Receipts

Profit on Catering – Catering Receipts	6,650	
Catering Costs	4,460	
Income and Expenditure Account		2,190

Chapter **5**
Service Firms

Questions on this topic may appear in section 1 or section 2 of the examination paper.

The method is the same as with club accounts.

Enter all the figures as they come up, but do not try to complete any section of the question until you come to the end.

The unique point in these questions is that accumulated depreciation on all the fixed assets must be calculated. Sometimes this information is only disclosed at the very end of the question.

In the longer version of the questions, expenses will have to be allocated between the main profit and loss account and the subsidiary account – usually a health shop.

You will be asked to complete four sections:

1. Calculate the company's reserves.
2. Prepare a health shop account.
3. Prepare a profit and loss account.
4. Prepare a balance sheet.

These should be laid out blank on four separate pages. Make sure to show all workings.

Service Firm

Included in the assets and liabilities of the Looking Good Health Centre on 1/1/2008 were the following: buildings and grounds at cost €850,000; equipment at cost €80,000; furniture at cost €30,000; stock of health food €1,800; stock of heating oil €700; contract cleaning prepaid €400; creditors for supplies €2,100; clients' fees paid in advance €6,000; investments €100,000; authorised capital €950,000; issued capital €650,000.

All fixed assets have two years' accumulated depreciation on 1/1/2008.

Receipts and Payments Account for the Year Ending 31/12/2008

Receipts	€	Payments	€
Current A/C 1/1/2008	8,600	Wages and Salaries	90,150
Clients' Fees	251,500	Insurance	6,300
Interest	2,500	Light and Heat	3,200
Shop Receipts	72,400	Purchases – Shop	39,500
		Purchases – Supplies	27,800
		Laundry	3,600
		New Extension 1/1/2008	50,000
		Contract Cleaning	2,900
		Telephone and Postage	1,900
		Equipment 1/1/2008	18,000
		Repayment of €70,000 Loan on	
		30/6/2008 with 18 Months' Interest	76,000
		Balance	15,650
	335,000		335,000

You are given the following additional information:
1. Closing stock: shop €1,900; heating oil €400.
2. Electricity due 31/12/2008 €300.
3. Contract cleaning prepaid €500.
4. Clients' fees prepaid €3,000. Fees in arrears €2,000.
5. Wages and salaries include €18,000 paid to the receptionist who also runs the shop. It is estimated that 50 per cent of this salary and €300 of the light and heat, €500 of the insurance and €400 of the telephone is attributable to the shop.
6. The health centre revalued the buildings and grounds at €950,000 on 31/12/2008.
7. Depreciation is to be provided as follows:
   Buildings – 2 per cent of cost for a full year.
   Equipment – 20 per cent of cost per annum.
   Furniture – 20 per cent of cost per annum.
8. Creditors for supplies €1,700.

Prepare all the accounts.

Looking Good Health Centre

Reserves at 1/1/2008	Dr €	Cr €
Buildings and Grounds	850,000	
Acc Depn.: Buildings		34,000
Equipment	80,000	
Acc Depn.: Equipment		32,000
Furniture	30,000	
Acc Depn.: Furniture		12,000
Stock: Health Food	1,800	
Stock: Heating Oil	700	
Contract Cleaning Prepaid	400	
Creditors for Supplies		2,100
Clients' Fees in Advance		6,000
Investments	100,000	
Share Capital (950,000)		650,000
Bank	8,600	
Loan		70,000
Interest		4,000
Reserves at 1/1/2008		261,400
	1,071,500	1,071,500

Health Shop Profit and Loss Account for the Year Ending 31/12/2008

	€	€
Sales		72,400
Less Cost of Sales		
Opening Stock	1,800	
Purchases	39,500	
	41,300	
Less Closing Stock	1,900	39,400
Gross Profit		33,000
Less Expenses		
Wages	9,000	
Light and Heat	300	
Insurance	500	
Telephone	200	10,200
Net Profit		22,800

Looking Good Health Centre
Profit and Loss Account for the Year Ending 31/12/2008

	€	€	
Income			
Clients' Fees	6000 + 251,500 – 3,000 + 2,000	256,500	
Interest	2500	2,500	
Profit from Shop		22,800	
			281,800
Less Expenditure			
Light, Heat and Fuel	3200 + 700 – 400 + 300 – 300	3,500	
Contract Cleaning	400 + 2,900 – 500	2,800	
Supplies	– 2,100 + 27,800 + 1,700	27,400	
Wages	90,150 – 9,000	81,150	
Insurance	6,300 – 500	5,800	
Laundry	3,600	3,600	
Telephone & Postage	1,900 – 400	1,500	
Interest	**Note 4**	2,000	
Depreciation:	Buildings **Note 1**	18,000	
	Equipment **Note 2**	19,600	
	Furniture **Note 3**	6,000	
			171,350
Net Profit			110,450
Plus Reserves 1/1/2008			261,400
Profit and Loss 31/12/2008			371,850

Note 1.	Buildings	850,000	(34,000)	
	Extension	50,000		
	× 2%	900,000	(18,000)	
	Revaluation	50,000	52,000	102,000
		950,000	—	
Note 2.	Equipment	80,000	(32,000)	
	Addition	18,000		
	× 20%	98,000	(19,600)	
			(51,600)	
Note 3.	Furniture	30,000	(12,000)	
	× 20%		(6,000)	
		30,000	(18,000)	
Note 4.	Loan Amount Repaid		76,000	
	Loan Amount Borrowed		70,000	
	Interest for 18 Months		6,000	
	Interest for 6 Months (P&L)		2,000	
	Interest for 12 Months Reserves 1/1		4,000	

Looking Good Health Centre
Balance Sheet as at 31/12/2008

	€	€	€
Fixed Assets			
Buildings and Grounds	950,000	–	950,000
Equipment	98,000	51,600	46,400
Furniture	30,000	18,000	12,000
	1,078,000	69,600	1,008,400
Investments			100,000
			1,108,400
Current Assets			
Bank	15,650		
Stock: Health Shop	1,900		
Heating Oil	400		
Cleaning Prepaid	500		
Clients' Fees Due	2,000		
		20,450	
Less Creditors: Amounts Falling Due within One Year			
Electricity Due	300		
Clients' Fees Prepaid	3,000		
Creditors for Supplies	1,700		
		5,000	
			15,450
Net Current Assets			1,123,850
Financed by	Auth.	Issued	
Share Capital and Reserves			
Ordinary Shares	950,000	650,000	650,000
Revaluation Reserve **Note 1**			102,000
Profit and Loss Balance			371,850
			1,123,850

Question 5.1

Included in the assets and liabilities of the Slimline Health Centre Ltd on 1/1/2008 were the following: buildings and grounds at cost €520,000; equipment at cost €90,000; furniture at cost €25,000; stock of health food for sale €1,500; heating oil €1,660; contract cleaning prepaid €300; creditors for supplies to health centre €1,450; clients' fees paid in advance €5,500, investments €80,000; authorised capital €450,000; issued capital €320,000;

All fixed assets have three years' accumulated depreciation on 1/1/2008.

Receipts and Payments Account of Slimline Health Centre Ltd for the Year Ended 31/12/2008

Receipts	€	Payments	€
Current A/C Balance	7,560	Wages and Salaries	88,240
Client's Fees	262,600	Insurance	6,300
Interest	2,160	Light and Heat	2,900
Shop Receipts	67,000	Purchases – Shop	41,300
Balance	9,500	Purchases – Supplies	38,600
		Laundry	4,100
		New Extension 1/1/2008	80,000
		Contract Cleaning	2,700
		Telephone and Postage	1,880
		Equipment	16,000
		Repayment of €60,000 Loan	
		on 1/6/2008 with 17 Months' Interest	66,800
	€348,820		€348,820

You are given the following additional information and instructions:

1. Closing stock at 31/12/2008: shop €1,800; heating oil €360; electricity due 31/12/2008 €290.
2. Cleaning is done by contract payable monthly in advance and includes a payment of €400 for January 2009.
3. Clients' fees include fees for 2009 of €4,000.
4. Clients' fees in arrears at 31/12/2008 €650.
5. Wages and salaries include €16,000 per annum paid to the receptionist who also runs the shop. It is estimated that 60 per cent of this salary and €220 of the light and heat, €600 of the insurance and €360 of the telephone is attributable to the shop.
6. Slimline Health Centre Ltd decided to revalue buildings and grounds at €700,000 on 31/12/2008.
7. Depreciation to be provided as follows:
   Buildings – 2 per cent of cost for a full year.
   Equipment – 20 per cent of cost per annum.
   Furniture – 20 per cent of cost per annum.
8. Creditors for supplies to health centre at 31/12/2008 €1,600.

You are required to:

(a) Calculate the company's reserves on 1/1/2008. **(20)**
(b) Calculate the profit/loss from the health shop for the year ended 31/12/2008. **(12)**
(c) Prepare a profit and loss account for the year ended 31/12/2008. **(36)**
(d) Prepare a balance sheet on 31/12/2008. **(32)**

(100 marks)

Solution to Q 5.1

(a)   **20**

Statement of Capital and Reserves on 1/1/2008

Assets		€		€
Buildings and Grounds	(520,000 – 31,200)	488,800	❷	
Equipment	(90,000 – 54,000)	36,000	❷	
Furniture	(25,000 – 15,000)	10,000	❷	
Investment		80,000	❶	
Stock – Health Food for Resale		1,500	❶	
Stock – Oil		660	❶	
Contract Cleaning Prepaid		300	❶	
Cash at Bank		7,560	❶	624,820
Less Liabilities				
Creditors for Supplies		1,450	❶	
Customers' Advance Deposits		5,500	❶	
Loan		60,000	❷	
Interest on Loan	(12 months @ €400 per month)	4,800	❷	
Issued Capital		320,000	❶	391,750
Reserves				233,070 ❷

(b)   **12**

Health Shop Profit and Loss Account for Year Ended 31/12/2008

		€		€
Shop Receipts – Sales				67,000 ❷
Less Expenses				
Cost of Goods Sold	(1,500 + 41,300 – 1,800)	41,000	❺	
Light and Heat		220	❶	
Insurance		600	❶	
Telephone		360	❶	
Wages and Salaries	(60% of 16,000)	9,600	❷	51,780
Contribution from Health Shop				15,220

(c)   **36**

Profit and Loss Account for Year Ended 31/12/2008

Income			€		€
Interest Received			2,160	❶	
Profit on Health Shop			15,220	❶	
Customers' Fees		W 1	264,750	❹	282,130
Less Expenses					
Wages and Salaries	(88,240 – 9,600)		78,640	❷	
Insurance	(6,300 – 600)		5,700	❶	
Light and Heat		W 2	3,270	❺	
Purchases – Supplies		W 3	38,750	❸	

Profit and Loss Account for Year Ended 31/12/2008 (Continued)

Loan Interest	W 4	2,000 ❸		
Laundry		4,100 ❶		
Postage and Telephone		1,520 ❶		
Depreciation – Buildings	W 5	12,000 ❶		
– Equipment		21,200 ❶		
– Furniture		5,000 ❶		
Contract Cleaning	W 6	2,600 ❸	174,780	
Net Profit for Year			107,350 ❼	
Add Reserve 1/1/2008			233,070 ❶	
Profit and Loss Balance 31/12/2008			340,420	

(d)

36

Balance Sheet as at 31/12/2008

Fixed Assets	Cost €	Depreciation €	Net €
Buildings and Grounds	700,000 ❶		700,000
Equipment (90,000 + 16,000)	106,000 ❷	75,200 ❷	30,800
Furniture	25,000 ❷	20,000 ❷	5,000
	692,000	107,600	735,800
Investments			80,000 ❷
			815,800
Current Assets			
Closing Stock– Shop Goods	1,800 ❷		
– Oil	360 ❷		
Cleaning Prepaid	400 ❷		
Customers' Fees Due	650 ❷	3,210	
Less Creditors: Amounts Falling Due within One Year			
Bank Overdraft	9,500 ❷		
Electricity Due	290 ❷		
Customers' Advance Deposits	4,000 ❷		
Creditors for Supplies	1,600 ❷	(15,390)	(12,180)
			803,620

Financed by			
Share Capital and Reserves	**Authorised**	**Issued**	
Ordinary Shares	450,000 ❶	320,000 ❶	
Revaluation Reserve W 7		143,200 ❸	
Profit and Loss Balance		340,420	803,620
			803,620

Workings

1	**Customers' Fees** – Amount Received	262,600	
	Add Advance Deposits	5,500	
	Add Fees Due	650	
	Less Fees Prepaid 31/12/2008	(4,000)	264,750
2	**Light and Heat** – Amount Paid	2,900	
	Add Stock – Heating Oil 1/1/2008	660	
	Add Electricity Due 31/12/2008	290	
	Less Stock – Heating Oil 1/1/2008	(360)	
	Less Charge to Shop	(220)	3,270
3	**Purchases** (38,600 + 1,600 – 1,450)		38,750
4	**Loan Interest** – Paid	6,800	
	Less Interest Due 1/1/2008 for 1 year @ €400 per month	4,800	2,000
5	**Depreciation** – Buildings and Grounds 2% × (520,000 + 80,000)		12,000
	– Equipment 20% × (90,000 + 16,000)		21,200
	– Furniture 20% × (25,000)		5,000
6	**Contract Cleaning** – Amount Paid	2,700	
	Add Amount Prepaid 1/1/2008	300	
	Less Amount 31/12/2008	(400)	2,600
7	**Revaluation Reserve**		
	Buildings (700,000 – 600,000 including extension)	100,000	
	Depreciation (31,200 + 12,000)	43,200	143,200

Chapter **6**

Correction of Errors and Suspense Accounts

Correction of errors and suspense accounts are regarded as the most difficult topic on the course. A good knowledge of basic bookkeeping is essential. All the questions require very careful reading and should never be rushed. You should use T accounts to record what actually happened and what should have been entered, and you should then compare this to what has been entered. The real key to success is plenty of practice, but the following basic hints will be helpful.

1. When doing the journal entries, never just enter a single entry. Always complete the double entry.
2. Always write the narration under each entry.
3. As you go down through the journal entries, indicate beside each whether it is to go into the profit and loss account or the balance sheet.
4. In writing up the suspense account, simply follow your own instructions, i.e. where you indicated debit in the journal entry, do the same in the suspense and likewise with the credits.
5. In amending the profit and loss account, the debit items in the journal will be minuses and the credit items will be pluses.
6. In amending the balance sheet, debits on assets will be pluses, debits on liabilities minuses and vice versa with credits. Where you have, for example, a debit with a person's name, determine whether you are increasing a debtor or decreasing a creditor.

Question 6.1
The trial balance of J. Nolan, a clothes shop owner, failed to agree, and the difference was placed in the suspense account. The following balance sheet was then prepared.

Balance Sheet at 31 December 2007

	(€)	(€)	(€)
Fixed Assets			
Premises		80,000	
Furniture and Equipment		60,000	140,000
Current Assets			
Stock (including suspense)		35,000	
Debtors		12,000	
		47,000	
Less Current Liabilities			
Creditors	15,000		
Bank	7,000	22,000	
Net Current Assets			25,000
			165,000
Financed by			
Capital	125,000		
Plus Net Profit	60,000		
	185,000		
Less Drawings	20,000	165,000	

When the books were checked, the following errors were discovered.

1. A private debt of €1,200 owed to Nolan had been offset in full against a business debt of €1,400 owed by Nolan.
2. Furniture sold on credit to P. Dolan for €2,760 had been entered in both the sales account and the wrong side of Dolan's account as €2,670.
3. A credit note received from a creditor for €456 had been entered in the purchases returns account as €465 and on the wrong side of the creditor's account as €546.
4. Goods previously sold to a debtor for €760 had been returned and entered in the books as €670. Subsequently Nolan decided to apply a restocking charge of 10 per cent of this amount, and credited the debtor with €603. No other entry had been made in the books in respect of the restocking charge.
5. Payments from the business bank account of €300 for private repairs and €250 for equipment repairs had been credited to creditors and equipment, respectively.

You are required to:

(a) Journalise the necessary corrections.
(b) Show the suspense account.
(c) Prepare a statement showing the correct net profit.
(d) Prepare the corrected balance sheet.

Solution to Q 6.1(a)

J. Nolan

	Entry	Debit (€)	Credit (€)
Creditor (i)	b	1,400	
Capital	b		1,200
Discount Received	p		200

Private debt used to offset business debt of €1,400.

	Entry	Dr (€)	Cr (€)
Sales (ii)	p	2,670	
P. Dolan (debtor)	b	5,430	
Furniture	b		2,760
Suspense			5,340

Disposal of furniture entered as sales and on wrong side of Dolan's account.

	Entry	Dr (€)	Cr (€)
Creditors (iii)	b	1,002	
Purchases Returns	p	9	
Suspense			1,011

Wrong figure for credit note entered in accounts.

	Entry	Dr (€)	Cr (€)
Debtor (iv)	b	589	
Sales Returns	p	14	
Suspense			603

	Entry	Dr (€)	Cr (€)
Drawings (v)	b	300	
Equipment Repairs	p	250	
Creditors	b	300	
Equipment	b	250	
Suspense			1,100

Solution to Q 6.1(b)

Suspense Account

	(€)			(€)
Difference	8,054	(ii)	Sales, etc.	5,340
		(iii)	Creditors, etc.	1,011
		(iv)	Debtors, etc.	603
		(v)	Drawings, etc.	1,100
	8,054			8,054

Solution to Q 6.1(c)

Amended Net Profit

	Minus (€)	Plus (€)	(€)
Net Profit per Accounts			60,000
Discount Received		200	
Sales	(2,670)		
Purchases Returns	(9)		
Sales Returns	(14)		
Repairs	(250)		
	(2,943)	200	(2,743)
Corrected Profit			57,257

Solution to Q 6.1(d)

Corrected Balance Sheet

	(€)	(€)
Fixed Assets		
Premises	80,000	
Furniture and Equipment (60,000 – 2,760 + 250)	57,490	
		137,490
Current Assets		
Stock (35,000 – 8,054)	26,946	
Debtors (12,000 + 5,430 + 589)	18,019	
	44,965	
Less Current Liabilities		
Creditors (15,000 – 1,400 – 1,000 – 300) 12,298		
Bank 7,000	19,298	
Working Capital		25,667
		€163,157
Financed by		
Capital (125,000 + 1,200)		126,200
Add Net Profit		57,257
		183,457
Less Drawings (20,000 + 300)		(20,300)
		163,157

Question 6.2

The trial balance of R. Gillen, a grocer, failed to agree on 31 December 2008. The difference was entered in the suspense account, and the following balance sheet was prepared.

Balance Sheet at 31 December 2008

	(€)	(€)	(€
Fixed Assets			
Premises		165,000	
Fixtures and Equipment		33,000	198,000
Current Assets			
Stock		94,000	
Debtors		10,600	
Cash		400	
		105,000	
Less Current Liabilities			
Creditors (incorporating suspense)	72,000		
Bank	19,000	91,000	14,000
			212,000
Financed by			
Capital		176,000	
Add Net Profit		42,000	
		218,000	
Less Drawings		6,000	212,000
			212,000

On checking the books, the following errors were revealed.

1. Gillen sent a cheque for €520 in full settlement of a business debt of €560, and this was recorded correctly in the books. However, no entry has been made in the books of the subsequent dishonouring of this cheque and the payment on account of €300 cash by Gillen.
2. Repairs to premises €600 and repairs to private dwelling house €360 were paid out of the business bank account and credited to premises account.
3. A private debt of €390 owed by Gillen to a debtor of the business had been offset in full settlement against a business debt of €400 owed to Gillen. No entry had been made in the books.
4. Gillen had given a private car, valued at €4,500, to a creditor of the business to offset, in full, a debt of €4,700. This transaction had been treated in error as a credit purchase of stock for €4,500.
5. Goods previously sold to a debtor for €530 had been returned to Gillen and entered in the books in error as €350. Subsequently, Gillen decided to apply a restocking charge of 10 per cent to these returns, and he immediately credited the debtor with €315. No other entry was made in the books in respect of the restocking charge.

You are required to:

(a) Journalise the necessary corrections.
(b) Show the suspense account.
(c) Prepare a statement showing the correct net profit.
(d) Prepare the corrected balance sheet.

Solution to Q 6.2(a)

R. Gillen

	Dr (€)	Cr (€)
Bank Account	520	
Discount	40	
Creditors Account		260
Cash		300

Being the recording of a dishonoured cheque issued by Gillen and payment on account of €300 in cash.

	Dr (€)	Cr (€)
Premises Account	960	
Drawings Account	360	
Repairs Account	600	
Suspense Account		1,920

Being cancellation of entry in premises account and recording of payments in drawings and repairs accounts.

	Dr (€)	Cr (€)
Drawings/Capital Account	390	
Discount Account	10	
Debtors Account		400

Being a private debt of €400 owed by Gillen offset against a business debt of €530 owed to Gillen.

	Dr (€)	Cr (€)
Creditors Account	9,200	
Purchase Account		4,500
Discount Received Account		200
Capital Account		4,500

Being recording of €4,500 introduced as capital by Gillen and cancellation of incorrect entries in creditors and purchases accounts.

	Dr (€)	Cr (€)
Debtors Account	188	
Sales Returns Account	127	
Suspense Account		315

Being the recording of restock charge and correction of incorrect entry in sales returns and debtors accounts.

Solution to Q 6.2(b)

Suspense Account

	(€)		(€)
Difference	2,235	Premises	960
		Drawings	360
		Repairs	600
		Debtors	315
	2,235		2,235

Solution to Q 6.2(c)

Statement of Corrected Net Profit

	(€)	(€)
Net Profit as per Books		4,200
Add Purchases	4,500	
Discount Received	200	
		4,700
		46,700
Deduct Discount	40	
Repairs	600	
Discount	10	
Sales Returns	127	777
		45,923

Solution to Q 6.2(d)

Corrected Balance Sheet at 31 December 2008

	(€)	(€)	(€)
Fixed Assets			
Premises		165,960	
Fixtures and Equipment		33,000	198,960
Current Assets			
Stock		94,000	
Debtors		10,388	
Cash		100	
		104,488	
Less Current Liabilities			
Creditors	65,295		
Bank	18,480	83,775	20,713
			219,673
Financed by			
Capital		180,500	
Add Net Profit		45,923	
		226,423	
Less Drawings	6,750	219,673	
			219,673

Question 6.3

The trial balance of P. Morgan, a garage owner, failed to agree on 31/12/2007. The difference was placed in a suspense account and the following balance sheet was prepared.

Balance Sheet as at 31/12/2007

	(€)	(€)	(€)
Fixed Assets			
Premises		250,000	
Equipment		72,000	322,000
Current Assets			
Stock (including suspense)		86,000	
Debtors		36,000	
		122,000	
Less Creditors: Amounts Falling Due within One Year			
Creditors	54,000		
Bank	29,000	83,000	39,000
			361,000
Financed by			
Capital		320,000	
Add: Net Profit		56,000	
		376,000	
Less: Drawings		15,000	361,000

On checking the books, the following errors were discovered:

1. A motor car purchased on credit from P. Bourke for €13,000 had been entered on the incorrect side of Bourke's account and credited as €1,300 in the equipment account.
2. A private debt of €1,470 owed by Morgan had been offset in full against a business debt of €1,500 owed to the firm for car repairs previously carried out. No entry had been made in the books in respect of this offset.
3. Morgan had won a private holiday for two worth €9,000 in total. One ticket had been given to a salesperson as part payment of sales commission for the year, and the other to an advertising firm as payment in full of a debt of €4,750. No entry had been made in the books.
4. Morgan had returned a motor car previously purchased on credit from a supplier for €13,400 and had entered this transaction in the relevant ledger accounts as €14,300. However, a credit note subsequently arrived from the supplier in respect of the return showing a transport charge of €300 to cover the cost of the return. The only entry in respect of this credit note was a credit in the creditors account of €13,100.
5. Car parts previously sold on credit for €350 were returned to Morgan. These goods had been incorrectly entered as €35 on the credit of the equipment account and as €53 on the debit of the purchases account.

You are required to:

(a) Journalise the necessary corrections.
(b) Show the suspense account.
(c) Prepare a statement showing the correct net profit.
(d) Prepare a corrected balance sheet.

Solution to Q 6.3

P. Morgan, Garage Owner

Corrections	Dr €	Cr €
(i) Purchases	13,000	
Creditors		26,000
Equipment	1,300	
Suspense	11,700	
Purchase of car incorrectly recorded.		
(ii) Drawings	1,470	
Debtors		1,500
Discount Allowed	30	
Offset of private debt against business debt.		
(iii) Capital		9,000
Sales Commission	4,500	
Creditors	4,750	
Discount Received		250
Capital introduced in prizes used in business.		
(iv) Purchases Returns	1,200	
Creditors	11,900	
Suspense		13,100
Incorrect recording of credit and returns.		

(v) Sales Returns		350	
Debtors			350
Equipment		35	
Purchases			53
Suspense		18	
Car parts incorrectly entered.			

Suspense Account

(i) Equipment	11,700	(iv) Creditors	13,100
(v) Purchases	18		
Difference	1,382		
	13,100		13,100

Statement of Corrected Net Profit

			€
Net Profit per Accounts			56,000
Purchases	13,000		
Discount Allowed	30		
Sales Commission	4,500		
Discount Received		250	
Purchases Returns	1,200		
Sales Returns	350		
Purchases		53	
	19,080	303	18,777
Corrected Profit			37,223

Corrected Balance Sheet

Fixed Assets		€	€	€
Premises	250,000		250,000	
Equipment	72,000 + 1,300 + 35		73,335	
				323,335
Current Assets				
Stock	86,000 – 1,382	84,618		
Debtors	36,000 – 1,500 – 350	34,150		
			118,768	
Creditors: Amounts Falling Due within One Year				
Creditors	54,000 + 26,000 – 4,750 – 11,900	63,350		
Bank	29,000	29,000		
			92,350	
Net Current Assets				26,418
				349,753
Financed by				
Capital	320,000 + 9,000		329,000	
Plus Correct Profit			37,223	
			366,223	
Less Drawings	15,000 + 1,470		16,470	
				349,753

Question 6.4

The trial balance of S. Craddock, a furniture and carpet trader, failed to agree on 31/12/2009. The difference was entered in a suspense account and the following balance sheet was prepared.

Balance Sheet as at 31/12/2009

Fixed Assets	€	€
Premises	650,000	
Fixtures and Fittings	72,000	722,000
Current Assets		
Stock (including suspense)	88,600	
Debtors	33,300	
Cash	400	
	122,300	
Less: Current Liabilities		
Creditors	52,000	
Bank	27,000	79,000	43,300
		765,300
Financed by:		
Capital	730,000	
Add: Net Profit	63,300	
	793,300	
Less: Drawings	28,000	765,300
		765,300

On checking the books, the following errors were discovered:

1. Furniture, purchased on credit from J. Dolan for €16,500, had been entered as €6,500 on the incorrect side of Dolan's account and credited as €1,650 in the fixtures and fittings account.

2. A debtor who owed Craddock €900 sent a cheque for €750 and €100 in cash in full settlement. This was correctly recorded in the books. However, no entry had been made in the books of the subsequent dishonouring of this cheque or of the writing off of the remaining debt in full because of bankruptcy.

3. Bedside lockers previously sold on credit for €340 had been returned to Craddock. These goods had been incorrectly entered as €34 on the credit of the fixtures and fittings account and as €40 on the debit of the purchases account.

4. A private debt for €1,600, owed by Craddock, had been offset in full against a business debt of €1,700, owed to the firm for carpet repairs previously carried out. No entry had been made in the books in respect of this offset.

5. Craddock had returned furniture, previously purchased on credit from a supplier for €8,800, and had entered this transaction in the relevant ledger accounts incorrectly as €8,880. However, a credit note subsequently arrived from the supplier in respect of the return showing a transport charge of €200 to cover the cost of the return. The only entry made in respect to this credit note was a credit of €8,600 in the creditors account.

You are required to:

(a) Journalise the necessary corrections.   **(55)**
(b) Show the suspense account.   **(10)**
(c) Prepare a statement showing the correct net profit.   **(15)**
(d) Prepare a corrected balance sheet.   **(20)**

                                                                          (100 marks)

Solution to Q 6.4

(a)   55

Journal Entries

		Dr €	Cr €
(i)	Fixture and Fittings	1,650 ❸	
	Purchases	16,500 ❸	
	Creditors/Dolan		23,000 ❸
	Suspense	4,850 ❸	
	Being correction of incorrect recording of the purchase of furniture on credit.		
(ii)	Debtor Account	800 ❷	
	Bank Account		750 ❷
	Discount Allowed Disallowed		50 ❸
	Bad Debts Account	800 ❸	
	Debtor		800 ❷
	Being recording of dishonouring a cheque and recording of a bad debt.		
(iii)	Fixtures and Fittings	34 ❸	
	Purchases		40 ❸
	Suspense	6 ❸	
	Sales Returns	340 ❷	
	Debtors		340 ❷
	Being lockers returned by a customer entered incorrectly in the books.		
(iv)	Drawings	1,600 ❸	
	Discount Allowed	100 ❸	
	Debtors		1,700 ❸
	Being recording of an offset of a private debt owed by Craddock against a debt owed by a customer to the firm.		
(v)	Creditors	8,320 ❸	
	Suspense		8,600 ❸
	Purchases Returns	280 ❸	
	Being correction of incorrect recording of a credit not and recording of a charge for returns		

Penalty of 5 × 1 mark for each narrative omitted

(b)　　　　　　　　　　　　　　　　　　　　　　　　　　　　　　10

Suspense Account

		€			€
Purchases	(i)	4,850 ❸			
Purchases	(ii)	6 ❸			
*Original Difference		3,744 ❶	Creditors	(v)	8,600 ❸
		8,600			8,600

*Originally included in stock. The stock figure is now €88,600 – €3,744 = €84,856

(c)　　　　　　　　　　　　　　　　　　　　　　　　　　　　　　15

Statement of Correct Net Profit

	€	€
Original Net Profit as per Books		63,300 ❶
Add Discount Disallowed		50 ❷
Purchases		40 ❷
		63,390
Less Purchases	16,500 ❶	
Bad Debts	800 ❶	
Sales Returns	340 ❶	
Discount Allowed	100 ❶	
Purchases Returns	280 ❷	18,020
Correct Net Profit		45,370 ❹

(d)　　　　　　　　　　　　　　　　　　　　　　　　　　　　　　20

Balance Sheet as at 31/12/2009

Fixed Assets	€	€	€
Premises			650,000 ❶
Fixtures and Fittings (72,000 + 1,650 + 34)			73,684 ❸
			723,684
Current Assets			
Stock (88,600 – 3,744)		84,856 ❷	
Debtors (33,300 – 1,700 – 340)		31,260 ❸	
Cash		400 ❶	
		116,516	
Less Creditors: Amounts Falling Due within One Year			
Creditors (52,000 – 8,320 + 23,000)	66,680 ❸		
Bank (27,000 + 750)	27,750 ❷	94,430	22,086
			745,770 ❶
Financed by			
Capital		730,000 ❶	
+ Net Profit		45,370	
		775,370	
– Drawings (28,000 + 1,600)		29,600 ❷	745,770
			745,770 ❶

Chapter **7**
Tabular Statements

When answering questions regarding tabular statements, you should:

1. Think through each figure before you write it down.
2. Make sure each column agrees before you proceed to the next one.
3. Remember that you are applying knowledge you have already learned in another area.

Question 7.1

The financial position of Macken Ltd on 1 January 2007 is shown in the following balance sheet.

Balance Sheet at 1 January 2007

	Cost (€)	Accumulated Depreciation (€)	Net (€)
Fixed Assets			
Land and Buildings	175,000		175,000
Motor Vehicles	69,000	29,000	40,000
	24,000	29,000	215,000
Current Assets			
Stock		56,000	
Debtors		39,000	
Insurance Prepaid		3,000	
		98,000	
Less Current Liabilities			
Creditors	46,000		
Bank Overdraft	24,000		
Expenses Due	1,500	71,500	26,500
			241,500
Financed by			
Share Capital			
Authorised: 250,000 Ordinary Shares @ €1 Each			
Issued: 160,000 Ordinary Shares @ €1 Each			160,000
Reserves			
Share Premium		40,000	
Profit and Loss		41,500	81,500
			241,500

January:	Macken Ltd purchased an adjoining business which included buildings €85,000; stock €34,000; creditors €25,000. The purchase price was discharged by granting the seller 60,000 shares in Macken Ltd at a premium of 30 cent and €25,000 by cheque.
February:	The remaining shares were issued at a premium of 30 cent.
March:	Sold goods on credit for €72,000, which is cost price plus 20 per cent.
April:	Goods originally costing €500 were returned. Owing to their condition, a credit note for 20 per cent less than the selling price was issued.
May:	€500 was received from a debtor previously written off as bad. This represented 25 per cent of the original amount, and the debtor has undertaken to pay the balance in September.
June:	Paid a creditor a cheque for €600, having received a €30 discount.
September:	Received balance of previously written-off debt as agreed in May.
October:	Disposed of van for €9,000, which originally cost €17,000. The book value of the disposed van was €8,000. Acquired new van for €20,000. Depreciation for the year on all vehicles was €11,000.
November:	Purchased goods from supplier for a total cost price of €10,000. Paid half by cheque less 5 per cent discount. The other half was on credit.

You are required to:

Record on a tabular statement the effects each of these transactions had on the relevant asset and liability and to ascertain the total assets and liabilities on 31 December 2007.

Solution to Q 7.1

Macken Ltd Tabular Statement

	(€)	Jan (€)	Feb (€)	Mar (€)	Apr (€)	May (€)	June (€)	Sept (€)	Oct (€)	Nov (€)	Total (€)
Assets											
Land and Buildings	175,000	85,000									260,000
Motor Vehicle	69,000								3,000		72,000
Depreciation	(29,000)								(2,000)		(31,000)
Stock	56,000	34,000		(60,000)	*480					10,000	40,480
Debtors	39,000			72,000	(480)	1,500		(1,500)			110,520
Insurance Prepaid	3,000										3,000
Goodwill		9,000									9,000
	313,000	128,000	0	12,000	0	1,500	0	(1,500)	1,000	10,000	464,000
Creditors	46,000	25,000					(630)			5,000	75,370
Bank	24,000	25,000	(39,000)			(500)	600	(1,500)	11,000	4,750	24,350
Expenses Due	1,500										1,500
Share Capital	160,000	60,000	30,000								250,000
Shared Return	40,000	18,000	9,000								67,000
Profit and Loss	41,500					2,000	30		(10,000)	250	45,780
	313,000	128,000	0	12,000	0	1,500	0	(1,500)	1,000	10,000	464,000

Working

*W1

500 + 20% = €600

€600 − 20% = €480

Cost of Goods = €500

Value = €480

Use €480 as lower price – condition of goods.

Question 7.2

The financial position of CMW Ltd on 1 January 2007 is shown in the following balance sheet.

Balance Sheet at 1 January 2007

	Cost (€)	Depreciation (€)	Net (€)
Fixed Assets			
Land and Buildings	150,000		150,000
Vehicles	88,000	18,000	70,000
Goodwill	50,000		50,000
	288,000	18,000	270,000
Current Assets			
Stock		60,000	
Debtors		44,000	
		104,000	
Current Liabilities			
Creditors	37,000		
Bank	19,000		
Expenses Due	600	56,600	47,400
			317,400
Financed by			
Capital			
Authorised: 330,000 @ €1			
Issued: 220,000 @ €1			220,000
Reserves			
Share Premium		45,000	
Profit and Loss Balance		52,400	97,400
			317,400

The following transactions took place during 2007.

January: Goods were sold on credit at a mark-up of 20 per cent for €6,000.

February: CMW Ltd purchased an adjoining business made up of buildings €65,000 and stock €15,000. The purchase price was discharged by granting the seller 70,000 shares at a premium of 20 cent per share.

April: Received a cheque for €400 from a debtor and allowed a discount of €20.

June: Delivery van originally costing €15,000 was traded against a new van costing €24,000. An allowance of €9,500 was made for the old van. Depreciation to date on the old van was €6,500, and the depreciation for the year was €15,000.

August: Paid by cheque a creditor's account of €800 and received a 5 per cent discount.

September: Received first and final dividend of €80 from a debtor who was declared bankrupt. This amounted to 40 cent in the euro.

November: Goods previously sold for €120 were returned. Because of the delay in returning the goods, a credit note for only €110 was issued.

December: Received €50,000 from issue of remaining shares.

You are required to:

Record on a tabular statement the effect each of these transactions had on the relevant asset and liability and to ascertain the total assets and liabilities on 31 December 2007.

Solution to Q 7.2

CMW Ltd Tabular Statement

	€	Jan (€)	Feb (€)	Apr (€)	June (€)	Aug (€)	Sept (€)	Nov (€)	Dec (€)	Total (€)
Assets										
Land and Buildings	150,000		65,000							215,000
Vehicles	88,000				9,000					97,000
Depreciation	(18,000)				(8,500)					(26,500)
Goodwill	50,000		4,000							54,000
Stock	60,000	(5,000)	15,000					100		70,100
Debtors	44,000	6,000		(420)	500		(200)	(110)		49,270
	374,000	1,000	84,000	(420)	500	0	(200)	(10)	0	458,870
Liabilities										
Bank	19,000			(400)	14,500	760	(80)		(50,000)	(16,220)
Creditors	37,000					(800)				36,200
Expenses Due	600									600
Share Capital	220,000		70,000						40,000	330,000
Share Premium	45,000		14,000						10,000	69,000
Profit and Loss	52,300	1,000		(20)	500	40	(120)	(10)		39,290
	374,000	1,000	84,000	(420)	500	0	200	(10)	0	458,870

Question 7.3

The financial position of Casey Ltd on 1/1/2009 is shown in the following balance sheet.

Balance Sheet as at 1/1/2009

	Cost €	Dep. to Date €	Net €
Fixed Assets			
Land and Buildings	460,000	13,800	446,200
Delivery Vans	76,000	33,000	43,000
	536,000	46,800	489,200
Current Assets			
Stock	59,800		
Insurance Prepaid	1,500		
Debtors	61,700	123,000	
Less Creditors: Amount Falling Due within One Year			
Creditors	62,500		
Bank	10,100		
Wages Due	2,400	75,000	
Net Current Assets			48,000
			537,200
Financed by			
Capital and Reserves			
Authorised – 850,000 Ordinary Shares @ €1 Each			
Issued – 430,000 Ordinary Shares @ €1 Each		430,000	
Share Premium		40,000	
Profit and Loss Balance		67,200	
		537,200	

The following transactions took place during 2009.

Jan: Casey Ltd decided to revalue the land and buildings at €580,000 on 1/1/2009, which includes land now valued at €100,000.

Feb: On 1/2/2009 Casey Ltd bought an adjoining business which included buildings €360,000, delivery vans €58,000, stock €25,000 and creditors €33,000. The purchase price was discharged by granting the seller 400,000 shares in Casey Ltd at a premium of 20c per share.

March: Goods previously sold by Casey Ltd for €1,800 were returned. The selling price of these goods was cost plus 20 per cent. Owing to the delay in returning these goods, a credit note was issued showing a deduction of 10 per cent of invoice price as a restocking charge.

April: A delivery van which cost €20,000 was traded in against a new van costing €36,000. An allowance of €12,500 was made for the old van. Depreciation to date on the old van was €6,600.

May: Received a bank statement on 31 May showing a direct debit of €4,800 to cover fire insurance for year ended 31/5/2010.

July: A payment of €720 was received from a debtor whose debt had been previously written off and who now wishes to trade with Casey Ltd again. This represents 60 per cent of the original debt and the debtor had undertaken to pay the remainder of the debt in January 2010.

Dec: The buildings depreciation charge for the year to be 2 per cent of book value. The depreciation charge to be calculated from date of valuation and date of purchase. The total depreciation charge on delivery vans for the year was €22,000.

You are required to:

Record on a tabular statement the effect each of the above transactions had on the relevant asset and liability and ascertain the total assets and liabilities on 31/12/2009.

(60 marks)

Solution to Q 7.3

60

	1/1/2009 €	January €	February €	March €	April €	May €	July €	December €	Total €
Assets									
Land and Buildings	460,000	120,000 ②	360,000 ②						940,000
Accumulated Depreciation	(13,800)	(13,800) ②						(16,200) ②	(16,200)
Delivery Vans	76,000		58,000 ②		16,000 ②			(22,000) ①	150,000
Accumulated Depreciation	(33,000)				6,600 ②				(48,400)
Stock	59,800		25,000 ②	1,500 ③					86,300
Debtors	61,700			(1,620) ②			480 ③		60,560
Insurance A/C (Prepaid)	1,500					4,800 ③		(4,300) ①	2,000 ①
Goodwill			70,000 ③						70,000
TOTAL	**612,200**	**133,800**	**513,000**	**(120)**	**22,600**	**4,800**	**480**	**(42,500)**	**1,244,260** ①
Liabilities									
Share Capital	430,000		400,000 ②						830,000
Share Premium	40,000		80,000 ②						120,000
Revaluation Reserve		133,800 ③							133,800
Profit and Loss	67,200			(120) ①	(900) ③		1,200 ②	(42,500) ③	24,880 ②
Creditors	62,500		33,000 ②		23,500 ①				95,500
Wages due	2,400								2,400
Bank	10,100					4,800 ②	(720) ①		37,680 ①
TOTAL	**612,200**	**133,800**	**513,000**	**(120)**	**22,600**	**4,800**	**480**	**(42,500)**	**1,244,260** ①

Question 7.4

The financial position of Sadler Ltd on 1/1/2007 is shown in the following balance sheet.

Balance Sheet as at 1/1/2007

	Cost €	Dep. to Date €	Net €
Fixed Assets			
Land and Buildings	250,000	20,000	230,000
Equipment	40,000	15,000	25,000
	290,000	35,000	255,000
Current Assets			
Stock		65,000	
Debtors (less provision 5%)		76,000	
		141,000	
Less Creditors: Amount Falling Due within One Year			
Creditors	59,000		
Bank	21,000		
Expenses Due	2,000	82,000	
Net Current Assets			59,000
			314,000
Financed by:			
Capital and Reserves			
Authorised – 400,000 Ordinary Shares @ €1 Each			280,000
Issued – 280,000 Ordinary Shares @ €1 Each			12,000
Share Premium			22,000
Profit and Loss Balance			314,000

The following transactions took place during 2007.

Jan: Sadler Ltd bought an adjoining business which included buildings €110,000, debtors €15,000 and creditors €35,000. The purchase price was discharged by granting the seller 80,000 shares in Sadler Ltd at a premium 25c per share.

Feb: Sadler Ltd decided to revalue the land and buildings at €500,000, which includes land valued at €50,000 on 28/2/2007.

March: A payment of €900 was received from a debtor whose debt had been previously written off and who now wishes to trade with Sadler Ltd again. This represents 60 per cent of the original debt and the debtor had undertaken to pay the remainder of the debt by December 2007.

April: Goods previously sold for €720 were returned. The selling price of these goods was cost plus 20 per cent. Owing to the delay in returning these goods, a credit note was issued showing a deduction of 10 per cent of selling price as a restocking charge.

May: Received a bank statement on 31 May showing a direct debit of €1,800 to cover van insurance for year ended 31/3/2008 and a credit transfer received of €3,600 representing nine months' rent in advance from 1 May.

June: A creditor who was owed €400 by Sadler Ltd accepted equipment, the book value of which was €300, in full settlement of the debt. This equipment had cost €800.

July: An interim dividend of 6c per share was paid.

Oct: Received €50,000 from the issue of the remaining shares.

Nov: Received balance of previously written-off bad debt as agreed in March.

Dec: The buildings are to be depreciated at the rate of 2 per cent per annum of value at 28/2/2007.

You are required to:

Record on a tabular statement the effect each of the above transactions had on the relevant asset and liability and ascertain the total assets and liabilities on 31/12/2007.

(100 marks)

Solution to Q 7.4

	1/1/2007	Jan	Feb	Mar	April	May	June	July	Oct	Nov	Dec	31/12/2007
Land and Buildings	250,000	+10,000	+140,000									500,000
Depreciation	(20,000)	(−20,000) [2]									(7,500)	(7,500)
Equipment	40,000		[3]				−800 [3]				[4]	39,200
Depreciation	(15,000)				+600 [4]		(−500) [3]					(14,500)
Stock	65,000			+600			[3]		[3]			65,600
Debtors	80,000	+15,000 [2]		+600 [3]	(648) [4]					(600)		94,352
Bad Debts Provision	(4,000)									[3]		(4,000)
Goodwill	10,000	+10,000 [2]										10,000
Insurance A/C (prepaid)			+160,000 [2]	+600	(48)	+1,800 [3]	(300)		[3]	(600)	(1,350) [1]	450 [2]
	396,000	+135,000 [3]	+160,000	+600	(48)	+1,800	(300)			(600)	(8,850)	683,602
Ordinary Shares	280,000	+80,000 [3]							+40,000 [3]			400,000
Share Premium	12,000	+20,000							+10,000 [1]			42,000
Profit and Loss Balance	22,000	[3]		+1,500 [1]	(48) [1]		+100 [1]	(21,600) [1]	[3]		(7,500) [1] (1,350) [1] 3,200 [1]	(3,698) [5]
Creditors	59,000			(900) [3]		(3,600) [3]	(400) [3]		(50,000) [2]	(600)		93,600
Bank	21,000	+35,000 [3]				+1,800 [3]		+21,600 [3]	[2]	[2]		(10,700) [2]
Expenses Due									[2]	[2]		2,000
Revaluation Reserve	2,000		+160,000 [4]									160,000
Rent Receivable						+3,600 [3]				[1]	(3,200)	400 [2]
	396,000	+135,000	+160,000	+600	(48)	+1,800	(300)			(600)	(8,850)	683,602

Chapter 8
Depreciation and Revaluation

Questions on depreciation have always been popular with examiners and students. Questions on revaluation will also be easy to introduce into the examination. The key to success in both areas is to read through the questions carefully and to have a systematic approach.

1. It is vital that you show all your calculations, as most of the marks are allocated for these.
2. With depreciation questions, determine immediately whether the depreciation is to be calculated from cost price or the written-down value.
3. Calculate carefully the total amount of depreciation written off from date of purchase to the beginning of the question for each fixed asset separately, showing all your figures.
4. With mid-year acquisitions/disposals, slowly count off on your fingers the number of months the asset was in the company's possession during the year in question.

To answer revaluation questions, consider the following:

1. This will involve land and buildings. Always remember that land is not depreciated. When land is revalued, this will simply mean an increase in the asset value.
2. When buildings are revalued, the asset value is increased to the relevant amount and the accumulated depreciation is eliminated.
3. Further depreciation on the buildings is usually calculated based on the remaining useful life of the buildings.

Question 8.1
Mooney Transport Ltd prepares its final accounts to 31 December each year. The company's policy is to depreciate its vehicles at the rate of 20 per cent of book value per annum calculated from date of purchase to date of disposal and to accumulate this depreciation in the provision for depreciation account.

On 1 January 2007 the company owned the following vehicles:

> Vehicle No. 1 purchased on 1 January 2003 for €35,000.
> Vehicle No. 2 purchased on 1 January 2004 for €40,000.
> Vehicle No. 3 purchased on 1 January 2005 for €44,000.

On 1 October 2007 vehicle No. 1 was traded against a new vehicle costing €50,000. Vehicle No. 1 had had a tachograph, which cost €6,000, fitted on 1 January 2005. The trade-in allowance was €15,000.

On 1 May 2008 vehicle No. 2 was crashed and traded against a new vehicle costing €55,000. The company received compensation of €12,000 and the cheque paid for the new vehicle was €43,000.

Show, with workings, to the nearest euro for 2007 and 2008:

(a)   The vehicles account.
(b)   The provision for depreciation account.
(c)   The disposal account.

Solution to Q 8.1(a)

Vehicles Account

2007			(€)	2007		(€)
1 Jan	Balance B/D		125,000	1 Oct	Disposal	41,000
1 Oct	Trade-in	15,000				
	Bank	35,000	50,000	31 Dec	Balance C/D	134,000
			175,000			175,000
2008			(€)	2008		(€)
1 Jan	Balance B/D		134,000	1 May	Disposal	40,000
1 May	Trade-in	12,000				
	Bank	43,000	55,000	31 Dec	Balance C/D	149,000
			189,000			189,000

Solution to Q 8.1(b)

Provision for Depreciation Account

2007		(€)	2007		(€)
1 Oct	Disposal	25,550	1 Jan	Balance B/D	58,184
31 Dec	Balance C/D	47,588	31 Dec	Profit and Loss	14,954
		73,138			73,138
2008		(€)	2008		(€)
1 May	Disposal	24,707	1 Jan	Balance B/D	47,588
31 Dec	Balance C/D	45,311	31 Dec	Profit and Loss	22,430
		70,018			70,018
			2003		
			1 Jan	Balance B/D	45,311

Solution to Q 8.1(c)

Disposal Account

2007		(€)	2007		(€)
1 Oct	Vehicle 1 + Tachograph	41,000	1 Oct	Depreciation	25,550
				Trade-in	15,000
				Profit and Loss	450
		41,000			41,000
2008		(€)	2008		(€)
1 May	Vehicle	40,000	1 May	Depreciation	24,706
	Profit and Loss	8,706		Trade-in	12,000
				Insurance Company	12,000
		48,706			48,706

Workings
W1

Vehicle 1

	Cost/Net (€)	Depreciation (€)	Net (€)
2003	35,000	7,000	28,000
2004	28,000	5,600	22,400
2005	22,400	4,480	17,920
2006	17,920	3,584	14,336
		(i) 20,664	
2007	(iii) $14,336 \times 20\% \times 0.75$	2,150	
		(ii) 22,814	

W2

Vehicle 2

	Cost/Net (€)	Depreciation (€)	Net (€)
2004	40,000	8,000	32,000
2005	32,000	6,400	25,600
2006	25,600	5,120	20,480
		(i) 19,520	
2007	(iii) 20,480	4,096	
2008	(iv) $16,384 \times 20\% \times \frac{1}{3}$	1,091	
	Total to disposal		24,707

W3

Vehicle 3

	Cost/Net (€)	Depreciation (€)	Net (€)
2005	44,000	8,800	35,200
2006	35,200	7,040	28,160
		(i) 15,840	
2007	(iii) 28,160	5,632	
2008	(iv) 22,528	4,506	

W4

Tachograph

	Cost/Net (€)	Depreciation (€)	Net (€)
2005	6,000	1,200	4,800
2004	4,800	960	
		(i) 2,160	
2007	(iii) $3840 \times 20\% \times \frac{3}{4}$	576	
		(ii) 2,736	

W5

Vehicle 4

	Cost/Net (€)	Depreciation (€)	Net (€)
2007	(iii) 50,000		2,500
2008	(iv) 47,500	9,500	

W6

Vehicle 5

	Cost/Net (€)	Depreciation (€)	Net (€)
2008	(iv) $55,000 \times 20\% \times \frac{2}{3}$	7,333	

(i) Depreciation to 2007	(ii) Depreciation Disposal 1	(iii) Depreciation 2007	(iv) Depreciation 2008
20,664	22,814	2,150	1,091
19,520	2,736	4,096	4,506
15,840		5,632	9,500
2,160	25,550	576	7,333
		2,500	
58,184			22,430
		14,954	

Question 8.2

High 'n' Mighty Plc purchased property on 1 January 1997 consisting of land €150,000 and buildings €340,000. The estimated useful life of the buildings was fifty years with a nil residual value at the end of the period. Depreciation is provided on a straight-line basis.

On 1 January 2007 the property was revalued to €960,000. Of this revaluation €300,000 was attributed to the land. (Land is not depreciated.) The remaining useful life of the buildings at the date of revaluation is to be left unchanged at forty years.

Show:

(a) (i)   Land and buildings account.

(ii)   Provision for depreciation account.

(iii)   Revaluation reserve account all for 2007.

(b)   The relevant extracts from the final accounts relating to 2007.

Solution to Q 8.2(a) (i)

High 'n' Mighty Ltd
Land and Buildings Accounts

2007		(€)	2007		(€)
1 Jan	Balance B/D	490,000	31 Dec	Balance C/D	960,000
1 Jan	Revaluation Reserve	470,000			
		960,000			960,000
2008		**(€)**			
1 Jan	Balance B/D	960,000			

Solution to Q 8.2(a) (ii)

Provision for Depreciation Account

2007		(€)	2007		(€)
1 Jan	Revaluation Reserve	68,000	1 Jan	Balance C/D	68,000
31 Dec	Balance C/D	16,500	31 Dec	Profit and Loss	16,500
		84,500			84,500
			2008		**(€)**
			1 Jan	Balance C/D	16,500

Solution to Q 8.2(a) (iii)

Revaluation Reserve Account

2007		(€)	2007		(€)
31 Dec	Balance C/D	438,000	1 Jan	Land and Buildings	470,000
			1 Jan	Provision for Depreciation	68,000
		438,000			438,000
			2008		**(€)**
			1 Jan	Balance C/D	438,000

Solution to Q 8.2(b)

Balance Sheet at 31 December 2007

	(€)
Tangible Fixed Assets	
Land and Buildings	960,000
Less Depreciation	16,500
	943,000
Reserves	
Revaluation Reserve	438,000

Question 8.3

Moroney Ltd acquired property on 1 January 1998 consisting of land €200,000 and buildings €420,000. The estimated useful life of the buildings was forty years with a nil residual value at the end of the period. Depreciation is provided for on a straight-line basis.

On 1 January 2007 the property was revalued at €870,000. Of this, €350,000 was attributable to the land. Land is not depreciated. The remaining useful life of the buildings at the date of revaluation is to be left unchanged.

Show:

(a) The land and buildings account.
(b) The revaluation reserve account.
(c) The provision for depreciation account.

Solution to Q 8.3(a)

Moroney Ltd
Land and Buildings Account

2007		(€)	2007		(€)
1 Jan	Balance B/D	620,000	31 Dec	Balance C/D	870,000
1 Jan	Revaluation Reserve	250,000			
		870,000			870,000
2008		**(€)**			
1 Jan	Balance B/D	870,000			

Solution to Q 8.3(b)

Revaluation Reserve Account

2007		(€)	2007		(€)
31 Dec	Balance C/D	344,500	1 Jan	Provision for Depreciation	94,500
				Land and Buildings	250,000
		344,500			344,500
			2008		**(€)**
			1 Jan	Balance B/D	344,500

Solution to Q 8.3(c)

Provision for Depreciation Account

2007		(€)	2007		(€)
1 Jan	Revaluation Reserve	94,500	1 Jan	Balance B/D	94,500
31 Dec	Balance C/D	16,744	31 Dec	Profit and Loss	16,744
		111,274			111,274
			2008		(€)
			1 Jan	Balance B/D	16,744

Question 8.4

Midwest Transport Ltd prepares its final accounts to 31 December each year. The company's policy is to depreciate its vehicles at the rate of 20 per cent of book value per annum calculated from the date of purchase to the date of disposal and to accumulate this depreciation in the provision for depreciation account.

On 1 January 2006 Midwest Transport Ltd owned the following vehicles:

> Vehicle No. 1 purchased on 1 January 2003 for €40,000.
> Vehicle No. 2 purchased on 1 January 2004 for €39,000.
> Vehicle No. 3 purchased on 1 January 2005 for €42,000.

On 1 September 2006 Vehicle No. 1 was traded for €16,000 against a new vehicle costing €54,000. Vehicle No. 1 had had a tachograph fitted on 1 January 2004 costing €6,000. On 1 April 2007 Vehicle No. 3 was crashed and traded against a new vehicle costing €64,000. The company received compensation to the value of €8,000, and the cheque paid for the new vehicle which was €53,000.

You are required to show, with workings, to the nearest €1, for each of the two years 2006 and 2007:

(a) The vehicles account.
(b) The provision for depreciation account.
(c) The vehicles disposal account.

Solution to Q 8.4(a)

Midwest Transport Ltd
Vehicle Account

2006		(€)	2006		(€)
1 Jan	Balance	127,000	1 Sept	Disposal	46,000
1 Sept	Bank	54,000	31 Dec	Balance	135,000
		181,000			181,000
2007		(€)	2007		(€)
1 Jan	Balance	135,000	1 Apr	Disposal	42,000
1 Apr	Bank	64,000	31 Dec	Balance	157,000
		199,000			199,000

Solution to Q 8.4(b)

Provision for Depreciation Account

2006		Workings	(€)	2006		Workings	(€)
1 Sept	Disposal	W4	24,923	1 Jan	Balance	W1	44,120
31 Dec	Balance		37,752	31 Dec	Profit and Loss	W2	18,555
			62,675				62,675
2007		Workings	(€)	2007		Workings	(€)
1 Apr	Disposal	W5	16,464	1 Jan	Balance		37,752
31 Dec	Balance		46,306	31 Dec	Profit and Loss	W3	25,018
			62,770				62,770

Solution to Q 8.4(c)

Disposal Account

2006		(€)	2006		(€)
1 Sept	Vehicle No. 1	46,000	1 Sept	Provision Account	24,923
				Allowance	16,000
			31 Dec	Profit and Loss	5,077
		€46,000			€46,000
2007		(€)	2007		(€)
1 Apr	Vehicle No. 3	42,000	1 Apr	Provision Account	16,464
				Compensation	8,000
				Allowance	11,000
			31 Dec	Profit and Loss	6,536
		42,000			42,000

Workings

W1

Depreciation Balance 1 January 2006

Vehicle No.	(€)	(€)
1	21,680	
2	14,040	
3	8,400	44,120

W2

Depreciation for 2006

Vehicle No.	(€)	(€)
1	3,243	
2	4,992	
3	6,720	
4	3,600	18,555

W3

Depreciation for 2007

Vehicle No.	(€)	(€)
2	3,994	
3	1,344	
4	10,080	
5	9,600	25,018

W4

Total Depreciation on Vehicle No. 1

Depreciation	(€)	(€)
To 1 January 2006	21,680	
For 2006	3,243	24,923

W5

Total Depreciation on Vehicle No. 3

Depreciation	(€)	(€)
To 1 January 2006	8,400	
For 2006	6,720	
For 2007	1,344	16,464

Question 8.5

On 1 January 2003 Quinn Ltd purchased buildings for €120,000. These buildings were expected to have a useful life of fifty years. During the year ended 31 December 2005, €38,000 was paid to a building contractor for an extension to the buildings. The company's own employees worked on the extension, and they were paid wages amounting to €10,000 by the company for this work. On 14 July 2006 the building was partially damaged by a storm, and the company spent €2,000 on repairs. On 1 January 2007 the building was valued by professional valuers at €230,000, and it was agreed to incorporate this revaluation into the company's accounts. It is the company's policy to apply a full year's depreciation in the year of acquisition.

The expected useful life of the extension was to be the same as the remaining useful life of the original building.

You are required to prepare the relevant ledger accounts in respect of the above transactions for the years ended 31 December 2003 to 31 December 2007.

Solution to Q 8.5

Buildings Account

Year		(€)	Year		(€
2003			2003		
1 Jan	Bank	120,000	31 Dec	Balance C/D	120,000
2004			2004		
1 Jan	Balance B/D	120,000	31 Dec	Balance C/D	120,000
2005			2005		
1 Jan	Balance B/D	120,000	31 Dec	Balance C/D	168,000
	Bank	38,000			
	Wages	10,000			
		168,000			168,000
2006			2006		
1 Jan	Balance B/D	168,000	31 Dec	Balance C/D	168,000
2007			2007		
1 Jan	Balance B/D	168,000	31 Dec	Balance C/D	230,000
1 Jan	Revaluation Reserve	62,000			
		230,000			230,000

Buildings Accumulated Depreciation Account

Year		(€)	Year		(€
2003 31 Dec	Balance C/D	2,400	2003 31 Dec	Profit and Loss	2,400
2004 31 Dec	Balance C/D	4,800	2004 1 Jan	Balance B/D	2,400
			31 Dec	Profit and Loss	2,400
		4,800			4,800
2005 31 Dec	Balance C/D	8,300	2005 1 Jan	Balance B/D	4,800
			31 Dec	Profit and Loss	3,500
		8,300			8,300
2006 31 Dec	Balance C/D	11,800	2006 1 Jan	Balance B/D	8,300
			31 Dec	Profit and Loss	3,500
		11,800			11,800
2007 1 Jan	Revaluation Reserve	11,800	2007 1 Jan	Balance B/D	11,800
31 Dec	Balance C/D	5,000	31 Dec	Profit and Loss	5,000
		16,800			16,800

Building Repairs Account

2006		(€)	2006		(€)
1 Jan	Bank	2,000	31 Dec	Profit and Loss	2,000

Revaluation Reserve Account

2007		(€)	2007		€
31 Dec	Balance C/D	73,800	1 Jan	Buildings	62,000
			1 Jan	Building Accumulated Depreciation	11,800
		73,800			73,800

Chapter 9
Control Accounts

It is vital to know where the figures in the control accounts come from. The figures in the actual control account do not originate in the personal accounts; they are, in fact, taken from the nominal/general ledger accounts. In appearance the control is just the same as a personal account, and this causes confusion for some students. You must go back to basic book-keeping.

Let's go through the steps affecting debtors. The approach is then the same for creditors.

1. All credit sales are entered individually in the debtors accounts and the total is entered in the sales accounts.
2. This is the same for returns, payments, discounts, etc.
3. At the end of the period, the accounts are balanced, and a list of all the debtors is drawn up.
4. At this stage only the control account is drawn up. This is done as a check/control on the accuracy of the list of debtors.
5. We go back to the accounts in the nominal ledger and take out the various total figures for the debtors' items. These are then entered in the control account, which is balanced.
6. The balance on the control account is then compared with the total of the list of debtors.

In these questions, differences have arisen, and as in suspense accounts, we must reconcile the figures.

Question 9.1
On 31 December 2007 the creditors ledger control account of F. Short showed the following balances: €19,560 and €360. These did not agree with the list of balances because of the following.

1. An invoice received from K. Fahy for the purchase of goods at €900 less a trade discount of 30 per cent had been omitted from the books. (An item omitted will affect both the list of creditors and the control account, both of which should be increased.)
2. A credit note had been received from a supplier for €245. The only entry made in the books was €254 credited to the creditors account. (This is missing from the purchases returns account, and the figure in the creditors account is both incorrect and on the wrong side.)
3. A discount of €85 was received and omitted from the books. (An omission means both sides must be reduced.)
4. A cash purchase of €300 had been credited to a supplier's account. (Cash purchases do not belong here at all.)
5. A creditor had charged Short €75 interest on an overdue account. The only entry made in the books had been €57 credited in the creditors account. Following a complaint made by

Short, this charge was reduced to €40 but had not been entered in the books. (In interest account, enter €40, and reduce creditors account to €40.)

6. A credit note received from a supplier for €150 had been debited twice in the purchases returns account but omitted from the creditors account. (With purchases returns on the wrong side twice, a correction is then needed, and a reduction in creditors account must be entered.)

You are required to show:

(a) The adjusted creditors control account.
(b) The adjusted list of creditors.
(c) A journal entry to correct error 5.

Solution to Q 9.1(a)

F. Short
Adjusted Creditors Control Account

	(€)		(€)
Balance	360	Balance	19,560
Credit Note (2)	245	K. Fahy (1)	630
Discount Received (3)	85	Interest (5)	40
Balance C/D	20,050	Credit Note (6)	150
		Balance	360
	20,740		20,740
Balance C/D	360	Balance B/D	20,050

Solution to 9.1(b)

Adjusted List of Creditors

	Plus (€)	Minus (€)	(€)
Original Balance			20,111
K. Fahy (1)	630		
Credit Note (2)		(499)	
Discount Received (3)		(85)	
Cash Purchases (4)		(300)	
Interest (5)		(17)	
Credit Note (6)		(150)	
	+630	(1,051)	(421)
Corrected Balance			19,690

Solution to 9.1(c)

Journal Entry

	Dr (€)	Cr (€)
Creditors	17	
Interest	40	
Suspense		57

Interest omitted from interest account and inverted figure in creditors account.

Question 9.2

On 31 December 2006 the creditors ledger control account of P. Flynn showed the following balances: €26,940 and €140. These figures did not agree with the schedule (list) of creditors drawn up. An examination of the books revealed the following.

1. A credit note received for €340 had been entered in the books as €430.
2. Goods purchased on credit for €1,800 had been omitted from the books.
3. A discount received of €70 had been entered correctly. This had been subsequently disallowed, and the only entry made in the books had been €70 debited to the creditors account.
4. A cash purchase of €300 had been credited to the creditors account.
5. Bills payable accepted of €900 had been entered twice in the creditors account.
6. Flynn won a holiday voucher valued at €3,000. She gave half of this to a creditor as part-payment of her account. No entry had been made in the books.

You are required to show:

(a) The adjusted creditors control account.
(b) The adjusted list of creditors.

Solution to Q 9.2(a)

P. Flynn
Adjusted Creditors Control Account

	(€)		(€)
Balance	140	Balance	26,940
Holiday Voucher (6)	1,500	Credit Note (1)	90
Balance C/D	27,400	Purchases (2)	1,800
		Discount Received (3)	70
		Balance C/D	140
	29,040		29,040
Balance B/D	140	Balance B/D	27,400

Solution to Q 9.2(b)

Adjusted List of Creditors

	Plus (€)	Minus (€)	(€)
Original Balance			26,130
Credit Note (1)	90		
Purchases (2)	1,800		
Discount Received (3)	140		
Cash Purchases (4)		300	
Bills Payable (5)	900		
Holiday Voucher (6)		1,500	
	2,930	(1,800)	+1,130
Correct Balance			27,260

Question 9.3

On 31 December 2007 the debtors ledger control account of B. Cunningham showed balances of €25,560 and €80. These figures did not agree with the list of debtors drawn up on the same date. An examination of the books revealed the following.

1. An invoice sent to a customer for €750 had been entered in the day books as €570.
2. Interest of €85 had been charged to a customer but had been entered as €95 in the customer's account. Following a complaint by the customer, this had been reduced to €40 but had not been entered in the books.
3. Cash sales of €6,000 had been debited to a customer's account.
4. A discount of €30 was disallowed but had been treated as allowed in the customers account.
5. Sales returns of €400 had been omitted from the books.
6. A credit note for €150 was sent to a customer and entered in the books. The clerk forgot to deduct 10 per cent for a restocking charge and then sent and entered a second credit note for €135.

You are required to show:

(a) The adjusted debtors ledger control account.
(b) The adjusted schedule of debtors.

Solution to Q 9.3(a)

B. Cunningham
Adjusted Debtors Control Account

	(€)		(€)
Balance	25,560	Balance	80
Credit Note (6)	150		
Invoice (1)	180	Interest (2)	45
		Sales Returns (5)	400
		Balance C/D	25,365
	25,890		25,890
Balance B/D	25,365		

Solution to Q 9.3(b)

Adjusted List of Debtors

	Plus (€)	Minus (€)	(€)
Original Balance			31,430
Invoice (1)	180		
Interest (2)		(55)	
Cash Sales (3)		(6,000)	
Discount Disallowed (4)	60		
Sales Returns (5)		(400)	
Credit Note (6)	150		
	(390)	(6,455)	(6,065)
Correct Balance			25,365 (starting point)

Question 9.4

The debtors ledger control account of R. Gilmartin showed the following balances: €18,840 debit and €390 credit on 31 December 2007. These figures did not agree with the schedule (list) of debtors balances extracted on the same date. An examination of the books revealed the following.

1. Interest amounting to €64, charged to a customer's overdue account, had been entered as €46 in the interest account. Following a complaint by the customer, this charge was reduced to €36, but this reduction had not been entered in the books.
2. A discount to a customer of €15 was disallowed and had been treated as a discount allowed in the discount account.
3. Gilmartin had sent an invoice to a customer for €870. This had been entered in the appropriate day book as €780. However, when posting from this book to the ledger, no entry had been made in the personal account.
4. Bills payable of €750 had been entered on the debit side of a debtor's account.
5. A credit note was sent to a customer for €105. The only entry made in the books was €15 debited to the debtors account.
6. A customer's account had been credited with cash sales of €425.
7. A credit note for €160 was sent to a customer and entered in the books. However, the accounts clerk forgot to deduct a restocking charge of 10 per cent. When the error was realised, the clerk immediately sent another credit note for €144 and debited it to the debtors account.

You are required to show:

(a) The adjusted debtors ledger control account.
(b) The adjusted schedule of debtors showing the original balance.

Solution to Q 9.4(a)

Adjusted Debtors Ledger Control Account

	(€)		(€)
Balance	18,840	Balance	390
Discount Disallowed (2)	30	Interest (1)	10
Invoice Error (3)	90	Credit Note Omitted (5)	105
Credit Note Error (7)	16	Balance	18,861
Balance	390		
	€19,366		€19,366
Balance B/D	18,861	Balance B/D	390

Solution to Q 9.4(b)

Adjusted Schedule of Debtors

	(€)	(€)
Balance as per List		18,202
Add Invoice Omitted (3)	870	
Cash Sales (6)	425	1,295
		19,497
Deduct Interest (1)	28	
Bills Payable (4)	750	
Credit Note Error (6)	120	
Restocking Error (7)	128	1,026
Balance as per Adjusted Control Account		18,471

Question 9.5

On 31 December 2007 the creditors ledger control account of K. Cruise showed a credit balance of €19,955. This did not agree with the list of balances because of the following.

1. A discount disallowed of €80 had been omitted from the creditors account but adjusted properly in the discount account.
2. Interest charged by a creditor of €95 had been entered only in the creditors account and as €59.
3. Cruise returned goods of €320 to a supplier and entered this correctly in the books. However, a credit note arrived showing a deduction of 10 per cent for a restocking charge. The only entry for this was €280 debited to the creditors account.
4. Bills payable accepted of €1,100 had been omitted from the books.
5. Cruise received an invoice from a supplier for €675. This had been entered in the day book as €765.
6. Goods returned to P. Murphy of €450 had been entered in the books as €540.

You are required to show:

(a) The adjusted creditors control account
(b) The adjusted schedule of creditors.

Solution to Q 9.5(a)

K. Cruise
Adjusted Creditors Control Account

	(€)		(€)
Bills Payable (4)	1,100	Balance	19,955
Purchases (5)	90	Interest (2)	95
Balance	18,982	Purchases Returns (3)	32
		P. Murphy (6)	90
	20,172		20,172
		Balance C/D	18,982

Solution to Q 9.5(b)

Adjusted List of Creditors

	Plus (€)	Minus (€)	(€)
Balance per Accounts			19,654
Discount Disallowed (1)	80		
Interest (2)	36		
Purchases Returns (3)	312		
Bills Payable (4)		(1,100)	
Purchases (5)		(90)	
P. Murphy (6)	90		
	518	(1,190)	(672)
Correct Balance			18,982

Chapter 10
Cash Flow Statements

It is essential that you know the layout for cash flow statements. The layout used is provided in the solutions. Write it out blank first when answering these questions.

In Section 2, i.e. the 100-mark question, you may also be required to prepare an abridged profit and loss account, in which case, write out the layout first. You then start at the bottom figure, which is the retained profit at year end, and work backwards to find the operating profit figure. Remember to add back the figures that you would normally subtract.

In reconciling the operating profit to the net cash flow, the following always apply:

1. Always add back depreciation.
2. Profit on disposal is a minus and loss is a plus.
3. Increase in stock and debtors is a minus and decrease is a plus.
4. Increase in creditors is a plus and decrease is a minus.

In the cash flow statement itself, all the figures are payments or receipts. The interest figure is calculated as a percentage of the loan figure. The taxation and dividends are best calculated using T accounts. The rest of the figures are the difference between the two balance sheets.

In reconciling the net cash and net debt, start with the final figure in the cash flow statement, i.e. the increase/decrease in cash, and adjust this with the increase/decrease in debentures. The final figure is the net debt at the end of the year, which is checked by comparing the loans and cash at end of year.

There is usually a short theory question to finish, typically something like:

1. Why prepare cash flow statements?
2. What are non-cash items?
3. Why does an increase in profit not mean an increase in cash?

These are dealt with in the sample questions.

Question 10.1

The following are the balance sheets of McGarry Plc as at 31/12/2007 and 31/12/2008.

Balance Sheets as at

	31/12/2008		31/12/2007	
	€	€	€	€
Fixed Assets				
Cost	600,000		520,000	
Less Accumulated Depreciation	140,000		120,000	
	460,000		400,000	
Quoted Investments	150,000		80,000	
		610,000		480,000
Current Assets				
Stock	390,000		310,000	
Debtors	190,000		210,000	
	580,000		520,000	
Less Creditors Amounts Falling Due within One Year				
Trade Creditors	200,000		170,000	
Bank	20,000		35,000	
Taxation	40,000		25,000	
Dividends	70,000		60,000	
	330,000		290,000	
Net Current Assets		250,000		230,000
		860,000		710,000
Financed by				
Creditors: Amounts Falling Due after More Than One Year				
8% Debentures	240,000		200,000	
Capital and Reserves				
Ordinary Share	350,000		300,000	
Share Premium	10,000		—	
Profit and Loss Account	260,000		210,000	
		860,000		710,000

The following information is also available:

1. 50,000 shares were issued at €120 per share.
2. €40,000 debentures were issued on 30/6/2007.
3. Fixed assets which cost €60,000 and on which total depreciation of €40,000 had been provided were sold for €30,000.
4. Dividends due and taxation due on 31/12/2007 were paid. Interim dividends for 2008 of €50,000 were also paid.

You are required to:

(a) Prepare an abridged profit and loss account for the year ending 31/12/2008.
(b) Reconcile the operating profit to net cash inflow from operating activities.
(c) Prepare the cash flow statement for the year ending 31/12/2008.
(d) Explain why cash flow statements are prepared.

Solution to Q 10.1(a)

Abridged Profit and Loss Account for the Year Ending 31 December 2008

	€000	€000	
Operating Profit		227.6	last figure
Less Interest **Note 1**		(17.6)	
		210	
Less Taxation		(40)	
		170	
Less Dividends: Interim	(50)		
Proposed	(70)	(120)	
Retained Profit		50	
Balance 1/1/2008		210	2nd figure
Balance 31/12/2008		260	1st figure

Note 1

Interest	€200,000 × 8% × 6/12 = €8,000
	€240,000 × 8% × 6/12 = €9,600
Total	€17,600

Solution to Q 10.1(b)

Reconciliation of Operating Profit to Net Cash Inflow from Operating Activities

Operating Profit	227.6
Plus Depreciation	60
Less Profit on Disposal	(10)
Less Increase in Stock	(80)
Plus Decrease in Debtors	20
Plus Increase in Creditors	30
Net Cash Inflow from Operating Activities	247.6

Note: Net debt at 1/1/2008 = Debentures 200 + Bank 35
Net debt at 31/12/2008 = Debentures 240 + Bank 20

Notes

Fixed Asset Account

1/1	Balance	520		Disposal		60
	Bank cfs	140	31/12	Balance		600
		660				660

Accumulated Depreciation Account

	Disposal	40	1/1	Balance		120
31/12	Balance	140		Profit and Loss cfs		60
		180				180

Disposal Account

Fixed Assets	60	Acc. Depn.	40
Profit and Loss cfs	10	Bank cfs	30
	70		70

Theory

Why prepare cash flow statements?

1. Because they may be compulsory.
2. Because profits do not equal cash.
3. To find out what happened to cash during the year.
4. To help predict future cash flows.

What are non-cash items?

These are things that do not affect cash. These include depreciation, provisions for bad debts, either an increase or decrease and profits or losses on disposals.

Why does profit not always equal cash?

1. Goods may be sold on credit at a profit.
2. Non-cash items affect profit but not cash.
3. Acquisitions and disposals may affect cash but not profit.

Question 10.2

The following are the balance sheets of Experience Plc as at 31/12/2007 and 31/12/2006.

Balance Sheets as at

	31/12/2007		31/12/2006	
Fixed Assets	€	€	€	€
Cost	500,000		480,000	
Less Accumulated Depreciation	(120,000)	380,000	(110,000)	370,000
Current Assets				
Stock	369,000		310,000	
Debtors	181,000		118,000	
	550,000		428,000	
Less Creditors: Amounts Falling Due within One Year				
Trade Creditors	170,000		190,000	
Bank	10,000		34,000	
Taxation	38,000		29,000	
Dividends	52,000		65,000	
	270,000		318,000	
Net Current Assets		280,000		110,000
		660,000		480,000

Financed by		
Creditors: Amounts Falling Due after More than One Year		
10% Debentures	150,000	100,000
Capital and Reserves		
€1 Ordinary Shares	260,000	200,000
Share Premium	12,000	–
Profit and Loss Account	238,000	180,000
	660,000	480,000

The following information is also available:

1. 60,000 shares were issued at €1.20 per share.
2. Fixed assets, which cost €50,000 and on which total depreciation of €25,000 had been provided, were sold for €30,000.
3. €50,000 debentures were issued on 1/1/2007.
4. Dividends due and taxation due on 31/12/2006 were paid.

You are required to:

(a) Prepare an abridged profit and loss account to ascertain the operating profit for the year ending 31/12/2007. **(25)**
(b) Reconcile the operating profit to net cash inflow from operating activities. **(25)**
(c) Prepare the cash flow statement for Experience Plc for the year ended 31/12/2007. **(35)**
(d) Explain why cash flow statements are prepared. **(15)**

100 marks

Solution to Q 10.2(a)

25

Abridged Profit and Loss Account for the Year Ended 31/12/2007

	€	
Operating Profit	163,000	5
Interest Paid	(15,000)	4
Profit before Taxation	148,000	
Taxation	(38,000)	4
Profit after Taxation	110,000	
Proposed Dividends	(52,000)	
Retained Profits for the Year	58,000	3
Profit and Loss Balance 1/1/2007	180,000	
Profit and Loss Balance 31/12/2007	238,000	

Solution to Q 10.2(b)

25

Reconciliation of Operating Profit to Net Cash Flow from Operating Activities

			€
Operating Profit			163,000 ❸
Depreciation Charges for Year	W 1		35,000 ❺
Profit on Sale of Fixed Assets	W 2		(5,000) ❺
Increase in Stocks			(59,000) ❸
Increase in Debtors			(63,000) ❸
Decrease in Creditors			(20,000) ❸
Net Cash Inflow from Operating Activities			51,000 ❸

Solution to Q 10.2(c)

35

Cash Flow Statement of Plc for the Year Ended 31/12/2007

		€	€
Operating Activities			
Net Cash Inflow from Operating Activities			51,000 ❶
Returns on Investment and Servicing of Finance ❷			
Interest Paid		(15,000) ❷	
Dividends Paid		(65,000) ❸	(80,000)
Taxation ❷			
Corporation Tax Paid			(29,000) ❸
Investing Activities ❷			
Payments to Acquire Tangible Fixed Assets	W 3	(70,000) ❹	
Receipts from Sale of Fixed Assets		30,000 ❷	(40,000)
Net Cash Outflow before Financing ❶			(98,000)
Financing ❷			
Receipts from Issue of Debentures		50,000 ❸	
Receipts from Issue of Shares		60,000 ❸	
Receipts from Share Premium		12,000 ❸	122,000
Increase in Cash ❶			**24,000** ❶

Solution to Q 10.2(d)

15

3 × 5 marks (15)

- To show the cash inflows and outflows during the past year.
- To help predict future cash flows.
- To help financial planning.
- To provide information to assess liquidity.
- To show that profits do not equal cash.
- To comply with legal requirements.

Workings

1 Depreciation

Depreciation Provision at 31/12/2007	120,000
Less Depreciation Provision at 1/1/2007	110,000
Increase in Provision	10,000
Depreciation Transferred to Disposal	25,000
Depreciation for Year	35,000

2 Profit on Disposal of Fixed Assets

Net Book Value of Fixed Assets Sold (50,000 – 25,000)	25,000
Proceeds on Disposal	30,000
Profit on Disposal of Fixed Assets	5,000

3 Assets Purchased

Fixed Assets at the Beginning of the Year	480,000
Less Fixed Assets Sold during Year	50,000
	430,000
Add Fixed Assets Purchased during the Year	70,000
Fixed Assets at the End of the Year	500,000

Question 10.3

The following are the balance sheets of Creation Plc as at 31/12/2008 and 31/12/2009, together with an abridged profit and loss account for the year ended 31/12/2009.

Abridged Profit and Loss Account for the Year Ended 31/12/2009

		€
Operating Profit		150,600
Interest for Year		(10,600)
Profit before Taxation		140,000
Taxation for Year		(47,000)
Profit after Taxation		93,000
Dividends – Interim	23,000	
– Proposed	48,000	(71,000)
Retained Profits for the Year		22,000
Retained Profits on 1/12/2009		189,000
Retained Profits on 31/12/2009		211,000

Balance Sheets as at

	31/12/2009		31/12/2008	
	€	€	€	€
Fixed Assets				
Land and Buildings at Cost	800,000		725,000	
Less Accumulated Depreciation	(75,000)	725,000	(60,000)	665,000
Machinery at Cost	380,000		450,000	
Less Accumulated Depreciation	(190,000)	190,000	(170,000)	280,000
		915,000		945,000
Financial Assets				
Quoted Investments		120,000		90,000
Current Assets				
Stock		225,000		208,000
Debtors		212,000		184,000
Bank		–		12,000
Cash		3,000		1,000
		440,000		405,000
Less Creditors: Amounts Falling Due within One Year				
Trade Creditors	253,000		230,000	
Interest Due	1,400		–	
Taxation	51,000		44,000	
Dividends	48,000		37,000	
Bank	8,600		–	
	(362,000)		(311,000)	
Net Current Assets		78,000		94,000
		1,113,000		1,129,000
Financed by				
Creditors: Amounts Falling Due after More than One Year				
8% Debentues		50,000		160,000
Capital and Reserves				
€1 Ordinary Shares	840,000		780,000	
Share Premium	12,000		–	
Profit and Loss Account	211,000	1,063,000	189,000	969,000
		1,113,000		1,129,000

The following information is also available:

1. There were no disposals of buildings during the year, but new buildings were acquired.
2. There were no purchases of machinery during the year. Machinery was disposed of for €24,000.
3. Depreciation charged for the year on machinery in arriving at the operating profit was €55,000.

You are required to:

(a) Reconcile the operating profit to net cash inflow from operating activities. **(20)**

(b) Prepare the cash flow statement of Creation Plc for the year ended 31/12/2009. **(30)**

(c) Explain why profit does not always mean a corresponding increase in cash and list two non-cash items. **(10)**

(60 marks)

Solution to Q 10.4(a)

20

Reconcilliation of Operating Profit to Net Cash Flow from Operating Activities

			€	
Operating Profit			150,600	2
Depreciation Charges for Year	W 1		70,000	4
Loss on Sale of Machinery	W 2		11,000	6
Increase in Stocks			(17,000)	2
Increase in Stocks			(28,000)	2
Increase in Creditors			23,000	2
Net Cash Inflow from Operating Activities			209,600	2

Solution to Q 10.4(b)

30

Cash Flow Statement of Creation Plc for the Year Ended 31/12/2009

		€	
Operating Activities			
Net Cash Inflow from Operating Activities		209,600	1
Returns on Investment and Servicing of Finance 1			
Interest Paid		(9,200)	3
Taxation 1			
Corporation Tax Paid		(40,000)	3
Capital Expenditure and Financial Investment 1			
Investments	(30,000) 2		
Payments to Acquire Tangible Fixed Assets	(75,000) 2		
Receipts from Sale of Fixed Assets	24,000 2	(81,000)	
Equity Dividends Paid 1			
Dividends Paid during Year	W 3	(60,000)	4
Net Cash **Inflow** before Liquid Resources and Financing		19,400	
Financing			
Repayment of Debentures	(110,000) 2		
Receipts from Issue of Shares	60,000 1		
Receipts from Share Premium	12,000 1	(38,000)	
Decrease in Cash 2		**(18,600)**	
Reconciliation of Net Cash Flow to Movement in Net Debt			
Decrease in Cash during Period		(18,600)	1
Cash Used to Purchase Debentures		110,000	1
Change in Net Debt		91,400	
Net Debt at 1/1/2009		(147,000)	
Net Debt at 31/12/2009		555,600	1

Solution to Q 10.4(c) **10**

- Credit sales/purchases affect profit but do not affect cash.
- Non-cash losses and gains affect profit but not cash.
- Purchase and sale of fixed assets by cash affect cash but not profit.
- Introduction or withdrawal of capital in cash affects cash but not profit.
- Non-cash items – depreciation, provisions against losses, losses/profits from sale of assets.

Chapter 11
Published Accounts

The layout of these questions must be exactly followed. This should be written out in blank form first. The layout is as shown in the sample questions.

1 Profit and Loss Account

(a)   The title is profit and loss account.
(b)   The word 'turnover', not 'sales', is to be used.
(c)   Cost of sales is calculated separately and is shown as one figure.
(d)   Distribution and administrative expenses are shown each as one figure.
(e)   The dividends must be shown as paid and proposed.
(f)   The other figures are usually quite straightforward.

2 Balance Sheet

(a)   Fixed assets must be shown under intangible, tangible and financial.
(b)   Current assets must be listed in full.
(c)   Liabilities are shown under creditors due within one year and after more than one year.
(d)   The capital section is shown as usual.

3 Notes to the Accounts

There are a lot of marks for this section. The usual notes asked for are:

(a)   Accounting policy.
(b)   Operating profit.
(c)   Tangible fixed assets.
(d)   Dividends.

There is usually a fifth note required, which is often an explanation in simple English of what is asked. Learn them from the solutions. In the note on dividends, you are required to show the amount in cents per share and in total.

Theory

The theory questions are dealt with in Chapter 16. Some of them are shown with the solutions.

Question 11.1

Gayle Plc has an authorised capital of €800,000 divided into 600,000 ordinary shares at €1 each and 200,000 9 per cent preference shares at €1 each. The following trial balance was extracted from its books at 31/12/2009.

	€	€
Vehicles at cost	220,000	
Vehicles – Accumulated Dep on 1/1/2009		33,000
Investment Income		10,000
Buildings at Cost	700,000	
Buildings – Accumulated Dep on 1/1/2009		42,000
Debtors and Creditors	289,000	163,000
9% Investments	240,000	
Stock at 1/1/2009	73,000	
Patent at 1/1/2009	40,000	
Administration Expenses	172,000	
Purchases and Sales	1,150,000	1,880,000
Rental Income		60,000
8% Debentures 2008/2009		200,000
Distribution Costs	248,000	
Profit on Sale of Land		65,000
Bank	48,000	
VAT		71,000
Interim Dividends	24,000	
Profit and Loss at 1/1/2009		52,000
Issued Capital		
Ordinary Shares		400,000
Preference Shares		200,000
Provision for Bad Debts		27,000
Debenture Interest Paid	12,000	
Discount		13,000
	3,216,000	3,216,000

The following information is relevant:

1. Stock on 31/12/2009 is €96,000.
2. The patent was acquired on 1/1/2010 for €80,000. It is being amortised over eight years in equal instalments. The amortisation is to be included in cost of sales.
3. On 1/7/2009, the ordinary shareholders received an interim dividend of €15,000 and the preference shareholders received €9,000. The directors propose the payment of the preference dividend due and a final dividend on ordinary shares to bring that total dividend up to 7c per share.
4. Provide for debenture interest due, investment interest due, auditors' fees €9,500, directors' fees €50,000 and corporation tax €87,000.
5. Depreciation is to be provided for on buildings at a rate of 2 per cent straight line and is to be allocated 20 per cent on distribution costs and 80 per cent on administration expenses. There was no purchase or sale of buildings during the year. Vehicles are to be depreciated at the rate of 20 per cent of cost.

6. During the year, land adjacent to the company's premises, which had cost €80,000, was sold for €145,000. At the end of the year the company revalued its buildings at €900,000. The company wishes to incorporate this value in this year's accounts.
7. Included in administration expenses is the receipt of €12,000 for patent royalties.

You are required to:

(a) Prepare the published profit and loss account for the year 31/12/2009 and a balance sheet as at that date, in accordance with the Companies Acts and appropriate accounting standards, showing the following notes:
   1. Accounting policy note for tangible fixed assets and stock.
   2. Operating profit.
   3. Interest payable.
   4. Dividends.
   5. Tangible fixed assets. **(84)**
(b) State three items of information that must be included in a directors' report. **(9)**
(c) Explain the term 'exceptional item' and give an example. **(7)**

(100 marks)

Solution to Q 11.1(a)

Profit and Loss Account of Gayle Plc for Year Ended 31/12/2009

	€	
Turnover	1,880,000	❷
Cost of Sales	(1,137,000)	❹
Gross Profit	743,000	
Distribution Costs	(294,800)	❸
	448,200	
Administrative Expenses	(254,700)	❺
	193,500	
Other Operating Income	85,000	❸
Operating Profit ❶	278,500	
Investment Income	21,600	❷
Profit on Sale of Land	65,000	❷
	365,100	
Interest Payable	(16,000)	❸
Profit on Ordinary Activities before Tax	349,100	
Taxation	(87,000)	❷
	262,100	
Dividend Paid	(24,000) ❸	
Dividend Proposed	(22,000) ❸	(46,000)
	216,100	
Profit Brought Forward at 1/1/2009	52,000	❷
Profit Carried Forward at 31/12/2009	268,100	❶

Workings

Cost of Sales	73,000 + 1,150,000 + 10,000 – 96,000	=	1,137,000
Distribution Costs	248,000 + 2,800 + 44,000	=	294,800
Administrative Expenses	172,000 + 9,500 + 50,000 + 11,200 + 12,000	=	254,700
Other Operating Income	60,000 + 13,000 + 12,000	=	85,000
Debtors	289,000 – 27,000 +11,600	=	273,600

27

Balance Sheet of Gayle Plc as at 31/12/2009

			€
Fixed Assets			
Intangible Assets			30,000 ❷
Tangible Assets			1,043,000 ❷
Financial Assets			240,000 ❶
			1,313,000
Current Assets			
Stock	96,000 ❶		
Debtors	273,600 ❸		
Bank	48,000 ❶	417,600	
Creditors: Amounts Falling Due within One Year: ❶			
Trade Creditors	163,000 ❶		
Dividends Due	22,000 ❷		
Taxation	158,000 ❷		
Other Creditors	63,500 ❹		
		(406,500)	
Net Current Assets			11,100
Total Assets less Current Liabilities			1,324,100
Creditors: Amounts Falling Due after More than One Year			
8% Debentures			200,000 ❶
Capital and Reserves			
Issued Shares	600,000 ❷		
Revaluation Reserve	256,000 ❸		
Profit Carried Forward	268,100 ❶		
			1,124,000
			1,324,100

Notes to the Accounts

Accounting Policy Notes   **21**

1. **Tangible Fixed Assets** ❻

   Buildings were revalued at the end of 2009 and have been included in the accounts at their revalued amount. Vehicles are shown at cost. Depreciation is calculated in order to write off the value of the tangible assets over their estimated useful economic life, as follows:

- Buildings: 2 per cent per annum – straight line basis.
- Delivery vans: 20 per cent of cost.
- Stocks: Stocks are valued on a first in, first out basis at the lower of cost and net realisable value.

2. Operating Profit ❸
Operating profit is arrived at after charging:

Depreciation on Tangible Assets	58,000
Patent Amortised	10,000

3. Interest Payable ❷

Interest payable on debentures (repayable by 2013/2014)	16,000

4. Dividends ❹
Ordinary Dividends

Interim/Paid 3.75c per share	15,000	
Final Proposed 3.25c per share	13,000	28,000
Preference Dividends		
Interim/Paid 4.5c per share	9,000	
Final Proposed 4.5c per share	9,000	18,000

5. Tangible Fixed Assets ❻

	Land and Buildings	Vehicles	Total
1/1/2009	780,000	220,000	1,000,000
Disposal	(80,000)		(80,000)
Revaluation Surplus 31/12/2009	200,000		200,000
Value at 31/12/2009	900,000	220,000	1,120,000
Depreciation 1/1/2009	42,000	33,000	75,000
Depreciation Charge for Year	14,000	44,000	58,000
	56,000	77,000	133,000
Transfer on Revaluation	(56,000)		(56,000)
Depreciation 31/12/2009	Nil	77,000	77,000
Net Book Value 1/1/2009	738,000	187,000	925,000
Net Book Value 31/12/2009	900,000	143,000	1,043,000

Solution to Q 11.1(b)

Directors' Report (3 × 3 marks)   9

A directors' report must contain the following:

- The dividends recommended for payment.
- The amount to be transferred to reserves.
- A report of any changes in the nature of the company's business during the year.
- A fair review of the development of the business of the company during the year and of the position at the end of the year.
- The principal activities of the company and any changes therein.
- Details of any important events affecting the company since the end of the year.
- Any likely future developments in the business.
- An indication of activities in the field of research and development.
- Significant changes in fixed assets.

- Details of own shares purchased.
- A list of the company's subsidiaries and affiliates.
- Evaluation of company's compliance with its safety statement.
- Details of directors' shareholdings and dealings during the year.

Solution to Q 11.1(c)

Exceptional Item 9
This is a material item of significant size. It is a profit or loss that must be shown separately in the profit and loss account because of size. ❹
Example: Profit or loss on sale of fixed asset or large bad debt. ❸

Question 11.2
The following is the trial balance of Thompson Plc as at 31/12/2007.

	Dr €	Cr €
Fixed Asset Investments	300,000	
Patent at 1/1/2007	168,000	
Building – Cost at 1/1/2007	700,000	
Building – Accumulated Depreciation at 1/1/2007		48,000
Stock at 1/1/2007	650,000	
Debtors and Creditors	139,000	241,000
8% Debentures 2011/2012		400,000
Purchases and Sales	6,150,000	7,988,000
Distribution Costs	610,000	
Administration Expenses	742,000	
Rental Income		52,000
Provision for Bad Debts		23,000
Debenture Interest Paid	12,000	
Interim Dividends	24,000	
Profit on the Sale of Land		80,000
Bank	179,000	
VAT		82,000
Authorised and Issued Share Capital:		
Ordinary Shares @ €1 Each		400,000
7% Preference Shares @ €1 Each		300,000
Profit and Loss at 1/1/2007		60,000
	9,674,000	9,674,000

The following additional information is provided:

1. Stock at 31/12/2007 is €690,000.
2. Depreciation is to be provided for as follows:
   Building: 2 per cent straight line (There were no purchases or sales of buildings during the year).
   During the year, land adjacent to the company's building which had cost €55,000 was sold for €135,000. At the end of the year the company revalued its building at €750,000. The company wishes to incorporate this value in this year's accounts.

3.	Provision is to be made for:
	Directors' remuneration €80,000.
	Auditors' remuneration €9,000.
	Corporation tax €170,000.
	Debenture interest due at 31/12/2007.
4.	The patent was acquired on 1/1/2004 for €240,000. It is being amortised over ten years in equal instalments. The amortisation should be included in cost of sales.
5.	On 1 July 2007 interim dividends of €10,500 and €13,500 were paid to the ordinary and preference shareholders, respectively. The directors propose the payment of the preference dividend due and a final dividend on ordinary shares of 6c per share.
6.	The fixed asset investments are in listed companies. The market value of these investments at 31/12/2007 was €480,000. There were no purchases or sales of investments during the year.
7.	The debentures are secured by a fixed charge over the company's tangible fixed assets.
8.	On 12/12/2007 the company received a letter from a former employee who was dismissed on 1/10/2007. The employee is claiming compensation for unlawful dismissal. The company's legal advisers believe that the company is unlikely to be liable under the terms of the employment contract and they estimate the maximum amount of the liability will be legal costs of €25,000.

You are required to:

(a) Prepare the published profit and loss account for the year ended 31/12/2007 and a balance sheet as at that date in accordance with the Companies Acts and latest accounting standards, showing the following notes:
	1.	Accounting policy note for tangible fixed assets and stock.
	2.	Operating profit.
	3.	Contingent liabilities.
	4.	Dividends.
	5.	Tangible fixed assets.	**(85)**
(b) State the difference between an auditor's qualified and unqualified report.	**(15)**
					(100 marks)

Solution to Q 11.2(a)

Profit and Loss Account of Thompson Plc for the Year Ended 31/12/2007   **45**

	Notes	€
Turnover ❶		7,988,000 ❷
Cost of Sales	1	6,134,000 ❻
Gross Profit		1,854,000
Distribution Costs		(610,000) ❶
Administrative Expenses		(845,000) ❽
		399,000
Other Operating Income		
Rental Income		52,000 ❷
Operating Profit ❶	2	451,000
Profit on Sale of Land		80,000 ❷
		531,000
Interest Payable	3	(32,000) ❹
Profit on Ordinary Activities before Taxation ❶		499,000
Taxation on Profit on Ordinary Activities		(170,000) ❷
Profit on Ordinary Activities after Taxation		329,000
Dividends Paid	4	(24,000) ❹
Dividends Proposed	4	(31,500) ❹
Profit Retained for Year		273,500
Profit Brought Forward at 1/1/2007		60,000
Profit Carried Forward at 31/12/2007		333,500 ❹

Balance Sheet as at 31/12/2007   **22**

	Notes		
Fixed Assets			
Intangible Assets		144,000 ❸	
Tangible Assets	5	750,000 ❷	
Financial		300,000 ❶	1,194,000
Current Assets			
Stock		690,000 ❶	
Debtors		116,000 ❶	
Cash at Bank and On Hand		179,000 ❶	985,000
Creditors: Amounts Falling Due within One Year			
Trade Creditors		241,000 ❶	
Other Creditors		109,000 ❶	
Taxation and Social Welfare		252,000 ❷	
Proposed Dividends		31,500 ❶	633,500
Net Current Assets			351,500
Total Assets less Current Liabilities			1,545,500 ❷
Creditors: Amounts Falling Due after More than One Year			
8% Debentures 2011/2012			400,000 ❷
Capital and Reserves			
Called-Up Share Capital		700,000 ❷	
Revaluation Reserve		112,000 ❸	
Profit and Loss Account		333,500 ❶	145,500
			1,545,500

Notes to the Accounts   🔳18
Accounting policy notes ❺

1. **Tangible Fixed Assets**
    Buildings were revalued at the end of 2007 and have been included in the accounts at their revalued amount. Depreciation is calculated in order to write off the value or cost of tangible fixed assets over their estimated useful economic life, as follows:
    * Buildings: 2 per cent per annum – straight line basis.
    * Stocks: Stocks are valued on a first in, first out basis at the lower of cost and net realisable value.

2. **Operating profit ❸**
    The operating profit is arrived at after charging:

Depreciation on Tangible Fixed Assets	14,000
Patent Amortised	24,000
Directors' Remuneration	80,000
Auditors' Remuneration	9,000

3. **Contingent Liability ❷**
    The company is being sued by a former employee for unlawful dismissal. The company's legal advisers have advised that the company will probably *not* be liable under the terms of the employment contract. They have estimated the maximum amount of liability at €25,000.

4. **Dividends ❹**

Ordinary Dividends		
Interim Paid 2.625c per Share	10,500	
Final Proposed 60c per Share	24,000	34,500
Preference Dividends		
Interim Paid 45c per Share	13,500	
Final Proposed 2.5c per Share	7,500	21,000
		55,500

5. **Tangible Fixed Assets ❹**

	Land and Buildings	Total
Cost/Valuation at 1/1/2007	755,000	755,000
Disposal	55,000	55,000
Revaluation Surplus at 31/12/2007	50,000	50,000
	750,000	750,000
Depreciation at 1/1/2007	48,000	48,000
Charge for Year	14,000	14,000
Transfer on Revaluation	(62,000)	(62,000)
Net Book Values at 31/12/2006	707,000	707,000
Net Book Values at 31/12/2007	750,000	750,000

Workings

Cost of Sales	6,150,000 + 650,000 – 690,000 + 24,000 =	6,134,000
Administrative Expenses	742,000 + 14,000 + 80,000 + 9,000 =	845,000
Revaluation Reserve	48,000 + 50,000 + 14,000 =	112,000

Solution to Q 11.2(b)   **15**

Unqualified Auditor's Report

An unqualified auditor's report is often referred to as a clean report. **5** This is when the auditor's report states that in his/her opinion the following apply:

- The financial statements *give a true and fair view* **3** of the state of affairs of the company at the end of the year and of its profit and loss account for the year.
- The financial statements are prepared in accordance with the Companies Acts. **5**
- All the information necessary for the audit was available.
- The information given by the directors is consistent with the financial statements.
- The net assets are more than 50 per cent of the called-up capital.

Qualified Auditor's Report

A qualified auditor's report is when an auditor in his/her opinion is *not satisfied* or is unable to conclude that all or any of the following apply: **2**

- The financial statements give a *true and fair view* of the state of affairs of the company at the end of the year and of its profit and loss account for the year.
- The financial statements are prepared in accordance with the Companies Acts.
- All the information necessary for the audit was available.
- The information given by the directors is consistent with the financial statements.
- The net assets are more than 50 per cent of the called-up capital.

The report will state the elements of the accounts or of the directors' report that are unsatisfactory.

Question 11.3

Oatfield Plc has an authorised capital of €900,000 divided into 700,000 ordinary shares at €1 each and 200,000 8 per cent preference shares at €1 each. The following trial balance was extracted from its books on 31/12/2008.

	€	€
Patent	56,000	
9% Investments 1/1/2008	120,000	
Land and Buildings (revalued on 1/7/2008)	880,000	
Revaluation Reserve		260,000
Delivery Vans at Cost	145,000	
Delivery Vans – Accumulated Depreciation on 1/1/2008		68,000
Debtors and Creditors	187,000	98,000
Purchases and Sales	696,000	1,105,000
Stocks 1/1/2008	75,000	
Directors' Fees	84,000	
Salaries and General Expenses	177,000	
Discount		6,160
Advertising	21,000	
Investment Income		8,100
Profit on Sale of Land		85,000
Rent	32,000	
Interim Dividends for First 6 Months	27,000	

Question 11.3 (Continued)

	€	€
Profit and Loss Balance 1/1/2008		73,700
8% Debentures (2014/2015) including €120,000 8%		
Debentures Issued on 1/8/2008		270,000
Bank		17,740
VAT		8,300
Issued Capital		
350,000 Ordinary Shares at €1 Each		350,000
150,000 8% Preference Shares		150,000
	2,500,000	2,500,000

The following information is also relevant:

1. Stock on 31/12/2008 was valued on a first in, first out basis at €77,000.
2. The patent was acquired on 1/1/2005 for €80,000. It is being amortised over ten years in equal instalments. The amortisation should be included in cost of sales.
3. On 1/7/2008 the ordinary shareholders received an interim dividend of €21,000 and the preference shareholders received €6,000. The directors propose the payment of the preference dividend due and a final dividend on ordinary shares, bringing the total ordinary dividend up to 16c per share for the year.
4. On 1/7/2008 land which had cost €90,000 was sold for €175,000. On this date the remaining land and buildings were revalued at €880,000. Included in this revaluation is land now valued at €180,000 but which originally cost €70,000. The revalued buildings had cost €550,000.
5. Depreciation is to be provided as follows:
    Delivery vans at the rate of 20 per cent of cost. Buildings at the rate of 2 per cent of cost per annum until date of revaluation and thereafter at 2 per cent per annum of revalued figure.
6. Provide for debenture interest due, investment income due, auditors' fees €7,700 and taxation €33,000.

You are required to:

(a) Prepare the published profit and loss account for the year ended 31/12/2008 in accordance with the Companies Acts and financial reporting standards, showing the following notes:
    1. Accounting policy note for stock and depreciation.
    2. Dividends.
    3. Interest payable.
    4. Operating profit.
    5. Profit on sale of property. **(50)**
(b) Name the agencies that regulate the production, content and presentation of company financial statements. **(10)**
(60 marks)

Solution to Q 11.3(a) 50

Profit and Loss Account of Oatfield Plc for the Year Ended 31/12/2008

	Notes		€
Turnover			1,105,000 ❶
Cost of Sales (75,000 + 696,000 – 77,000 + 8000)	1		702,000 ❼
Gross Profit			403,000
Distribution Cost	W 1	50,000 ❷	
Administrative Expenses	W 2	313,200 ❼	363,200
			39,800
Other Operating Income			
Discount			6,160 ❶
Operating Profit	2		45,960
Profit on Sale of Land			85,000 ❷
Investment Income			10,800 ❸
			141,760
Interest Payable	3		16,000 ❸
Profit on Ordinary Activities before Taxation ❶			125,760
Taxation			33,000 ❶
Profit after Taxation			92,760
Dividends Paid	4	27,000 ❷	
Dividends Proposed	4	41,000 ❸	68,000
Profit Retained for Year			24,760
Profit Brought Forward at 1/1/2008			73,700 ❶
Profit Carried Forward at 31/12/2008			98,460 ❹

Notes to the Accounts

1. **Accounting Policy Notes ❸**

   Tangible Fixed Assets

   Depreciation is calculated in order to write off the value or cost of tangible fixed assets over their estimated useful economic life, as follows:

   Buildings: 2 per cent per annum – straight line basis.

   Delivery vans: 20 per cent cost.

   Stocks: Stocks are valued on a first in, first out basis at the lower of cost and net realisable value.

2. **Dividends ❹**

Ordinary Dividends		
Interim Paid 6.0c per Share	21,000	
Final Proposed 10.0c per Share	35,000	56,000
Preference Dividends		
Interim Paid 4.0c per Share	6,000	
Final Proposed 4.0c per Share	6,000	12,000

3. **Interest Payable** ❶

Interest Payable on Debentures Repayable during Years 2014/2015 16,000

4. **Operating Profit** ❸

The operating profit is arrived at after charging:

Depreciation on Tangible Fixed Assets	41,500
Patent Amortised	8,000
Directors' Remuneration	84,000
Auditors' Fees	7,700

5. **Profit on Sale of Property** ❶

The company sold land for €85,000 greater than it cost. Cost was €90,000.

Workings

1. **Distribution costs**

Advertising	21,000	
Depreciation – Delivery Vans	29,000	50,000

2. **Administrative Expenses**

Directors' Fees	84,000	
Salaries and General Expenses	177,000	
Rent	32,000	
Auditors' Fees	7,700	
Depreciation – Buildings	12,500	313,200

(b)

Agencies

The Government – Legislation

The European Union – Directives

The Accountancy Profession – FRSs and SSAPs

The Stock Exchange – Listing Rules

10

Chapter **12**
Costing

1 Stock Valuation

'Stock should be valued at the lower of cost and net realisable value.' SSAP 9.

'Cost' is the expenditure incurred in bringing the stock to its location and condition.

'Net realisable value' is the estimated selling price less all further costs involved in getting it into saleable condition.

When materials are purchased at different prices during the year, a problem arises as to which price to use when valuing closing stocks. There are different methods, but FIFO is the only one which will be applied. This is also approved under SSAP 9.

2 Overheads and Absorption

The overhead absorption rates (OAR) to be used will be predetermined, based on machine hours, labour hours, etc.

$$OAR = \frac{\text{Total Overheads of Cost Centre}}{\text{Total Number of Absorption Units}}$$

Calculate the total overheads for the centre and then divide by the absorption units.

3 Apportionment

Where you have non-production departments, the overheads of these departments should be apportioned (allocated) among the various production departments. Build up the total overheads of all the departments in the first instance, and then proceed to eliminate the service departments among the other departments.

Service Department	Possible Basis of Apportionment
Canteen	Number of Employees
Maintenance	Value of Plant
Stores	Value of Materials
	Frequency of Requisitions

For example, if you have two production departments, a maintenance department and a canteen, the two service departments will be eliminated. Start with the canteen and eliminate its overheads among the two production departments and the maintenance department. Only then eliminate the maintenance department.

Question 12.1

The New Irish Manufacturing Co. Ltd has three separate workshops in one of its factories. The following data relate to this current year.

	Machine Shop	**Assembly Shop**	**Finishing Shop**
Direct Labour Hours	14,975	16,343	9,762
Hourly Wage Rates (€)	4.75	4.25	3.75
Variable Factory Overhead (€)	112,312.50	65,372	53,691

Total fixed factory overhead is expected to be €205,400.

A particular customer has requested a piece of specialist equipment, which will require materials from store of 1,000 kg at €4.173 per kilo together with components which will have to be purchased from outside suppliers amounting to €2,457. The packing and delivery costs will amount to €1,151. The following direct labour hours will be required to produce the equipment.

Shop	(hours)
Machine	140
Assembly	160
Finishing	100

Administration cost will be absorbed at 10 per cent of factory cost. For this type of job, it is the company practice to add 20 per cent of the selling price for profit.

You are required to:
Prepare the detailed cost estimate and proposed selling price for this piece of specialist equipment.

Solution to Q 12.1

Specialist Equipment

	Rate	(€)	(€)
Direct Materials			
Materials ex Stores	1,000 kg @ €4.173		4,173
Bought-out Components			2,457
			6,630
Direct Labour			
Machine Shop	140 hr @ €4.75	665	
Assembly Shop	160 hr @ €4.25	680	
Finishing Shop	100 hr @ €3.75	375	1,720
Variable Overhead			
Machine Shop	140 hr @ €7.50	1,050	
Assembly Shop	160 hr @ €4.00	640	
Finishing Shop	100 hr @ €5.50	550	2,240

Specialist Equipment *(Continued)*

	Rate	(€)	(€)
Fixed Overhead	400 hr @ €5.00		2,000
Factory Cost			12,590
Administration 10% of €12,590			1,259
Packing and Delivery			1,151
Total Cost			15,000
Profit			3,750
Selling Price			18,750

Calculations

	(€)	(€)
Variable Overhead Rates		
Machine Shop	$\dfrac{112,321.50}{14,975} = 7.50$	
Assembly Shop	$\dfrac{65,372}{16,343} = 4.00$	
Finishing Shop	$\dfrac{53,691}{9,762} = 5.50$	
Fixed Overhead Rate	$\dfrac{205,400}{14,975 + 16,343 + 9,762} = €5.00$	

Question 12.2

There are three departments in Timmons Ltd – manufacturing, polishing and packing. For the year 2008, the following are the budgeted costs.

	Total (€)	Manufacturing (€)	Polishing (€)	Packing (€)
Indirect Materials	180,000	110,000	40,000	30,000
Indirect Labour	240,000	120,000	70,000	50,000
Light and Heat	48,000			
Rent and Rates	27,000			
Machine Maintenance	16,000			
Plant Depreciation	80,000			
Factory Canteen	35,000			

The following information relates to the three departments.

	Total	Manufacturing	Polishing	Packing
Floor Space in Square Metres	9,000	4,000	3,000	2,000
Volume in Cubic Metres	24,000	12,000	8,000	4,000
Plant Valuation in € at book value	400,000	240,000	100,000	60,000
Machine Hours	60,000	30,000	15,000	15,000
Number of Employees	70	30	30	10
Labour Hours	160,000	80,000	60,000	20,000

Job no. 999 has just been completed. The details are:

	Direct Material	Direct Labour	Machine Hours	Labour Hours
Manufacturing	€7,500	€850	50	20
Polishing	€2,800	€3,900	15	90
Packing	–	€1,500	6	25

The company budgets for a profit margin of 20 per cent of sales.

You are required to:

(a) Calculate the overhead to be absorbed by each department. State clearly the basis of apportionment used.
(b) Calculate a suitable overhead absorption rate for each department.
(c) Compute the selling price of job no. 999.

(80 marks)

Solution to Q 12.2(a)   **31**

Overhead Analysis

Overhead	Basis of Apportionment	Total	Manufacturing	Polishing	Packing
Indirect Materials	Actual	180,000	110,000 ❶	40,000 ❶	30,000 ❶
Indirect Labour	Actual	240,000	120,000 ❶	70,000 ❶	50,000 ❶
Light and Heat	Volume ❶	48,000	24,000 ❶	16,000 ❶	8,000 ❶
Rent and Rates	Floor Space ❶	27,000	12,000 ❶	9,000 ❶	6,000 ❶
Machine Maintenance	Machine Hrs ❶	16,000	8,000 ❶	4,000 ❶	4,000 ❶
Plant Depreciation	Plant Valuation ❶	80,000	48,000 ❶	20,000 ❶	12,000 ❶
Factory Canteen	Employees ❶	35,000	15,000 ❶	15,000 ❶	5,000 ❶
		626,000	337,000 ❶	174,000 ❸	115,000 ❶

Solution to Q 12.2(b)   **21**

Overhead Recovery (Absorption) per	Machine Hours Manufacturing	Direct Labour Polishing	Hours Packing
Budgeted Overheads	337,000	174,000	115,000
Budgeted Hours	30,000	60,000	20,000
Overhead Absorption Rate per Machine Hour	€11.23 ❼		
Overhead Absorption Rate per Indirect Labour Hour	€4.21	€2.90 ❼	€5.75 ❼

Solution to Q 12.2(c)

Selling Price of Job No. 999

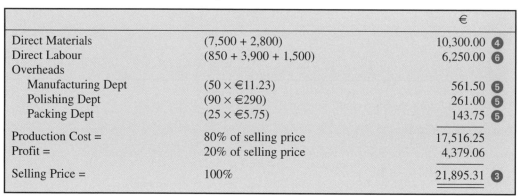

		€
Direct Materials	(7,500 + 2,800)	10,300.00 ④
Direct Labour	(850 + 3,900 + 1,500)	6,250.00 ⑥
Overheads		
Manufacturing Dept	(50 × €11.23)	561.50 ⑤
Polishing Dept	(90 × €290)	261.00 ⑤
Packing Dept	(25 × €5.75)	143.75 ⑤
Production Cost =	80% of selling price	17,516.25
Profit =	20% of selling price	4,379.06
Selling Price =	100%	21,895.31 ③

Question 12.3
(a) Valuation of Closing Stock

The following information relates to the purchases and sales (exclusive of VAT) of O'Leary Ltd for the year 2008.

Period	Details	Quantity and Price
01/01/08 to 31/03/08	Purchases on credit	4,200 @ €7 each
	Credit sales	1,300 @ €12 each
	Cash sales	1,200 @ €11 each
01/04/08 to 30/06/08	Purchases on credit	3,200 @ €7 each
	Credit sales	1,350 @ €12 each
	Cash sales	1,500 @ €12 each
01/07/08 to 30/09/08	Purchases on credit	2,700 @ €8 each
	Credit sales	1,400 @ €13 each
	Cash sales	1,200 @ €11 each
01/10/08 to 31/12/08	Purchases on credit	3,200 @ €9 each
	Credit sales	1,600 @ €13 each
	Cash sales	900 @ €13 each

On 1/1/2008 there was an opening stock of 4,400 units @ €7 each.

You are required to:

(i)   Calculate the value of the closing stock, using the first in first out (FIFO) method.
(ii) Prepare a trading account for the year ended 31/12/2008.

(b) Product Costing

O'Mahony Ltd is a small company with three departments. The following are the company's budgeted costs for the coming year.

Department	Variable Costs	Fixed Costs	Wage Rate per Hour
X	€18 per hour	€8.50 per hour	€11
Y	€16 per hour	€7.50 per hour	€12
Z	€20 per hour	€4.00 per hour	€10

General administration overhead absorption rate per hour is budgeted to be €74.50. The following are the specifications for a quotation for job no. 999:

Material costs €6,450.

Labour hours required in each department are:

Department	Hours
X	90
Y	180
Z	50

You are required to:

(i) Calculate the selling price of job no. 999 if the profit is set at 25 per cent of selling price.

(ii) State two reasons for product costing and explain each.

(80 Marks)

Solution to Q 12.3(a)(i) **30**

Purchases in Units		Cost Price	Purchases at Cost €
4,200	@	€7	29,400
3,200	@	€7	22,400
2,700	@	€8	21,600
2,300	@	€9	20,700
12,400			**94,100**

Sales in Units		Selling Price	Sales Value €
2,400	@	€11	26,400
4,150	@	€12	49,800
3,900	@	€13	50,700
10,450			**126,900**

Closing Stock in Units	
Opening Stock	4,400
Add Purchases	12,400
	16,800
Less Sales	10,450
Closing Stock	6,350

Closing Stock in €			€
2,300	@	€9	20,700
2,700	@	€8	21,600
1,350	@	€7	9,450
6,350			51,750

Solution to Q 12.3(a)(ii)

Trading Account for Year Ending 31 December 2008

	€	€
Sales		126,900 ❸
Less Cost of Goods Sold		
Opening Stock	30,800 ❷	
Purchases	94,100 ❸	
	124,900	
Less Closing Stock	51,750 ❸	73,150
Gross Profit		53,750 ❹

Solution to Q 12.3(b)(i)   50

		€	€
Direct Materials			6,450.00 ❸
Direct Wages			
Department X	(90 hours @ 11)	990 ❸	
Department Y	(180 hours @ 12)	2,160 ❸	
Department Z	(50 hours @ 10)	500 ❸	3,650.00
Variable Overheads			
Department X	(90 hours @ 18)	1,620 ❸	
Department Y	(180 hours @ 16)	2,880 ❸	
Department Z	(50 hours @ 20)	1,000 ❸	5,500.00
Fixed Overheads			
Department X	(90 hours @ 8.50)	765 ❸	
Department Y	(180 hours@ 7.50)	1,350 ❸	
Department Z	(50 hours @ 4.00)	200 ❸	2,315.00
General Administration Overhead (320 hours @ €4.50)			1,400.00 ❹
Total Cost	= 75% of selling price		19,355.00 ❷
Profit	= 25% of selling price		6,451.67
Selling Price	= 100%		25,806.67 ❷

Solution to Q 12.3(b)(ii)

- To establish the selling price for the purpose of tendering. ❼
- To control costs – budget versus actual.   ❺
- To help planning and decision-making.
- To ascertain the value of closing stock in order to prepare final accounts.

Question 12.4

Roversby Ltd produce a specialised component for the catering industry. The company has two production departments – machinery and assembly – and a service department that maintains the heavy machinery and the air tools used in the assembly section. Budgeted costs for the coming year are as follows.

	€
Rent and Rates	40,000
Insurance of Machinery	25,000
Depreciation of Machinery	440,000
Supervisory Salaries	97,000
Maintenance Supervisor	20,000
Factory Cleaning	18,000
Rubbish Removal Contract	6,000
Lighting and Heating	150,000
Building Insurance	25,000
Indirect Materials	78,000
Maintenance of Fire Prevention Equipment	2,000

The following information is also available.

	Machinery	Assembly	Maintenance
Floor Area (sq m)	4,000	2,500	150
Number of Employees	50	120	6
Value of Machinery (€)	900,000	120,000	

The factory works one seven-hour shift per day in the machinery department and one eight-hour shift per day in the assembly department (48 working weeks).

You are required to:

(a) Prepare an analysis of the overheads showing the basis of allocation and apportionment to the three departments.
(b) Reallocate the maintenance overheads to the production departments.
(c) Calculate an overhead absorption rate based on direct labour hours for each of the two departments.
(d) Calculate the cost of a job which has the following costs:

	Machinery	Assembly
Direct Materials (€)	300	100
Direct Labour (hr)	9	25
Wages Rate (€)	5.50	5.90

(e) Briefly state what problems can arise when using the above method of allocation and apportionment.

Solution to Q 12.4(a)

Roversby Ltd Overheads

	Percentage Apportioned	Machinery	Percentage Apportioned	Assembly	Percentage Apportioned	Maintenance	Total
Floor Area	60	4,000	37.5	2,500	2.5	150	6,650
Employees	28.5	50	68	120	3.5	6	176
Machinery	88	900,000	12	120,000			1,020

Solution to Q 12.4(b)

Roversby Ltd
Overhead Reallocation

	Machinery (€)	Assembly (€)	Maintenance(€)	Total (€)	Basis
Rent and Rates	24,000	15,000	1,000	40,000	FS
Insurance of Machinery	22,000	3,000		25,000	Value
Depreciation of Machinery	387,200	52,800		440,000	Value
Supervisory Salaries	58,200	36,375	2,425	97,000	FS
Maintenance Supervisor			20,000	20,000	
Factory Cleaning	10,800	6,750	450	18,000	FS
Rubbish Removal Contract	3,600	2,250	150	6,000	FS
Light and Heating	90,000	56,250	3,750	150,000	FS
Building Insurance	15,000	9,375	625	25,000	FS
Indirect Materials	46,800	29,250	1,950	78,000	FS
Maintenance of Fire Prevention Equipment	1,200	750	50	2,000	FS
	658,800	211,800	30,400	901,000	
	26,752	3,648	(30,400)		
	685,552	211,848			

Solution to Q 12.4(c)
Machinery
$7 \times 5 \times 48 = 1,680$ hrs; OAR = 685,552/1,680 = €408.07
Assembly
$8 \times 5 \times 48 = 1,920$ hrs; OAR = 211,848/1,920 = €110.34

Solution to Q 12.4(d)

Cost of Job

Direct Materials			
Machinery	300		
Assembly	200		400.00
Direct Labour			
Machinery	9×5.5	49.50	
Assembly	25×5.9	147.50	197.00
Overhead Maintenance	408.07×9	3,672.63	
Assembly	110.34×25	2,758.50	6,431.13
Budgeted Cost			7,028.13

Question 12.5

Ranelagh Ltd manufactures three products in two production departments, a machine shop and a fitting section; it also has two service departments, a canteen and a machine maintenance section. Shown below are next year's budgeted production data and manufacturing costs for the company.

Product	X	Y	Z
Production (units)	4,200	6,900	1,700
Prime Cost			
Direct Materials (€ per unit)	11	14	17
Direct Labour Machine Shop (€ per unit)	6	4	2
Fitting Section (€ per unit)	12	3	21
Machine Hours (per unit)	6	3	4

Budgeted Overheads

	Machine Shop (€)	Fitting Section (€)	Canteen (€)	Machine Maintenance Section (€)	Total (€)
Allocated Overheads	27,660	19,470	16,600	26,650	90,380
Rent, Rates and Light					17,000
Depreciation and Insurance of Equipment					25,000
Additional Data:					
Gross Book Value of Equipment	150,000	75,000	30,000	45,000	
Number of Employees	18	14	4	4	
Floor Space Occupied (sq m)	3,600	1,400	1,000	800	

It has been estimated that approximately 70 per cent of the machine maintenance section's costs are incurred servicing the machine shop and the remainder incurred servicing the fitting section.

You are required to:

(a) Calculate the following overhead absorption rates: a machine hour rate for the machine shop and a rate expressed as a percentage of direct wages for the fitting section. All workings and assumptions should be clearly shown.
(b) Calculate the budgeted manufacturing cost per unit of each product.

Solution to Q 12.5(a)

Overhead Schedule

Expense	Basis of Apportionment	Machine Shop (€)	Fitting Section (€)	Canteen (€)	Machine Maintenance Section (€)	Total (€)
Allocated		27,660	19,470	16,600	26,650	90,380
Rent etc.	Area	9,000	3,500	2,500	2,000	17,000
Depr and Insurance	Book Value	12,500	6,250	2,500	3,750	25,000
		49,160	29,220	21,600	32,400	132,380
Apportionments						
Canteen	Number of Employees	10,800	8,400	(21,600)	2,400	
Maintenance	70 : 30	24,360	10,440		(34,800)	
		84,320	48,060			132,380

Calculation of Total Machine Hours

Product	X	Y	Z	Total
Machine Hours (per unit)	6	3	4	
Production (units)	4,200	6,900	1,700	
Total Machine Hours	25,200	20,700	6,800	52,700

Total overhead apportioned to the machine shop is €84,320. Therefore, the absorption rate per machine hour is €1.60.

Calculation of Payroll Total for Fitting Section

Product	X	Y	Z	Total
Wages (€ per unit)	12	3	21	
Production (units)	4,200	6,900	1,700	
Payroll Total (€)	50,400	20,700	35,600	106,800

Total overhead apportioned to the fitting section is €48,060. Therefore, the absorption rate as a percentage of direct wages is $48,050/106,800 \times 100 = 45\%$.

Solution to Q 12.5(b)

Cost of Production (per unit)

	(€)	X (€)	(€)	Y (€)	(€)	Z(€)
Prime Cost						
Direct Materials		11		14		17
Direct Labour – Machine Shop		6		4		2
Direct Labour – Fitting Section		12		3		21
		29		21		40
Overhead						
Machine Shop (per machine hr)	9.6		4.80		6.40	
Fitting Section (per direct wages)	5.4		1.35		9.45	
		15		6.15		15.85
Cost of Production		44		27.15		55.85

Question 12.6

A picture-framing firm had the following transactions for the six months ended 31 December 2007. The figures are exclusive of VAT.

Purchases		Sales	
2007		2007	
25 July	Purchased 150 units @ €20 each	15 Sept	Sold 305 units @ €45 each
28 Aug	Purchased 225 units @ €30 each	4 Oct	Sold 50 units @ €45 each
10 Nov	Purchased 410 units @ €40 each	23 Dec	Sold 100 units @ €75 each

Additional information:

1. The balance sheet at 1 July 2007 was as follows:

Bank Balance	€10,000
Capital Account	€10,000

2. Two months' credit is taken from suppliers.
3. One month's credit is given to debtors.
4. Expenses of €1,400 are paid each month as incurred.
5. Assume that purchases are liable to VAT at 10 per cent. Assume that sales are liable to VAT at 20 per cent.

You are required to:

(a) Calculate the value of closing stock at the end of each month during the period 1 July 2007 to 31 December 2007, using the first in, first out method (FIFO).
(b) Prepare the trading and profit and loss accounts and balance sheet for the six months ended 31 December 2007 and the balance sheet at that date.

Solution to Q 12.6(a)

Stock Valuation – FIFO

Date 2007	Purchases			Sales			Balance	
	Units	€	Total	Units	€	Total	Units	Total
25 July	150	20	3,000				150	3,000
28 Aug	225	30	6,750				375	9,750
15 Sept				305				
				150	20	3,000		
				155	30	4,650	70	2,100
4 Oct				50	30	1,500	20	600
10 Nov	410	40	16,400				430	17,000
23 Dec				100				
				20	30	600		
				80	40	3,200	330	13,200

Solution to 12.6(b)

**Trading and Profit and Loss Accounts for Six Months Ended
31 December 2007**

	(€)	(€)
Sales		223,475
Less Costs Purchases	26,150	
Closing Stock	13,200	
Cost		12,950
Gross Profit		10,525
Less Expenses		8,400
Net Profit		€2,125

Balance Sheet at 31 December 2007

	(€)	(€)
Current Assets		
Stock	13,200	
Debtors $(100 \times 75 + 20\%)$	9,000	
Bank	7,825	
VAT Refund Due	140	
	30,165	
Less Current Liabilities		
Creditors $(410 \times 40 + 10\%)$	(18,040)	12,125
Financed by		
Capital	10,000	
Plus Net Profit	2,125	
		12,125

Chapter **13**
Marginal Costing

'Marginal costing' means finding the cost of producing $x + 1$ units instead of x units. It is also called 'variable costing' or 'contribution costing'.

It is not the cost of one unit or the cost of the first unit; rather it is the cost of producing 101 units instead of 100 units.

Costs are divided into two types: fixed and variable.

Fixed costs do not change with production and should be shown as one large figure. Variable costs alter with production and should be unitised.

Instead of sales, we take selling price per unit.

$$\text{Selling Price} - \text{Variable Costs} = \text{Contribution (per unit)}$$

$$\text{Contribution} \times \text{Units Sold} = \text{Total Contribution}$$

$$\text{Total Contribution} - \text{Fixed Costs} = \text{Profit}$$

$$\frac{\text{Fixed Costs}}{\text{Contribution (per unit)}} = \text{Breakeven}$$

$$\frac{\text{Contribution}}{\text{Sales Price}} = \text{Contribution Sales Ratio}$$

Breakeven Charts

There are different acceptable methods by which breakeven charts may be drawn up. The one shown could be referred to as the 'traditional method'.

1. Draw the X and Y axes. The X, or horizontal, axis is for units, and the Y, or vertical, axis is for monetary values.
2. Draw the fixed costs as a straight line parallel to the X axis.
3. Next draw the total costs line as a straight but sloping line, with the slope depending on the level of variable costs. (Note that you do not draw the variable costs as a separate line; rather they are the difference between fixed and total costs.)
4. Then draw the sales/revenue line as a straight/sloping line from the origin.
5. Where the sales line intersects the total costs line is the breakeven point.
6. The section above this represents profit and the section below loss.

Example

A company makes a product with a maximum capacity of €500,000 per annum. The unit selling price is €1, and the variable costs are €0.60 per unit. The fixed costs are €120,000. Draw a breakeven chart showing the profit at the projected sales/production level of 400,000.

$$\text{Selling Price} = 1.00$$
$$\text{Variable Costs} = 0.60$$
$$= \overline{}$$
$$\text{Contribution} = 0.40$$
$$\text{Breakeven} = \frac{120,000}{0.40}$$
$$= 3,000,000 \text{ units}$$

Question 13.1

The Irish Manufacturing Co. Plc produces a single product. The cost per unit is as follows.

	(€)
Direct Material	12
Direct Wages (10 hours @ €5)	50
Overhead	68
Total	130

The fixed overheads amount to €800,000 and the above calculation has been obtained by dividing the total overheads incurred in the last period by the actual production of 20,000 units. These 20,000 units represent the normal capacity, but the factory can produce 25,000 units in the same period with no additional increase in fixed overheads. The company has an agreement with the union that the guaranteed minimum wage per period for direct workers will not be less than 180,000 hours at €5 per hour and overtime will be worked only when an excess of 20,000 units are produced and will be paid at time plus one-half. The company sells the units for €140.

You are required to:

(a) Calculate the breakeven in units for the period.
(b) Calculate the profit at 15,000, 20,000 and 25,000 units per period.

Solution to Q 13.1(a)

Separate the fixed and variable costs:

$$\text{Overhead} \times \text{Units} = 68 \times 20,000 = 1,360,000$$
$$\text{Less Fixed Costs} = 800,000$$
$$\text{Total Variable Costs} = 560,000$$
$$\text{Unit Variable Cost} = \frac{560,000}{20,000} = €28$$

(Note: Regard labour as fixed.)

$$\text{Material} = \text{Unit Cost} = 12$$
$$\text{Overhead} = 28$$
$$\text{Total} = 40$$

$$\text{Selling Price} = 140$$
$$\text{Contribution} = 100$$
$$\text{Fixed Overheads} = 800,000$$
$$\text{Plus Labour} = 900,000$$
$$\text{Total} = 1,700,000$$
$$\frac{1,700,000}{100} = 17,000$$

Solution to Q 13.1(b)

Profit Calculation

		Units				
Profit		**@ 15,000**		**@ 20,000**		**@ 25,000**
Total Contribution		1,500,000		2,000,000		2,500,000
Fixed Costs						
Overheads	800,000		800,000		800,000	
Labour	900,000		1,000,000		1,375,000	
Total		1,700,000		1,800,000		2,175,000
Profit/(Loss)		(200,000)		200,000		325,000

Question 13.2

You work as a product accountant for Gene's Jeans and are working on the planned estimates for the next year of one of your company's products.

The following are the budgeted costs of producing 12,000 units:

	€
Direct Labour	156,000
Direct Material	228,000
Production Overheads:	
Indirect Labour	24,000
Indirect Expenses	66,000
Administration Overheads	246,000
	720,000

You also have the following information.

1. The maximum possible capacity is for 14,000 units.
2. To obtain the selling price, a mark-up of 25 per cent is used.
3. Your research into cost behaviour reveals that:
   (i) Indirect labour is 10 per cent variable.
   (ii) Indirect expenses are estimated to be €3.60 per unit variable with the balance being fixed.
   (iii) Direct labour and direct material are 100 per cent variable.
   (iv) All other costs are considered fixed.

You are required to:

(a) Prepare a suitable table to show fixed and variable costs based on an output of 12,000 units.

(b) Calculate:
    (i)   The selling price.
    (ii)   The contribution per unit.
    (iii) The breakeven point in units.

(c) Prepare a breakeven chart based on 12,000 units of output, clearly indicating:
    (i)   Area of loss.
    (ii)   Area of profit.
    (iii) Margin of safety.

(d) If the price were reduced by 5 per cent, output/sales would rise to 14,000 units. What would the profit be?

Solution to Q 13.2(a)

Gene's Jeans
Table of Costs

	Variable (€)	Fixed (€)	Total (€)
Direct Labour	156,000		156,000
Direct Material	228,000		228,000
Indirect Labour	2,400	21,600	24,000
Indirect Expenses	43,200	22,800	66,000
Administration Expenses		246,000	246,000
	429,600	290,400	720,000

Solution to Q 13.2(b)(i) Selling Price

$$\text{Total Costs} = 720,000$$

$$\text{Unit Costs} = \frac{720,000}{12,000} = €60$$

Selling Price = Cost + 25% = 60 + 15 = €75.

Solution to Q 13.2(b)(ii) Contribution per Unit

Contribution per Unit = Selling Price – Variable Costs

	(€)	(€)
Selling Price		75.00
Variable Costs		
Direct Labour	13.00	
Direct Material	19.00	
Indirect Labour	0.20	
Indirect Expenses	3.60	35.80
Contribution		39.20

Solution to Q 13.2(b)(iii) Breakeven Point

$$\text{Breakeven} = \frac{\text{Fixed Cost}}{\text{Contribution per Unit}}$$

$$= \frac{290{,}400}{39.20} = 7{,}408 \text{ Units}$$

Solution to 13.2(c)

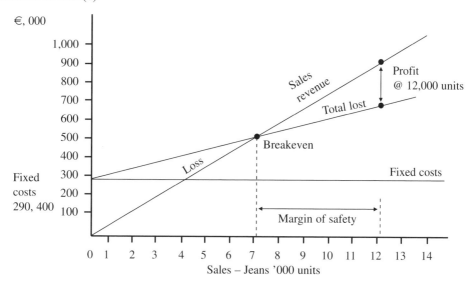

Solution to Q 13.2(d)

Selling Price – 5% = Units Sold
Selling Price = 75 – 5% = 71.25
Less Variable Costs = 35.80
Contribution = 35.45
Total Contribution = 35.45 × 14,000 = 496,300
Profit = Total Contribution – Fixed Costs
205,900 = 496,300 – 290,400
Profit @ 12,000 Units = (39.20 × 12,000) – 290,400 = 180,000

Question 13.3

The account of Astor Plc is currently evaluating three proposals put forward for discussion by the sales marketing team.

Current Position for 50,000 Units

	(€000s)	(€000s)
Sales (50,000 units)		2,500
Direct Materials	750	
Direct Labour	525	
Fixed Overheads	900	2,175
Profit		325

Proposal (i): To reduce the selling price by €5 per unit and increase advertising costs by €30,000. It is anticipated that this should increase sales volume by 15 per cent.

Proposal (ii): To use a better-quality material in the manufacturing process. This will increase the material costs by €3 per unit, but as it is easier to work with, there will be less reworking to be done, saving €1 per unit in labour costs. Additional advertising will be necessary to promote the 'new image' product. This will cost €60,000 and should result in an increase in sales of 5,000 units.

Proposal (iii): Install new computerised equipment which will cut labour costs by 50 per cent. This proposal will necessitate using better-quality material at an additional cost of €3 per unit. As a special introductory offer for the new product, the company would pass on 40 per cent of the labour cost's savings to the customers. Sales are expected to increase to 65,000 units with additional costs of €25,250.

You are required to:

Evaluate each proposal and recommend, with reasons, which one (if any) management should adopt.

Solution to Q 13.3

Contribution per Unit

			(€)
Selling Price		50.00	
Variable Costs			
Direct Materials	15.00		
Direct Labour	10.50	25.50	
Contribution		24.50	
Total Contribution (24.50 × 50,000)			1,225,000
Less Fixed Costs			900,000
Profit			325,000

Proposal (i)

	(€)
Selling Price	45.00
Less Variable Costs	25.50
Contribution	19.50
Total Contribution (19.50 × 57,500)	1,121,250
Less Fixed Costs	930,000
Profit	191,250

Proposal (ii)

	(€)	(€)
Selling Price		50.00
Direct Materials	18.00	
Direct Labour	9.50	
		27.50
Contribution		22.50
Total Contribution (22.50 × 55,000)		1,237,500
Less Fixed Costs		960,000
Profit		€277,500

Proposal (iii)

	(€)	(€)
Selling Price	50 – 2.10	47.90
Less Variable Costs		
Direct Materials	18.00	
Direct Labour	5.25	23.45
Contribution		24.65
Total Contribution (65,000 × 24.65)		1,602,250
Less Fixed Costs		925,250
Profit		677,000

Proposal (iii) should be adopted as this easily gives the highest profit. Proposals (i) and (ii) yield lower profits than the present position.

All of these computations assume that the figures are accurate and that agreement can be obtained for each proposal. If proposal (iii) leads to redundancy, a once-off figure for redundancy payment will have to be included.

Question 13.4

O'Connor produces a single product. The company's profit and loss account for the year ended 31/12/2008, during which 80,000 units were produced and sold, was as follows:

	€	€
Sales		960,000
Materials	320,000	
Labour	200,000	
Factory Overheads	120,000	
Administration Expenses	110,000	
Selling Expenses	90,000	
		840,000
Net Profit		120,000

The materials, labour and 60 per cent of the factory overheads are variable costs. Apart from the sale of 5 per cent of sales, selling and administration expenses are fixed.

You are required to calculate:

(a) The company's breakeven point and margin of safety.

(b) The number of units that must be sold in 2009 if the company is to increase its net profit by 20 per cent over the 2008 figure, assuming the selling price and cost levels and percentages remain unchanged.

(c) The profit the company would make in 2009 if it reduced its selling price to €11, increased fixed costs by €13,000 and thereby increased the number of units sold to 100,000, with all other cost levels and percentages remaining unchanged.

(d) The selling price the company must charge in 2009, if fixed costs are increased by 10 per cent but the volume of sales and the profit remain the same.

(e) The number of units that must be sold at €13 per unit to provide a profit of 10 per cent of the sales revenue from these same units.

(f) Explain two limitations of marginal costing.

Solution to Q 13.4

O'Connor Solution

80,000 units   Selling Price = 960,000/80,000 = €12 per Unit

Costs	Total	Fixed	Variable	Var. p.u.
Materials	320,000	–	320,000	4.00
Labour	200,000	–	200,000	2.50
Factory Overheads	120,000	48,000	72,000	0.90
Administration	110,000	110,000	–	
Selling	90,000	42,000	48,000	0.60
	840,000	200,000	640,000	8.00

Contribution = 1200 – 8.00 = 4.00

Solution to Q 13.4(a)

Breakeven = 200,000/4 = 50,000 units

Margin of Safety = 80,000 – 50,000 = 30,000 units

Solution to Q 13.4(b)

Selling Price = 12.00

Variable Cost = 8.00

Contribution = 4.00

Total Contribution = 4 × X = ?

Fixed Costs = 200,000

Profit = 120,000 + 20% = 144,000

Therefore (200,000 + 144,000)/4 = 86,000 units

Solution to Q 13.4(c)

Selling Price = 11.00

Variable Cost = 7.95 (selling exs   = 0.550)

Aug   A payment of €700 was received from a debtor whose debt had been previously written off and who now wishes to trade with Harris Ltd. again. This represents 70% of the original debt and the debtor had undertaken to pay the remainder of the debt in February 2007.

Dec   The Buildings depreciation charge for the year to be 2% of book value. The depreciation charge to be calculated from date of valuation and date of purchase. The total depreciation charge on vehicles for the year was €20,000.

You are required to:

Record on a tabular statement the effect each of the above transactions had on the relevant asset and liability and ascertain the total assets and liabilities on 31/12/2006.

(60 marks)

SECTION 2 (200 marks)

Answer any **TWO** questions

5. Interpretation of Accounts

The following are the actual figures for the year ended 31/12/2006 and the projected figures for the year ended 31/12/2007 of Mila Plc., a manufacturer in the pharmaceutical industry. Mila Plc. has an authorised capital of €900,000 made up of 650,000 ordinary shares at €1 each and 250,000 6% preference shares at €1 each. The firm has already issued 325,000 ordinary shares and all the preference shares.

Trading and Profit and Loss account for year ended 31/12/2006

	€	€
Sales		820,000
Opening Stock	50,000	
Closing Stock	55,000	
Costs of goods sold		615,000
Gross Profit		205,000
Operating expenses for year		145,000
		60,000
Interest		27,000
Dividends		31,000
Retained Profit		2,000
Profit and Loss Balance 1/1/2006		45,000
Profit and Loss Balance 31/12/2006		47,000

Balance Sheet as at 31/12/2006

		€
Fixed Assets		680,000
Investments (market value 31/12/2006 €210,000)		188,000
		868,000
Current Assets	187,000	
Current Liabilities		
Trade Creditors	(102,000)	
Proposed Dividends	(31,000)	54,000
		922,000
Financed by		
9% Debentures (2014 secured)		300,000
Capital and Reserves		
Ordinary Shares @ €1 each	325,000	
6% Preference Shares @ €1 each	250,000	
Profit and Loss Balance	47,000	622,000
		922,000

Projected ratios and figures for year ended 31/12/2007

Earnings per Ordinary Share	8c
Dividend per Ordinary Share	6.1c
Interest Cover	4 times
Quick Ratio	1.1 to 1
Price Earnings Ratio	14 to 1
Return on Capital Employed	8.5%
Gearing	58%

Market value of one Ordinary Share €1.20

You are required to calculate the following for 2006

(a) (i) The Cash Purchases if the period of credit received from Trade Creditors is 2.4 months.

(ii) The Interest Cover.

(iii) The Dividend Yield.

(iv) How long it would take one Ordinary share to recover its value at present pay out rate.

(v) The projected market value of one Ordinary share in 2007. **(45)**

(b) Indicate if the Ordinary shareholders would be satisfied with the performance, state of affairs and prospects of the company. Use relevant ratios and other information to support your answer. **(35)**

(c) Advise the bank manager as to whether a loan of €150,000, on which an interest rate of 10% would be charged, should be granted to Mila Plc. for future expansion. Use relevant ratios and other information to support your answer. **(20)**

(100 marks)

6. Service Firm

The following were included in the assets and liabilities of the Oak Health Centre Ltd., on 1/1/2006:

Buildings €500,000; Equipment €70,000; Furniture at cost €20,000; Stock of health food for sale €1,300; Heating oil €640; Creditors for supplies to Health Centre €1,250; 5% Investments €70,000; Contract cleaning prepaid €250; Clients' fees paid in advance €4,300; Authorised Capital €430,000 and Issued Capital €300,000.

All fixed assets have 2 years accumulated depreciation on 1/1/2006.

The following is the Receipts and Payments Account for the year ended 31/12/2006:

Receipts and Payments Account of Oak Health Centre for year ended 31/12/2006

	€		€
Balance at Bank 1/1/2006	7,250	Laundry	800
Clients' fees	252,600	Wages & Salaries	86,220
Investment Income	3,000	Repayment of €50,000 loan on	
Shop receipts	65,000	1/5/2006 with 18 months interest	57,200
		Equipment	14,000
		New extension	70,000
		Cleaning	2,600
		Light and heat	2,800
		Insurance	6,200
		Telephone	1,660
		Purchases – shop	42,100
		Purchases – supplies	36,800
		Balance at Bank 31/12/2006	7,470
	327,850		327,850

The following information and instructions are to be taken into account:

1. Closing stocks at 31/12/2006: Shop €1,600, Heating oil €250.
2. Cleaning is done under contract payable monthly in advance and includes a payment of €300 for January 2007.
3. Clients' fees includes fees for 2007 of €3,000. Clients' fees in arrears at 31/12/2006 €450.
4. The closing figure for bank does not take into account a dishonoured cheque €100 received from a client and lodged in late December.
5. Wages and Salaries include €12,000 per annum paid to the receptionist, who also runs the shop. It is estimated that 70% of this salary, €200 of the light and heat, €500 of the insurance and €340 of the telephone are attributable to the shop.
6. On 31/12/2006 the Oak Health Centre Ltd. decided to re-value Buildings at €680,000.
7. Electricity due 31/12/2006 €270.
8. Creditors for supplies to the Health Centre Ltd. at 31/12/2006 are €1,400
9. Depreciation to be provided as follows:
   Buildings 2% of cost for the full year.
   Equipment 15% of cost per annum.
   Furniture 25% of cost per annum.

You are required to:

(a) Calculate the company's reserves on 1/1/2006. **(20)**
(b) Calculate the Profit/Loss from the shop for the year ended 31/12/2006. **(12)**
(c) Prepare a Profit and Loss account for the year ended 31/12/2006. **(36)**
(d) Prepare a Balance Sheet on 31/12/2006. **(32)**

(100 marks)

7. Incomplete Records

On 1/1/2006, P. Lynch purchased a business for €590,000 which included the following tangible assets and liabilities: Premises €560,000; Stock €19,000; Debtors €12,000; 3 months Premises Insurance prepaid €1,600; Trade Creditors €18,200; Wages due €2,600 and Cash €200.

During 2006 Lynch did not keep a full set of accounts but was able to supply the following information on 31/12/2006.

Cash Payments: Lodgements €116,000, General Expenses €73,800, Purchases €105,200.
Bank Payments: Furniture €14,000, Creditors €38,800, Light and Heat €5,400, Interest €2,250, annual Premises Insurance Premium €6,800, Delivery Van €28,400.
Bank Lodgements: Debtors €61,000, Cash €116,000, Dividends €3,000.

Each week Lynch took goods from stock to the value of €150 and cash €200 for household expenses.

Lynch borrowed €180,000 on 1/9/2006, part of which was used to purchase an adjoining premises and residence costing €155,000. It was agreed that Lynch would pay interest on the last day of each month at a rate of 5% per annum. The capital sum was to be repaid in a lump sum in the year 2015 and to provide for this the bank was to transfer €1,200 on the last day of each month from Lynch's business bank account into an investment fund commencing on 30/9/2006.

Lynch estimated that 25% of the Furniture, 20% of interest *payable* for the year and 25% of Light and heat *used* should be attributed to the private section of the premises.

Included in the assets and liabilities of the firm on 31/12/2006 were: Stock €16,400, Debtors €20,200, Trade Creditors €30,400, Cash €400, Electricity due €480 and €25 interest earned by the fund to date.

You are required to:

(a) Prepare with workings the Trading and Profit and Loss Accounts for the year ended 31/12/2006. **(52)**
(b) Show the Balance Sheet with workings as at 31/12/2006. **(40)**
(c) (i) Explain the term Accounting Concept?
(ii) Name TWO fundamental accounting concepts.
(iii) Illustrate an accounting concept applying to the accounts of P. Lynch. **(8)**

(100 marks)

SECTION 3 (80 marks)

Answer **ONE** question

8. Costing and Stock Valuation

(a) Overhead Apportionment

Nevis Ltd. has two Production Departments, 1 and 2 and two ancillary Service Departments, A and B. The following are the expected overhead costs for the next period.

Overhead	Total
	€
Depreciation of equipment	16,000
Depreciation of factory buildings	20,000
Factory heating	9,600
Factory cleaning	2,000
Factory canteen	10,800

The following information relates to the Production and Service Departments of the factory.

	Production		Service	
	Dept. 1	Dept. 2	Dept. A	Dept. B
Volume in cubic metres	1,500	3,000	1,000	500
Floor area in square metres	600	800	400	200
Number of employees	60	60	30	30
Book value of equipment	€15,000	€10,000	€5,000	€10,000
Machine hours	3,000	1,000		

You are required to:

(i)   Calculate the overhead to be absorbed by each Department stating clearly the basis of apportionment used.

(ii) Transfer the Service Department costs to Production Departments 1 and 2 on the basis of machine hours.

(iii) Calculate machine hour overhead absorption rates for Departments 1 and 2.

(iv) Explain what is meant by 're-apportionment' of overheads.

(v)   Illustrate and explain 'over-absorption' of overheads.

(b) Stock Valuation

Cape Ltd. is a retail store that buys and sells one commodity. The following information relates to the purchases and sales of the firm for the year 2006.

Period	Purchases on credit	Credit Sales	Cash Sales
01/01/2006 to 31/03/2006	3,200 @ €5 each	800 @ €10 each	1,000 @ €11 each
01/04/2006 to 30/06/2006	2,100 @ €7 each	1,000 @ €11 each	1,200 @ €10 each
01/07/2006 to 30/09/2006	2,000 @ €8 each	1,200 @ €11 each	1,200 @ €12 each
01/10/2006 to 31/12/2006	1,400 @ €9 each	1,100 @ €13 each	1,000 @ €13 each

On 1/1/2006 there was opening stock of 3,500 units @ €5 each.

You are required to:

(i)   Calculate the value of closing stock using the 'first in first out' (FIFO) method.
(ii) Prepare a Trading Account for the year ended 31/12/2006.

(80 marks)

9. Cash Budgeting

Aisling Ltd. is preparing to set up business on 1/7/2007 and has made the following forecast for the first six months of trading:

	July €	August €	September €	October €	November €	December €	Total €
Sales	425,000	440,000	580,000	590,000	600,000	652,000	3,287,000
Purchases	200,000	215,000	252,000	260,000	350,000	356,000	1,633,000

(i)   The expected selling price is €50 per unit.
(ii)   The cash collection pattern from Sales is expected to be:
   Cash Customers –   30% of sales revenue will be for immediate cash and cash discount of 5% will be allowed.
   Credit Customers – 70% of sales revenue will be from credit customers. These debtors will pay their bills 50% in month after sale and the remainder in the second month after sale.
(iii) The cash payments pattern for purchases is expected to be:
   Credit Suppliers –   The purchases will be paid for 50% in month after purchase when 2% cash discount will be received.
   The remaining purchases will be paid for in the second month after purchase.
(iv)   Expenses of the business will be settled as follows:
   Expected Costs   Wages €35,000 per month payable as incurred.
   Variable overheads €10 per unit payable as incurred.
   Fixed overheads (including depreciation) €42,000 per month payable as incurred.
   Capital Costs   Equipment will be purchased in July costing €45,000 which will have a useful life of 5 years. To finance this purchase a loan of €40,000 will be secured at 10% per annum.
   Interest to be paid monthly, but capital loan repayments will not commence until January 2007.

You are required to:

(a)   Prepare a cash budget for the six months July to December 2007.
(b)   Prepare a budgeted Profit and loss account for the six months ended 31/12/2007.
(c)   Define 'cash budget' and describe two of its advantages.

(80 marks)

LEAVING CERTIFICATE ACCOUNTING

HIGHER LEVEL

Marking Scheme – 2007

Introduction

The solutions and marking scheme for Accounting, Higher Level is attached.

The solutions are printed and the marks allocated to each line/figure are highlighted and shown in a circle like this ❻ alongside.

These marks are then totalled for each section/page and shown in a square like this **40**.

Accounting solutions are mainly computational and most figures are made up of more than one component. If a figure is wrong per the solution, the examiners analyse the make-up of the candidate's figure and allocate some marks for each correct element included. To facilitate this, where relevant, the make-up of the figures is shown in workings attached to the solution.

In some Accounting questions there can be a number of alternative approaches and formats that can be validly used by candidates (e.g. a bank reconciliation statement can start with either the bank statement figure or the adjusted bank account balance). The solutions provided here are based on the approaches adopted by the vast majority of teachers/candidates and alternatives are not included. In cases where a valid alternative solution is required, it is provided for the examiners, so that full marks can be gained for correct accounting treatment.

Sometimes the solution to a part of a question may depend on the answer computed in another part of that question. Where a calculation in Section (a) is incorrect, allowance is made for this is subsequent sections.

Question 1 – Solution

(a)   **Trading and Profit and Loss Account for the Year Ended 31/12/2006**   **75**

		€	€	€
Sales				1,760,000 ❸
Less Cost of Sales				
Stock			75,200 ❸	
Add Purchases	W 1		1,211,000 ❽	
			1,286,200	
Less Stock 31/12/2006	W 2		(81,200) ❹	(1,205,000)
Gross Profit				555,000
Less Expenses				
Administration				
Patent written off	W 3	6,400 ❹		
Salaries and General expenses	W 4	180,600 ❸		
Directors fees		48,000 ❷		
Rent		19,600 ❷		
Depreciation – Buildings		18,640 ❸	273,240	
Selling and Distribution				
Bad Debts written off		1,750 ❸		
Advertising	W 5	15,700 ❻		
Depreciation – Delivery van	W 6	38,000 ❹		
Increase in bad debts provision	W 7	716 ❹	56,166	(329,406)
				225,594
Add Operating Income				
Discount	W 8		11,500 ❹	
Profit on Sale of Van	W 9		3,250 ❹	14,750
Operating Profit				240,344
Investment Income	W 10			28,800 ❸
				269,144
Debenture Interest	W 11			(14,400) ❸
Net Profit				254,744
Less Appropriations				
Preference Dividend paid			20,000 ❷	
Ordinary dividend paid			28,000 ❷	
Preference dividend due			20,000 ❷	
Ordinary dividend due			60,000 ❷	(128,000)
Retained Profit				126,744
Profit and Loss Balance 1/1/2006				(17,200) ❶
Profit and Loss Balance 31/12/2006				109,544 ❸

(b) **Balance Sheet as at 31/12/2006**

		Cost €	Acc. Dep. €	Net €	Total €
Intangible fixed assets					
Patents (32,000 – 6,400)					25,600 ❸
Tangible Fixed Assets					
Buildings	W12	932,000 ❸	18,640 ❶	913,360	
Delivery Vans	W13 & 14	312,000 ❸	110,750 ❸	201,250	
		1,244,000	129,390	1,114,610	1,114,610
Financial Assets					
9% Investments					320,000 ❷
					1,460,210
Current Assets					
Stock	W15			81,200 ❷	
Debtors		97,900 ❷			
Less provision		(3,916) ❶		93,984	
Insurance Company				52,000 ❶	
Investment income due				21,600 ❸	248,784
Creditors: Amounts falling due within one year					
Creditors	W16			86,690 ❸	
Bank	W17			43,160 ❺	
Preference dividend due				20,000 ❷	
Ordinary dividend due				60,000 ❷	
Debenture interest due				9,600 ❸ (219,450)	29,334
					1,489,544
Financed by					
Creditors: amounts falling due after more than one year					
8% Debentures					180,000 ❷
Capital and Reserves			Authorised	Issued	
Ordinary shares @ €1 each			1,200,000	800,000 ❷	
11% Preference shares @ €1 each			600,000	400,000 ❷	
			1,800,000	1,200,000	
Profit and Loss Balance				109,544	1,309,544
Capital Employed					1,489,544

Workings

1.	Purchases	$1,320,000 - 46,000 - 12,000 - 51,000$	1,211,000
2.	Closing stock	$85,200 - 4,000$	81,200
3.	Patent	$(24,800 + 7,200) \div 5$	6,400
4.	Salaries and Gen. expenses	$199,600 - 19,000$	180,600
5.	Advertising	$14,800 + 200 + 700$	15,700
6.	Depreciation Delivery van	$32,000 + 750 + 5250$	38,000
		$8,750 + 29,250$	
7.	Provision for bad debts	$3,912 - 3,200$	716 Dr
8.	Discount	$10,800 + 700$	11,500
9.	Profit on sale of van	$24,000 - 10,000 - 17,250$	3,250
10.	Investment Income	$21,600 + 7,200$	28,800
11.	Debenture Interest	$5,000 - 200 + 9,600$	14,400
12.	Buildings	$902,000 - 40,000 + 70,000$	932,000
13.	Delivery vans at cost	$280,000 + 56,000 - 24,000$	312,000
14.	Provision for Dep. – Vans	$90,000 + 38,000 - 17,250$	110,750
15.	Debtors	$100,400 - 2,500$	97,900
16.	Creditors	$86,600 + 90$	86,690
17.	Bank Overdraft as per trial balance	$44,000 - 90 - 750)$	
		$42,760 + 400$	43,160

Question 2 – Solution

22

(a)   **Adjusted Debtors Ledger Control Account**

	€			€	
Balance b/d	30,000	❶	Balance b/d	530	❶
Discount disallowed (i)	92	❸	Interest (ii)	70	❹
Restocking charge (vi)	12	❹	Credit note (iv)	520	❹
Balance c/d	530	❶	Sales overstated (v)	90	❹
			Balance c/d	29,424	
	30,634			30,634	
Balance b/d	29,424		Balance b/d	530	

30

(b)

Schedule of Debtors Accounts Balances

			€		€	
Balance as per list of debtors					24,734	❹
Add	Sales – cash and credit error	(iii)		3,240 ❺		
	Sales	(v)		1,560 ❺	4,800	
					29,534	
Deduct	Interest	(ii)		50 ❺		
	Credit note	(iv)		572 ❺		
	Reduction in charge	(vi)		18 ❺	640	
Net Balance as per adjusted Control Account					28,894	❶

8

(c)

(i) **Contra Item ❺**

A contra item is an offset of a debtor against a creditor where debtor and creditor are the same person

(ii) **Opening Balance €530 ❸**
   • A full payment of a debt followed by a credit note (returns or reduction)
   • Over payment of a debt
   • Full payment followed by discount

Question 3 – Solution

(a)   15

Land and Buildings Account

		€			€
01/01/02	Balance b/d	670,000 ❶			
01/01/02	Revaluation Res.	140,000 ❶	31/12/02 Balance c/d		810,000
		810,000			810,000
01/01/03	Balance b/d	810,000	01/01/03 Disposal		290,000 ❶
			31/12/03 Balance c/d		520,000
		810,000			810,000
01/01/04	Balance b/d	520,000 ❶	31/12/04 Balance c/d		1,220,000
	Bank	470,000 ❶			
	Bank	150,000 ❶			
	Wages	80,000 ❶			
		1,220,000			1,220,000
01/01/05	Balance b/d	1,220,000	31/12/05 Balance c/d		1,403,000
01/01/05	Revaluation Reserve	183,000 ❷			
		1,403,000			1,403,000
01/01/06	Balance b/d	1,403,000	01/01/06 Disposal		598,00 ❸
01/01/06	Revaluation Reserve	55,000 ❸	31/12/06 Balance c/d		860,000
		1,458,000			1,458,000

21

Provision for Depreciation on Buildings Account

	€				€	
01/01/02 Revaluation Res.	68,800	❷	01/01/02 Balance b/d		68,800	❷
31/12/02 Balance c/d	10,400		31/12/02 Profit and Loss		10,400	❷
	79,200				79,200	
31/12/03 Balance c/d	20,800		01/01/03 Balance b/d		10,400	
			31/12/03 Profit and Loss		10,400	❷
	20,800				20,800	
31/12/04 Balance c/d	45,200		01/01/04 Balance b/d		20,800	
			31/12/04 Profit and Loss		24,400	❷
	45,200				45,200	
01/01/05 Revaluation Res.	45,200	❷	01/01/05 Balance c/d		45,200	
31/12/05 Balance c/d	28,060		31/12/05 Profit and Loss		28,060	❷
	73,260				73,260	
01/01/06 Disposal	11,960	❷	01/01/06 Balance b/d		28,060	
01/01/06 Revaluation Res.	16,100	❸	31/12/06 Profit and Loss		17,200	❷
31/12/06 Balance c/d	17,200					
	42,400				42,400	
			01/01/07 Balance b/d		17,200	

3

Disposal of Land Account

	€			€	
01/01/03 Land and Buildings	290,000	❶	01/01/03 Bank	340,000	❶
31/12/03 P & L a/c (Profit)	50,000	❶			
	340,000			340,000	

4

Disposal of Buildings Account

	€			€	
01/01/06 Land and Buildings	598,000	❶	01/01/06 Depreciation	11,960	❶
31/12/06 P & L (Profit)	73,960	❶	01/01/06 Bank	660,000	❶
	671,960			671,960	

10

Revaluation Reserve Account

	€				€	
01/01/03 Revenue reserve	50,000	❶	01/01/02 Land and Buildings		140,000	❶
01/01/06 Revenue reserve	268,000	❶	Provision for Dep		68,800	❶
Balance	190,100	❷	01/01/05 Land and Buildings		183,000	❶
			Provision for Dep		45,200	❶
			01/01/06 Land and Buildings		55,000	❶
			Provision for Dep		16,100	❶
	508,100				508,100	

2

Revenue Reserve Account

	€	
01/01/03 Revaluation reserve	50,000	❶
01/01/06 Revaluation reserve	268,000	❶
	318,000	

5

(b)

Balance Sheet as at 31/12/2006

	€		€		€	
Fixed Assets						
Land and Buildings	860,000	❶	17,200	❶	842,800	❶
Capital and Reserves						
Revaluation Reserve					190,000	❶
Revenue reserve					318,000	❶

Question 4 - Solution

60

	1/1/2006 €	Jan €	Feb €	Mar €	Apr €	May €	Aug €	Dec €	31/12/2006 €
Land & Buildings	414,000	106,000 ②	300,000 ①						820,000
Depreciation	(12,420)	12,420 ②						(14,300) ③	(14,300)
Vehicles	68,400		50,000 ①		19,000 ②				137,400
Depreciation	(29,700)				4,500 ②			(20,000) ②	(45,200)
Goodwill				8,000 ②					8,000
Stock	53,820			12,500 ②					86,320
Debtors	55,530		20,000 ①	(13,500) ②			300 ②		42,330
Advertising prepaid	1,350				3,000 ②			(3,100) ②	1,250 ①
	550,980	118,420	378,000	(1000)	23,500	3,000	300	(37,400)	1,035,800
Ordinary Shares	387,000		290,000 ②						677,000
Share Prem.	36,000		58,000 ②						94,000
P&L Bal	58,050			(1000) ①	(500) ①		1,000 ②	(14,300) ① (20,000) ① (3,100) ① 2,000 ①	22,150 ③
Creditors	58,680		30,000 ①		24,000 ②				88,680 ③
Bank	9,090					500 ②	(700) ②		32,890 ②
Wages due	2,160								2,160
Revaluation Reserve		118,420 ③							118,420
Rent Rec.						2,500 ②	300	(2,000) ①	500 ①
	550,980	118,420	378,000	(1000)	23,500	3,000	300	(37,400)	1,035,800

Question 5 – Solution

(a) `45`

Cash Purchases

Credit Purchases	$=$	$\dfrac{102,000 \times 12}{2.4}$	$=$	€510,000
Cash Purchases	$=$	$620,000 - 510,000$	$=$	110,000 `9`

Interest Cover

$$\dfrac{\text{Net profit before interest}}{\text{Interest}} \quad = \quad \dfrac{60,000}{27,000} \quad = \quad 2.22 \text{ times} \quad \textbf{8}$$

Dividend Yield

$$\dfrac{\text{DPS} \times 100}{\text{Market Price}} \quad = \quad \dfrac{4.92c \times 100}{120c} \quad = \quad 4.1\% \quad \textbf{12}$$

Period to recoup price

$$\dfrac{\text{Market price}}{\text{Dividend per share}} \quad = \quad \dfrac{120}{4.92} \quad = \quad 24.39 \text{ years} \quad \textbf{8}$$

Projected Market Value of Ordinary Share

Price Earnings Ratio × Earnings per Share = $14 \times 8c$ $=$ €1.12   **8**

(b) `35`

Performance **15**

The ROCE and ROEF of 6.5% and 4.8% respectively are both disappointing. **8**
The ROCE of 6.5% is only marginally better than the return from risk free investments of around 5%. This indicates an inefficient use of funds and shareholders would be unhappy. The Return on Equity Funds of 4.8% is less than the Return from risk free investments.

The dividend per share is 4.92c and the dividend Yield is 4.1%. This yield is less than the Return from risk free investments of about 5%. **7**

Dividend Cover is 1.125 times indicating that a very small percentage of the profits is being retained. The Dividend Cover is low to maintain the yield at 4.1%.

State of Affairs **10**

Liquidity: The Acid Test ratio of 0.99 to 1 shows that the company is liquid. **5**
For every €1 of short-term debt, the company has 99c available in liquid assets.

Gearing: The company is highly geared at 59.6%. This indicates that the company is dependent on outside borrowings and therefore at risk from outside investors. The Interest Cover is 2.2 times. **5**

Prospects ⑩

1 point @ 4 marks is compulsory and 3 others at 2 marks each

Market Value: The Market value of Ordinary Share was 1.20 and is projected to fall to
€1.12 – a **fall** of 6.6% in value.   ④
The shareholders would be unhappy with this as it indicates a lack of market confidence
in the company.

ROCE: The ROCE of 6.5% is expected to rise to 8.5%.   ②
This represents an improving prospect.

Liquidity: The Acid Test figure of 0.99 to 1 is expected to rise to 1.1 to 1 a slight
improvement.   ②

Gearing: The company is highly geared at 59.6% indicating that it is dependent on
outside borrowing and therefore at risk. The gearing will improve in 2007, the
projected figure being 58% which is still high but the trend is good.   ②

Sector: The company is in the pharmaceutical sector. With an aging and increasingly
health conscious population, prospects are good.

(c)   **20**

Bank Loan Application

Yes/No ②
2 points at 5 marks each (Gearing and ROCE)
    2 points at 4 marks each

Gearing ⑤
The company is highly geared
The gearing will get worse with a further loan of 150,000.
The gearing with the loan will be 65%.
The Interest Cover will get worse

Return on Capital Employed ⑤
The ROCE will be 8.5% next year which is less than the 10% interest to be charged on the loan.

Dividend Cover/policy ④
The Dividend Cover is 1.1 times and is projected to increase to 1.31 times.
The Dividend Cover is low
Not enough of earnings are retained for repayment of the loan.

Purpose for which loan is required ④
The loan is required for future expansion and should generate extra income to service the loan.

Security
The Fixed Assets are valued at 680,000 but one should question depreciation policy to
ascertain the real value of the assets.
    The Investments alone have a market value of 210,000 which would provide security for the
loan of 150,000.
    The security is adequate.

Liquidity

The liquidity ratio of 0.99 to 1

It is expected to improve to 1.1 to 1 in 2007.

However the extra interest payment will cause this to be less favourable.

Question 6 – Solution

(a)   20

Statement of Capital and Reserves on 1/1/2006

Assets		€		€
Buildings and grounds	(500,000 – 20,000)	480,000 ②		
Equipment	(70,000 – 21,000)	49,000 ②		
Furniture	(20,000 – 10,000)	10,000 ②		
Investments		70,000 ①		
Stock – health food for resale		1,300 ①		
Stock – oil		640 ①		
Contract cleaning prepaid		250 ①		
Cash at bank		7,250 ①		618,440
Liabilities				
Creditors for supplies		1,250 ①		
Customers advance deposits		4,300 ①		
Loan		50,000 ②		
Interest on loan (14 months @ €400 per month)		5,600 ②		
Issued Capital		300,000 ①		(361,150)
Reserves 1/1/2006				**257,290** ②

(b)   12

Health Shop Profit and Loss Account for the year ended 31/12/2006

	€		€
Shop receipts			65,000 ②
Less expenses			
Cost of goods sold (1,300 + 42,100 – 1,600)	41,800 ⑤		
Light and heat	200 ①		
Insurance	500 ①		
Telephone	340 ①		
Wages and salaries (70% × 12,000)	8,400 ②		51,240
Profit from Health shop			13,760

(c)   36

Profit and Loss Account for year ended 31/12/2006

Income

Interest received		3,500 ❶	
Profit from health shop		13,760 ❶	
Customer's fees	W 1	254,350 ❺	271,610

Less Expenses

Wages and salaries (86,220 – 8,400)		77,820 ❷	
Insurance (6,200 – 500)		5,700 ❶	
Light and heat	W 2	3,260 ❺	
Purchases – supplies	W 3	36,950 ❸	
Loan interest	W 4	1,600 ❸	
Laundry		800 ❶	
Postage and telephone (1,660 – 340)		1,320 ❶	
Depreciation – Buildings		11,400 ❶	
Equipment		12,600 ❶	
Furniture		5,000 ❶	
Contract cleaning	W 5	2,550 ❸	(159,000)

Net Profit for year	112,610	❻
Add Reserves 1/1/2006	257,290	❶
Profit and Loss balance 31/12/2006	369,900	

(d)   **32**

Balance Sheet as at 31/12/2006

		Cost €	Depreciation €		Net €
Fixed Assets					
Buildings and grounds		680,000 ❶	-		680,000
Equipment (70,000 + 14,000)		84,000 ❷	33,600 ❷		50,400
Furniture		20,000 ❶	15,000 ❷		5,000
		784,000	48,600		735,400
Investments					70,000 ❷
					805,400
Current Assets					
Investment income due		500 ❷			
Closing stock – shop goods		1,600 ❶			
Oil		250 ❶			
Cleaning prepaid		300 ❷			
Customer's fees due (450 +100)		550 ❸			
Bank	W 6	7,370 ❷	10,570		
Less Creditors: amounts falling due within 1 year					
Electricity due		270 ❷			
Customer's advance deposits		3,000 ❷			
Creditors for supplies		1,400 ❷	(4,670)		5,900
					811,300

	Authorised	Issued	Net
Financed by			
Share Capital and Reserves			
Ordinary Shares	430,000 ❶	300,000 ❶	
Revaluation Reserve		141,400 ❸	
Profit and Loss balance		369,900	811,300
			811,300

Workings

W 1	**Customer's fees**	€	€	
	Amount received	252,600	252,600	
	Less Dishonoured cheque	(100)	–	
	Fees due	550	450	
	Advance deposits	4,300	4,300	
	Less fees prepaid	(3,000)	(3,000)	
				254,350
W 2	**Light and heat**			
	Amount paid		2,800	
	Stock oil 1/1/2006		640	
	Electricity due		270	
	Stock oil 31/12/2006		(250)	
	Charge to shop		(200)	3,260

W 3 **Purchases**	$36,800 + 1,400 - 1,250$	36,950
W 4 **Loan Interest**	$7,200/18 \times 4$	1,600
W 5 **Contract cleaning**	$2,600 + 250 - 300$	2,550
W 6 **Bank**	$7,470 - 100$	7,370

Question 7 – Solution

52

(a)   **Trading and Profit and Loss Account for the year ended 31/12/2006**

	€		€	
Sales			374,800	⑪
Less Cost of Sales				
Opening stock	19,000	②		
Purchases (156,200 – 7,800)	148,400	⑦		
	167,400			
Closing stock	(16,400)	②	(151,000)	
Gross Profit			223,800	
Less Expenses				
General expenses	71,200	⑤		
Insurance	6,700	⑥		
Interest	2,400	④		
Light and heat	4,410	⑥	84,710	
			139,090	
Add Income from Investment Fund			25	③
Net Profit			139,115	⑥

(b) `40`

Balance Sheet as at 31/12/2006

	€	€	€
Intangible Fixed Assets			
Goodwill			18,000 ❸
Tangible Fixed Assets			
Buildings	715,000 ❷		
Delivery Vans	28,400 ❶		
Furniture	10,500 ❷		753,900
Financial Assets			
Investment Fund			4,825 ❷
			776,725
Current Assets			
Stock	16,400 ❶		
Debtors	20,200 ❶		
Bank	104,550 ❺		
Cash	400 ❷		
Prepayments (Insurance)	1,700 ❸	143,250	
Creditors: amounts falling due within 1 year			
Creditors	30,400 ❶		
Interest due	750 ❸		
Electricity due	480 ❶	(31,630)	111,620
			888,345
Financed By			
Creditors: Amounts falling due after more than one year			
Loan			180,000 ❷
Capital		590,000 ❷	
Capital introduced		3,000 ❸	
Net Profit		139,115	
		732,115	
Less Drawings		(23,770) ❻	708,345
			888,345

(c) `8`

(i) **Accounting concepts**

Accounting concepts are the accounting practices or rules that are applied in the preparation of financial statements.

(ii) **Fundamental Accounting concepts**

Accruals, Going Concern, Consistency and Prudence

(iii) **The accruals Concept** – All expenses incurred in a particular period must be included in the accounts of that period regardless of whether they are paid or not. Similarly, all revenue income must be included in the accounts of that period whether received or not. E.g. Electricity due for the current year must be included in the accounts, although the bill may not be paid until the following year as the expense refers to the current year. Insurance prepaid should not be included in the current year's accounts as the payment refers to the following year.

Workings

1. **Sales** – Credit (61,000 + 20,200 – 12,000)   69,200
          – Cash (116,000 + 73,800 + 105,200 + 10,400 + 400 – 200)   305,600

   Total Sales   **374,800**

2. **Purchases**
   Credit purchases (– 18,200 + 30,400 + 38,800)   51,000
   Cash purchases   105,200

   Total Purchases   156,200
   Less drawings of stock   (7,800)

   Total purchases   **148,400**

3. **General Expenses** (73,800 – 2,600)   71,200

4. **Insurance** (1,600 + 6,800 – 1,700)   6,700

5. **Interest** (3,000 – 600)   2,400

6. **Light and heat** (5,400 + 480 – 1,470)   4,410

7. **Drawings** (7,800 + 10,400 + 1,470 + 600 + 3,500)   23,770

Question 8 – Solution

(a)

(i)   `29`

Overhead	Basis		Total	Production		Service	
				Dept 1	Dept 2	Dept A	Dept B
Dep of Equipment	Book value	①	16,000	6,000 ①	4,000 ①	2,000 ①	4,000 ①
Dep of Factory	Floor area	①	20,000	6,000 ①	8,000 ①	4,000 ①	2,000 ①
Factory heating	Volume	①	9,600	2,400 ①	4,800 ①	1,600 ①	800 ①
Factory cleaning	Floor area	①	2,000	600 ①	800 ①	400 ①	200 ①
Canteen	No. employees	①	10,800	3,600 ①	3,600 ①	1,800 ①	1,800 ①
			58,400	18,600 ①	21,200 ①	9,800 ①	8,800 ①

(ii)   `8`

	Production		Service	
	Dept 1	Dept 2	Dept A	Dept B
Total Cost	18,600	21,200	9,800	8,800
Apportion Dept A to Production	7,350 ②	2,450 ②	(9,800)	
Apportion Dept B to Production	6,600 ②	2,200 ②		(8,800)
	32,550	25,850		

(iii)   **8**

Machine hour absorption rate

Dept 1 $\dfrac{32,550}{3,000}$ = €10.85 per machine hour **④**

Dept 2 $\dfrac{25,850}{1,000}$ = €25.85 per machine hour **④**

(iv)   **2**

Re-apportionment:
This is the term used where Service Department costs are re-apportioned between production departments because overheads can only be recovered by being included as part of the cost of production.

(v)   **4**

Over-absorption:
Over-absorption is when costs are over recovered – budgeted costs are greater than actual costs. The cost of fuel/power reduced

(b)

(i)   **15**

Purchases in units	Cost	Purchases at cost
3,200	@ €5	16,000
2,100	@ €7	14,700
2,000	@ €8	16,000
1,400	@ €9	12,600
8,700 Total		**€59,300 Total**

Credit Sales Units	Credit Sales €	Cash Sales Units	Cash Sales €	Total Sales Units	Total Sales €
800 @ 10	8,000	1,000 @ 11	11,000	1,800	19,000
1,000 @ 11	11,000	1,200 @ 10	12,000	2,200	23,000
1,200 @ 11	13,200	1,200 @ 12	14,400	2,400	27,600
1,100 @ 13	14,300	1,000 @ 13	13,000	2,100	27,300
4,100	**46,500**	**4,400**	**50,400**	**8,500**	**96,900**

Closing Stock in Units = Opening Stock 3,500 + Purchases 8,700 – Sales 8,500
                                       = **3,700 units** **⑤**

Closing Stock in €
1,400	@ €9	=	12,600	❷
2,000	@ €8	=	16,000	❷
300	@ €7	=	2,100	❷
3,700			30,700	❹

(ii) ⬛14⬛

Trading account for the year ending 31/12/2006

	€	€	
Sales		96,900	❸
Less cost of Sales			
Opening Stock	17,500 ❷		
Purchases	59,300 ❸		
	76,800		
Closing Stock	30,700 ❷	(46,100)	
Gross Profit		50,800	❹

Question 9 – solution

(a) ⬛5⬛

Cash Budget – July to December

Receipts	Jul	Aug	Sept	Oct	Nov	Dec	Total
Cash Sales Rec	121,125 ❶	125,400 ❶	165,300 ❶	168,150 ❶	171,000 ❶	185,820 ❶	936,795
Credit Sales 1 month		148,750 ❶	154,000 ❶	203,000 ❶	206,500 ❶	210,000 ❶	922,250
Credit Sales 2 months			148,750 ❶	154,000 ❶	203,000 ❶	206,500 ❶	712,250
	121,125	**274,150**	**468,050**	**525,150**	**580,500**	**602,320**	**2,571,295**
Payments							
Purchases		98,000 ❶	105,350 ❶	123,480 ❶	127,400 ❶	171,500 ❶	625,730
Purchases		100,000 ❶	107,500 ❶	126,000 ❶	130,000 ❶	463,500	
Wages	35,000 ❸	35,000	35,000	35,000	35,000	35,000	210,000
Variable overhead	85,000 ❶	88,000 ❶	116,000 ❶	118,000 ❶	120,000 ❶	130,400 ❶	657,400
Fixed overhead	41,250 ❷	41,250 ❶	41,250 ❶	41,250 ❶	41,250 ❶	41,250 ❶	247,500
Equipment	45,000 ❶						45,000
Interest	333 ❷	333 ❶	333 ❶	333 ❶	333 ❶	333 ❶	1,998
	206,583	**262,583**	**397,933**	**425,563**	**449,983**	**508,483**	**2,251,128**
Net monthly cash flow	(85,458) ❶	11,567 ❶	70,117 ❶	99,587 ❶	130,517 ❶	93,837 ❶	320,167
Bank Loan	40,000 ❶						40,000
Opening balance		(45,458) ❶	(33,891)	36,226	135,813	266,330	
Closing balance	(45,458)	(33,891)	36,226	135,813	266,330	360,167 ❷	360,167

(b)   **14**

Budgeted Profit and Loss Account for 6 months ending 31/12/2007

	€		€	
Sales (65,740 @ 50)			3,287,000	❷
Less Cost of Sales				
Material	1,633,000	❶		
Labour (6 × 35,000)	210,000	❶		
Variable overhead	657,400	❶		
Fixed overhead (6 × €41,250)	247,500	❶	(2,747,900)	
Gross Profit			539,100	
Depreciation – equipment	4,500	❶		
Discount allowed (€3,287,000 × 30% × 5%)	49,305	❷	(53,805)	
			485,295	
Add Discount Received			12,770	❷
			498,065	
Less interest			(2,000)	❶
Net Profit			**496,065**	❷

(c)   **8**

A cash budget is a forecast or plan of cash inflow and cash outflow over a period
Advantages:
  Highlights whether enough cash will be available to meet future needs
  Helps to give advance knowledge so that overdraft can be arranged if shortfall occurs
  Helps to predict future surpluses so that short-term investment can be made

STATE EXAMINATIONS COMMISSION

Leaving Certificate Examination, 2006

Accounting – Higher Level

(400 marks)

Monday, 19ᵀᴴ June 2006 – Afternoon, 2.00 p.m. to 5.00 p.m.

This paper is divided into 3 Sections:

Section 1: Financial Accounting (120 marks).

This section has 4 questions (Numbers 1–4). The first question carries 120 marks and the remaining three questions carry 60 marks each.
 Candidates should answer either **QUESTION 1 only** OR else attempt any **TWO** of the remaining three questions in this section.

Section 2: Financial Accounting (200 marks).

This section has three questions (Numbers 5–7). Each question carries 100 marks.
Candidates should answer any **TWO** questions.

Section 3: Management Accounting (80 marks).

This section has two questions (Numbers 8 and 9). Each question carries 80 marks.
Candidates should answer **ONE** of these questions.

Calculators

Calculators may be used in answering the questions on this paper: however, it is very important that workings are shown in the answerbook(s) so that full credit can be given for correct work.

SECTION 1 (120 marks)

Answer **QUESTION 1** OR any **TWO** other questions

1. **Sole Trader – Final Accounts**

The following trial balance was extracted from the books of K. Kelly on 31/12/2005.

	€	€
Buildings (cost €900,000)	855,000	
Delivery Vans (cost €130,000)	60,500	
6% Investments 1/6/2005	160,000	
Patents (incorporating 3 months' investment income)	60,600	
5% Fixed Mortgage (including increase of €100,000 received on 1/4/2005)		300,000
Debtors and Creditors	76,500	85,500
Purchases and Sales	650,000	980,000
Stock 1/1/2005	65,700	
Commission	20,000	
Salaries and General Expenses (incorporating suspense)	192,500	
Provision for Bad Debts		3,900
Discount (net)		3,600
Rent		12,000
Mortgage Interest Paid for the First 3 Months	3,000	
Insurance	7,800	
VAT		4,300
PRSI		2,500
Bank		60,800
Drawings	36,000	
Capital		735,000
	2,187,600	2,187,600

The following information and instructions are to be taken into account:

(i) Stock at 31/12/2005 at cost was €72,500. No record had been made in the books for 'goods in transit' on 31/12/2005. The invoice for these goods had been received showing the recommended retail selling price of €7,000 which is cost plus 25 per cent.

(ii) Provide for depreciation on vans at the annual rate of 15 per cent of cost from the date of purchase to the date of sale.
NOTE: On 30/4/2005 a delivery van which cost €35,000 on 31/10/2002 was traded against a new van which cost €41,000. An allowance of €15,000 was made on the old van. The cheque for the net amount of this transaction was entered in the bank account but was incorrectly treated as a purchase of trading stock. These were the only entries made in the books in respect of this transaction.

(iii) The suspense figure arises as a result of the posting of an incorrect figure for mortgage interest to the mortgage interest account and discount received €700 entered only in the creditors account. The correct interest was entered in the bank account.

(iv) Patents, which incorporate three months' investment income, are to be written off over a five-year period, commencing in 2005.

(v) Provision to be made for mortgage interest due.

(vi) A new warehouse was purchased during the year for €200,000 plus VAT 12.5 per cent. The amount paid to the vendor was entered in the buildings account. No entry was made in the VAT account.

(vii) Provide for depreciation on buildings at the rate of 2 per cent *of cost* per annum. It was decided to revalue the buildings at €1,200,000 on 31/12/2005.

(viii) Provision for bad debts to be adjusted to 3 per cent of debtors.

You are required to prepare a:

(a) Trading and profit and loss account, for the year ended 31/12/2005. **(75)**

(b) Balance sheet as at 31/12/2005. **(45)**

(120 marks)

2. Farm Accounts

Among the assets and liabilities of Sean and Mary Kelly, who carry on a mixed farming business, on 1/1/2005 are: land and buildings at cost €290,000; machinery at cost €60,000; electricity due €400; value of cattle €60,000; milk cheque due €2,400; stock of fuel €800; and value of sheep €18,000.

The following is a summary taken from their cheque payments and lodgements books for the year ended 31/12/2005.

Lodgements	€	Cheque Payments	€
Balance	2,800	Fertilizer	3,000
Milk	28,000	General Farm Expenses	15,000
Sheep	22,000	Dairy Wages	1,500
Cattle	13,000	Sheep	19,000
Lambs	12,600	Cattle	14,000
Calves	5,900	Light, Heat and Fuel	3,400
EU Subsidy – Sheep	3,400	Machinery	6,500
EU Subsidy – Cattle	2,500	Repairs	6,300
Wool	1,800	Veterinary Fees and Medicines	1,750
Forestry Premium	2,100	Bank Loan Plus 18 Months' Interest	
Six Months' Interest from		at 6% per annum on 30/4/2005	16,350
4% Investment Bond	600	Balance	7,900
	€94,700		€94,700

The following information and instructions are to be taken into account:

		Cattle	Sheep
(i)	Value of livestock on 31/12/2005 was	€62,000	€25,000

(ii) Farm produce used by the family during the year – milk €700; lamb €300.

(iii) General farm expenses, fertilizer and veterinary fees and medicines are to be apportioned 60 per cent to 'Cattle and Milk' and 40 per cent to 'Sheep'.

(iv) Other expenses are to be apportioned 80 per cent to farm and 20 per cent to household.
(v) Depreciation to be provided on machinery at the rate of 10 per cent of cost per annum.
(vi) Veterinary fees and medicines include a cheque for family health insurance for €650.
(vii) On 31/12/2005 a milk cheque was due €1,800, creditors for fertilizers amounted to €400 and stock of fuel was €900.

You are required to:

(a) Prepare a statement of capital for the farm on 1/1/2005. **(20)**
(b) Prepare an enterprise analysis account for 'Cattle and Milk' and 'Sheep' for the year ended 31/12/2005. **(20)**
(c) Prepare a general profit and loss account for the year ended 31/12/2005. **(12)**
(d) Give three reasons why farmers should keep a full set of accounts. **(8)**

(60 marks)

3. Cash Flow Statement

The following are the balance sheets of Butler Plc as at 31/12/2004 and 31/12/2005, together with an abridged profit and loss account for the year ended 31/12/2005:

Abridged Profit and Loss Account for the Year Ended 31/12/2005

		€
Operating profit		140,000
Interest for year		(8,000)
Profit before taxation		132,000
Taxation for year		(45,000)
Profit after taxation		87,000
Dividends – Interim	21,000	
– Proposed	45,000	(66,000)
Retained profits for the year		21,000
Retained profits on 1/12/2005		191,000
Retained profits on 31/12/2005		212,000

Balance Sheets as at	31/12/2005		31/12/2004	
Fixed assets	€	€	€	€
Land and buildings at cost	825,000		750,000	
Less accumulated depreciation	(95,000)	730,000	(80,000)	670,000
Machinery at cost	400,000		470,000	
Less accumulated depreciation	(202,000)	198,000	(180,000)	290,000
		928,000		960,000
Financial assets				
Quoted investments		130,000		100,000
Current assets				
Stock	220,000		205,000	
Debtors	200,000		190,000	
Government securities	12,000		–	
Bank	–		10,000	
Cash	2,000		1,000	
	434,000		406,000	
Less creditors: amounts falling due within one year				
Trade creditors	250,000		228,000	
Interest due	1,200		–	
Taxation	50,000		43,000	
Dividends	45,000		34,000	
Bank	6,800		–	
	(353,000)		(305,000)	
Net current assets		81,000		101,000
		1,139,000		1,161,000
Financed by				
Creditors: amounts falling due after more than one year				
9% debentures		75,000		180,000
Capital and reserves				
€1 ordinary shares	830,000		790,000	
Share premium	22,000		–	
Profit and loss account	212,000	1,064,000	191,000	981,000
		1,139,000		1,161,000

The following information is also available:

(i) There were no disposals of buildings during the year but new buildings were acquired.

(ii) There were no purchases of machinery during the year. Machinery was disposed of for €35,000.

(iii) Depreciation charged for the year on machinery in arriving at the operating profit was €60,000.

You are required to:
(a) Prepare the cash flow statement of Butler Plc for the year ended 31/12/2005
 including reconciliation statement(s). **(48)**
(b) Explain why cash flow statements are prepared. **(8)**
(c) Identify a non-cash expense and a non-cash gain. **(4)**
 (60 marks)

4. Published Accounts

Ross Plc has an authorised capital of €800,000 divided into 600,000 ordinary shares at €1 each and 200,000 10 per cent preference shares at €1 each. The following trial balance was extracted from its books on 31/12/2005.

	€	€
9% investments 1/1/2005	200,000	
Patent	64,000	
Land and buildings (revalued on 1/7/2005)	860,000	
Delivery vans at cost	140,000	
Delivery vans – accumulated depreciation on 1/1/2005		64,000
Revaluation reserve		265,000
Debtors and creditors	200,000	95,000
Purchases and sales	700,000	1,221,000
Stock 1/1/2005	70,000	
Directors' fees	89,000	
Salaries and general expenses	175,000	
Discount		6,260
Advertising	23,000	
Investment income		9,000
Profit on sale of land		80,000
Rent	30,000	
Interim dividends	29,000	
Profit and loss balance 1/1/2005		78,000
6% debentures including €100,000		
issued on 1/8/2005		280,000
Bank		18,440
VAT		3,300
Issued capital		
300,000 ordinary shares at €1 each		300,000
160,000 10% preference shares		160,000
	2,580,000	2,580,000

The following information is also relevant:

(i) Stock on 31/12/2005 was valued on a first in first out basis at €72,000.
(ii) The patent was acquired on 1/1/2003 for €80,000. It is being amortised over ten years in equal instalments. The amortisation is to be included in cost of sales.
(iii) On 1/7/2005 the ordinary shareholders received an interim dividend of €21,000 and the preference shareholders received €8,000. The directors propose the payment of the preference dividend due and a final dividend on ordinary shares to bring the total ordinary dividend to 15c per share.

(iv) On 1/7/2005 land which cost €100,000 was sold for €180,000. On this date the remaining land and buildings were revalued at €860,000. Included in this revaluation is land now valued at €160,000 but which originally cost €50,000. The revalued buildings had cost €530,000.

(v) Depreciation is to be provided as follows:
Delivery vans at the rate of 20 per cent of cost.
Buildings at the rate of 2 per cent of cost per annum until date of revaluation and thereafter at 2 per cent per annum of revalued figure.

(vi) Provide for debenture interest due, investment income due, auditors' fees of €8,400 and taxation €40,000.

You are required to:

(a) Prepare the published **profit and loss account** for the year ended 31/12/2005, in accordance with the Companies Acts and appropriate reporting standards, showing the following notes:
1. Tangible fixed assets.
2. Stock.
3. Dividends.
4. Operating profit.
5. Profit on sale of property. **(48)**

(b) What is an audit? Describe an auditor's report that is 'qualified'. **(12)**

(60 marks)

SECTION 2 (200 marks)

Answer any **TWO** questions

5. Interpretation of Accounts

The following figures have been taken from the final accounts of Sawgrass Plc., a manufacturer in the dairy industry, for the year ended 31/12/2005. The company has an authorised capital of €500,000 made up of 400,000 €1 ordinary shares and 100,000 6 per cent preference shares.

Trading and Profit and Loss Account for Year Ended 31/12/2005

	€
Sales	890,000
Cost of sales	(695,000)
Total operating expenses for the year	(120,000)
Interest for year	(20,000)
Net profit for year	55,000
Proposed dividends	(48,000)
Retained profit for year	7,000
Profit and loss balance 1/1/2005	40,000 cr.
Profit and loss balance 31/12/2005	47,000

Ratios and Figures for Year Ended 31/12/2004

Interest cover	5 times
Quick ratio	1.2:1
Earnings per ordinary share	19c
Return on capital employed	14.2%
Market value of ordinary share	€2.10
Gearing	35%
P/E ratio	10 years
Dividend per ordinary share	18c

Balance Sheet as at 31/12/2005

	€	€
Intangible assets	150,000	
Fixed assets	320,000	
Investments (market value €90,000)	105,000	575,000
Current assets (including stock €45,000 and debtors €48,000)	98,000	
Creditors trade	(28,000)	
Proposed dividends	(48,000)	22,000
		597,000
10% debentures (2010/2011)		200,000
Issued capital		
300,000 ordinary shares @ €1 each	300,000	
50,000 6% preference shares @ €1 each	50,000	
Profit and loss balance	47,000	397,000
		597,000

Market value of one ordinary share is €2

You are required to provide answers to the following:

(a) Calculate the following for the year 2005:
1. Interest cover.
2. Earnings per share.
3. Cash sales if the average period of credit given to debtors is two months.
4. How long it would take one ordinary share to recoup (recover) its 2005 market price based on present dividend pay out rate.
5. Dividend yield on ordinary shares **for 2004.**   **(45)**
(b) Indicate whether the debenture holders would be satisfied with the policies and state of affairs of the company. Use available relevant information to support your answer. **(40)**
(c) What actions would you advise the company to take?   **(15)**

(100 marks)

6. Tabular Statement

The financial position of NSL Ltd on 1/1/2005 is shown in the following balance sheet:

Balance Sheet as at 1/1/2005

	Cost €	Dep. to date €	Net €
Fixed assets			
Land and buildings	260,000	25,000	235,000
Equipment	50,000	20,000	30,000
	310,000	45,000	265,000
Current assets			
Stock		70,000	
Debtors (less provision 5%)		85,500	
		155,500	
Less creditors: amounts falling due within one year			
Creditors	61,000		
Bank	23,000		
Expenses due	3,500	87,500	
Net current assets			68,000
			333,000
Financed by			
Capital and reserves			
Authorised – 400,000 ordinary shares @ €1 each			
Issued – 290,000 ordinary shares @ €1 each			290,000
Share premium			14,000
Profit and loss balance			29,000
			333,000

The following transactions took place during 2005:

Jan.   NSL Ltd. bought an adjoining business which included buildings €120,000, debtors €10,000 and creditors €38,000. The purchase price was discharged by granting the seller 80,000 shares in NSL Ltd. at a premium of 20 cent per share.

Feb.   NSL Ltd. decided to revalue land and buildings at €550,000 (which includes land valued at €70,000) on 28/2/2005.

March   Management decided that the provision for bad debts should be raised to 6 per cent of debtors.

April   Goods previously sold for €800 were returned. The selling price of these goods was cost plus 25 per cent. A credit note was issued showing a deduction of 10 per cent of the selling price as a restocking charge.

May   Received a bank statement on 31 May showing a credit transfer received of €4,800 to cover ten months' rent in advance from 1 May and a direct debit of €2,000 to cover fire insurance for the year ended 31/3/2006.

June   A payment of €630 was received from a debtor whose debt had been previously written off and who now wishes to trade with NSL Ltd. again. This represents 70 per cent of the original debt and the debtor had undertaken to pay the remainder of the debt by January 2006.

July   A creditor, who was owed €500 by NSL Ltd., accepted equipment, the book value of which was €400, in full settlement of the debt. The equipment cost €900.

Aug.   An interim dividend of 5c per share was paid on all paid up shares.

Oct.   Received €40,000 from the issue of the remaining shares.

Nov.   Received balance of previously written off bad debt as agreed in June.

Dec.   The buildings are to be depreciated at the rate of 2 per cent per annum of value at 28/2/2005. The total depreciation charge on equipment for the year was €9,700.

You are required to:

Record on a tabular statement the effect each of the above transactions had on the relevant asset, liability and capital accounts and ascertain the total assets and liabilities on 31/12/2005.

(100 marks)

7. Correction of Errors and Suspense Account

The trial balance of M. O'Meara, a garage owner, failed to agree on 31/12/2005. The difference was entered in a suspense account and the following balance sheet was prepared.

Balance Sheet as at 31/12/2005

	€	€	€
Fixed assets			
Premises		700,000	
Equipment		60,000	
Furniture		20,000	780,000
Current assets			
Stock (including suspense)		91,400	
Debtors		35,200	
Cash		500	
		127,100	
Less: current liabilities			
Creditors	54,000		
Bank	28,000	82,000	45,100
			825,100
Financed by:			
Capital		790,000	
Add: net profit		64,100	
		854,100	
Drawings		29,000	825,100
			825,100

On checking the books, the following errors were discovered:

(i)   A motor car, purchased on credit from D. Foran for €13,000, had been entered on the incorrect side of Foran's account as €1,300 and credited as €3,100 in the equipment account.

(ii)   O'Meara had returned a motor car, previously purchased on credit for €14,600 from a supplier.
O'Meara entered this transaction as €16,400 on the correct sides of the correct accounts in the ledger.
A credit note subsequently arrived from the supplier showing a restocking charge of €500 to cover the cost of the return. The only entry made in respect of this credit note was a credit of €14,100 in the creditor's account.

(iii) A debtor who owed O'Meara €1,000 sent a cheque for €800 and €150 in cash in full settlement. This was correctly recorded in the books. However, no entry has been made in the books of the subsequent dishonouring of this cheque or of the writing off of the remaining debt in full because of bankruptcy.

(iv) A private debt for €770, owed by O'Meara, had been offset in full against a business debt of €820 owed to the firm for car repairs previously carried out. No entry had been made in the books in respect of this offset.

(v) A cheque for €2,250 paid by O'Meara out of a private bank account for fifteen months' hire of diagnostic equipment up to 31/3/2006 had not been entered in the books.

You are required to:

(a) Journalise the necessary corrections.   **(50)**
(b) Show the suspense account.   **(6)**
(c) Prepare a statement showing the correct net profit.   **(14)**
(d) Prepare a corrected balance sheet.   **(20)**
(e) Explain with examples the difference between 'error of commission' and 'error of principle'.   **(10)**
                                                                              (100 marks)

SECTION 3 (80 marks)

Answer any **ONE** question

8. Marginal and Absorption Costing

A. Harrington Ltd produces a single product. The company's profit and loss account for the year ended 31/12/2005, during which 60,000 units were produced and sold, was as follows:

	€	€
Sales		720,000
Materials	288,000	
Direct labour	144,000	
Factory overheads	51,000	
Administration expenses	96,000	
Selling expenses	68,000	647,000
Net profit		73,000

The materials, direct labour and 40 per cent of the factory overheads are variable costs. Apart from sales commission of 5 per cent of sales, selling and administration expenses are fixed.

You are required to calculate:

(a) The company's breakeven point and margin of safety.
(b) The number of units that must be sold at €13 per unit to provide a profit of 10 per cent of the sales revenue received from these same units.

(c) The profit the company would make in 2006 if it reduced its selling price to €11, increased fixed costs by €10,000 and thereby increased the number of units sold to 80,000, with all other cost levels and percentages remaining unchanged.

B. Cloud Ltd produces 8,000 units of product Z during the year ended 31/12/2005. 6,000 of these units were sold at €6 per unit. The production costs were as follows:

Direct materials	€0.50 per unit
Direct labour	€0.80 per unit
Variable overhead	€0.50 per unit
Fixed overhead cost for the year	€3,000

You are required to:

(a) Prepare profit and loss statements under marginal and absorption costing principles.
(b) Outline the differences between marginal and absorption costing. Indicate which method should be used for financial accounting purposes and why.

(80 marks)

9. Flexible Budgeting

McGinley manufactures a component for the motor industry. The following flexible budgets have already been prepared for 50 per cent, 75 per cent and 85 per cent of the plant's capacity:

Output levels	50%	75%	85%
Units	10,000	15,000	17,000
Costs	€	€	€
Direct materials	140,000	210,000	238,000
Direct wages	110,000	165,000	187,000
Production overheads	73,000	108,000	122,000
Other overhead costs	39,000	54,000	60,000
Administration expenses	28,000	28,000	28,000
	390,000	565,000	635,000

Profit is budgeted to be 24 per cent of sales.

You are required to:

(a) (i)   Classify the above costs into fixed, variable and mixed costs.
     (ii)   Separate production overheads into fixed and variable elements.
     (iii) Separate other overhead costs into fixed and variable elements.
     (iv)   Prepare a flexible budget for 95 per cent activity level.
     (v)   Restate the budget, using marginal costing principles, and show the contribution.
(b) What is an adverse variance? State why adverse variances may arise in direct material costs.
(c) Explain, with examples, 'controllable' and 'uncontrollable' costs.

(80 marks)

LEAVING CERTIFICATE ACCOUNTING

Marking Scheme for the Examination

Introduction

The solutions and marking schemes for Accounting, Higher and Ordinary Levels, are attached.

The solutions are printed and the marks allocated to each line/figure are highlighted and shown in a circle like this ➏ alongside.

These marks are then totalled for each section/page and shown in a square like this ▪40▪.

Accounting solutions are mainly computational and most figures are made up of more than one component. If a figure is wrong per the solution, the examiners analyse the make-up of the candidate's figure and allocate some marks for each correct element included. To facilitate this, where relevant, the make-up of the figures is shown in workings attached to the solution.

In some Accounting questions there can be a number of alternative approaches and formats that can be validly used by candidates (e.g. a bank reconciliation statement can start with either the bank statement figure or the adjusted bank account balance). The solutions provided here are based on the approaches adopted by the vast majority of teachers/candidates and alternatives are not included. In cases where a valid alternative solution is required, it is provided for the examiners, so that full marks can be gained for correct accounting treatment.

Sometimes the solution to a part of a question may depend on the answer computed in another part of that question. Where their calculation in Section (a) is incorrect, but this inaccurate information is used in the answer to Section (b), examiners give credit for analysis/decisions correctly made by the candidate on the basis of the incorrect data in this section. In this way, candidates are not penalised twice for the same error.

Question 1 – Solution

(a) **Trading and Profit and Loss Account for the Year Ended 31/12/2005** **75**

		€	€	€
Sales				980,000 ❸
Less cost of sales				
Stock 1/1/2005			65,700 ❸	
Add purchases	W1		629,600 ❻	
			695,300	
Less stock 31/12/2005	W2		(78,100) ❻	(617,200)
Gross profit				362,800
Less Expenses				
Administration				
Patent written off	W3	12,600 ❺		
Salaries and general expenses	W4	193,700 ❼		
Insurance		7,800 ❸		
Depreciation – buildings	W5	17,500 ❹	231,600	
Selling and distribution				
Commission		20,000 ❸		
Loss on sale of van	W6	6,875 ❻		
Depreciation – delivery vans	W7	20,100 ❹	46,975	(278,575)
				84,225
Add operating income				
Discount	W8			4,300 ❺
Rent				12,000 ❸
Reduction in provision for bad debts	W9			1,605 ❹
Operating profit				102,130
Investment income	W10			5,600 ❺
				107,730
Mortgage interest	W11			(13,750) ❻
Net profit for year				93,980 ❷

(b) Balance Sheet as at 31/12/2005 **45**

		Cost €	Accumulated Depreciation €	Net €	Total
Intangible fixed assets					
Patents	(63,000 – 12,600)				50,400 ❹
Tangible fixed assets					
Buildings	W12	1,200,000 ❷		1,200,000	
Delivery vans	W13, W14	136,000 ❸	76,475 ❸	59,525	
		1,336,000	76,475	1,259,525	1,259,525
Financial assets					
6% investments					160,000 ❶
					1,469,925
Current assets					
Stock				78,100 ❷	
Debtors			76,500 ❷		
Less provision			(2,295) ❶	74,205	
VAT	W15			20,700 ❺	
Investment income due				3,200 ❸	
				176,205	
Creditors: amounts falling due within one year					
Creditors	W16		91,100 ❸		
Bank			60,800 ❷		
PRSI			2,500 ❷		
Mortgage interest due			11,250 ❸	(165,650)	10,555
					1,480,480
Financed by					
Creditors: amounts falling due after more than one year					
5% fixed mortgage					300,000 ❷
Capital and reserves					
Capital 1/1/2005				735,000 ❶	
Add net profit				93,980 ❶	
				828,980	
Less drawings				36,000 ❷	
				792,980	
Revaluation reserve	W17			387,500 ❸	
					1,180,480
Capital employed					1,480,480

Workings

1.	Purchases	650,000	
	Add goods in transit	5,600	
	Less payment for van	(26,000)	629,600
2.	Closing stock	72,500	
	Add goods in transit	5,600	78,100
3.	Patent (60,600 + 2,400) × 20%		12,600
4.	Salaries and general expenses	192,500	
	Add mortgage interest	500	
	Add discount	700	193,700
5.	Depreciation on buildings		
	(875,000 × 2%)		17,500
6.	Loss on sale of van		
	(35,000 − 15,000 − 13,125)		6,875
7.	Depreciation – delivery vans		
	(14,250 + 1,750 + 4,100)		20,100
	(19,500 + 600)		
	(6,500 + 13,600)		
8.	Discount	3,600	
	Add unrecorded discount	700	4,300
9.	Provision for bad debts		
	(3,900 − 2,295)		1,605 CR
10.	Investment income		
	(2,400 + 3,200)		5,600
11.	Mortgage interest		
	(3,000 − 500 + 11,250)		13,750
12.	Buildings	900,000	
	Less VAT	(25,000)	
	Add revaluation	325,000	1,200,000
13.	Provision for depreciation – vans		
	(69,500 + 20,100 − 13,125)		76,475
14.	Delivery vans		
	(130,000 − 35,000 + 41,000)		136,000
15.	VAT account	4,300	
	Less VAT on buildings	(25,000)	20,700
16.	Creditors	85,500	
	Add goods in transit	5,600	91,100
17.	Revaluation reserve		
	Land and buildings	325,000	
	Add provision for depreciation (45,000 + 17,500)	62,500	387,500

Question 2 – Solution

(a)   20

Statement of Capital 1/1/2005

		€	€
Assets			
Land and buildings		290,000 ❷	
Machinery		60,000 ❷	
Investments		30,000 ❸	
Milk cheque due		2,400 ❶	
Cattle		60,000 ❶	
Sheep		18,000 ❶	
Fuel		800 ❶	
Bank		2,800 ❷	464,000
Liabilities			
Electricity due		400 ❶	
Bank loan		15,000 ❷	
Loan interest due	**W1**	1,050 ❸	16,450
Capital			447,550 ❶

(b)   20

Enterprise Analysis Account – Cattle and Milk

Income			
Sales – Milk	**W2**	27,400 ❷	
– Cattle and calves (13,000 + 5,900)		18,900 ❶	
EU subsidy – cattle		2,500 ❶	
Increase in stock		2,000 ❶	
Drawings by family		700 ❶	51,500
Expenditure			
Purchases – cattle		14,000 ❶	
Dairy wages		1,500 ❶	
General farm expenses		9,000 ❶	
Fertilizer		2.040 ❶	
Vet fees		660 ❶	27,200
Gross profit			24,300

232

Enterprise Analysis Account – Sheep

Income			
Sales – sheep and lambs (22,000 + 12,600)		34,600 ❶	
EU subsidy – sheep		3,400 ❶	
Wool		1,800 ❶	
Increase in stock		7,000 ❶	
Drawings family		300 ❶	47,100
Expenditure			
Purchases – sheep		19,000 ❶	
General farm expenses		6,000 ❶	
Fertilizer	W3	1,360 ❶	
Vet fees	W4	440 ❶	26,800
Gross profit			20,300

(c)   **20**

General Profit and Loss Account for the Year Ended 31/12/2005

		€	€
Income			
Gross profit – Cattle and milk		24,300	
Sheep		20,300	
Interest	W5	1,200 ❶	
Forestry premium		2,100 ❶	47,900
Less expenditure			
Light, heat and fuel (80%)	W6	2,320 ❹	
Repairs (80%)		5,040 ❶	
Machinery depreciation		5,320 ❶	
Loan interest	W1	240 ❷	12,920
Net profit			34,980 ❷

(d)   **8**

- To find out the profit of the farm.
- To find out the net worth of the farm.
- To find out the profit of each section of the farm.
- To back up applications for grants and bank loans.
- To facilitate planning/budgeting.

Workings

1. Interest – 18 months' interest	=	$6\% \times 1.5 = 9\%$		
109%	=		16,350	
9%	=		1,350	
Interest for year 2005	=		300	
Less drawings			60	240

2. Milk sales		28,000	
Add due 31/12		1,800	
Less due 1/1		(2,400)	27,400

3. Fertilizer		3,000	
Add due 31/12		400	3,400

4. Veterinary fees		1,750	
Less VHI		(650)	1,100

5. Investment interest		600	
Interest due		600	1,200

6. Light, heat and fuel		3,400	
Add stock 1/1		800	
Less due 1/1		(400)	
Less stock 31/12		(900)	
Less drawings (20% of 2,900)		(580)	2,320

Question 3 – Solution

(a)
48

Reconciliation of Operating Profit to Net Cash Flow from Operating Activities

	€	
Operating profit	140,000	❷
Depreciation charges for the year	75,000	❹
Profit on sale of machinery	(3,000)	❻
Increase in stock	(15,000)	❷
Increase in debtors	(10,000)	❷
Increase in creditors	22,000	❷
Net cash inflow from operating activities	209,000	❷

Cash Flow Statement of Butler Plc for the Year Ended 31/12/2005

			€
Operating activities			
Net cash inflow from operating activities			209,000 ❶
Returns on investments and servicing of finance			
Interest paid			(6,800) ❸
Taxation			
Corporation tax paid			(38,000) ❸
Capital expenditure and financial investment			
Investments	(30,000)	❸	
Payments to acquire tangible fixed assets	(75,000)	❷	
Receipts from sale of fixed assets	35,000	❷	(70,000)
Equity dividends paid			
Dividends paid during the year			(55,000) ❸
Net cash **inflow** before liquid resources and financing			39,200
Management of liquid resources			
Purchase of government securities			(12,000) ❷
Financing			
Repayment of debentures	(105,000)	❶	
Receipts from issue of shares	40,000	❶	
Receipts from share premium	22,000	❶	(43,000)
Decrease in cash		❷	(15,800)
Reconciliation of net cash flow to movement in net debt			
Decrease in cash during period			(15,800) ❶
Cash used to purchase government securities			12,000
Cash used to purchase debentures			105,000 ❶
Change in net debt			101,200 ❶
Net debt at 1/1/2005			(169,000)
Net debt at 31/12 2005			(67,800) ❶

(b)   **8**

- To show the cash inflows and outflows during the past year.
- To help predict future cash flows.
- To help financial planning.
- To provide information to assess liquidity.
- To show that profits do not equal cash.
- To comply with legal requirements.

(c)   **4**

Non-cash expense	Depreciation, increase in provision for bad debts
Non-cash gain	Reduction in provision for bad debts, profit on sale of assets

Workings

Depreciation

Depreciation on machinery for year	60,000	
Depreciation on buildings for year	15,000	
Total depreciation for year		75,000

Profit/loss on disposal of fixed assets

Amount received for machine		35,000
Cost of machine disposed	70,000	
Depreciation on disposed machine		
[180,000 + 60,000 – 202,000]	38,000	
Book value	(32,000)	
Profit on sale of machinery		3,000

Dividends paid

Dividends due at 31/12/2004	34,000	
Add interim dividends 2005	21,000	
Amount paid during 2005		55,000

Taxation

Taxation due at 31/12/2004	43,000	
Taxation for year 2005	45,000	
	88,000	
Less taxation due 31/12/2005	(50,000)	
Taxation paid		38,000

Interest

Interest for year 2005	8,000	
Less interest due 31/12/2005	(1,200)	
Interest paid		6,800

Question 4 – Solution

(a)

4

Profit and Loss Account of Ross Plc for the Year Ended 31/12/2005

	Workings			**€**	
Turnover				1,221,000	❸
Cost of sales (70,000 + 700,000 – 72,000 + 8,000)				(706,000)	❻
Gross profit				515,000	
Distribution costs	**W1**	(51,000)	❷		
Administrative expenses	**W2**	(314,700)	❺	(365,700)	
				149,300	
Other operating income					
Discount				6,260	❶
Operating profit				155,560	
Profit on sale of land				80,000	❷
Investment income				18,000	❸
				253,560	
Interest payable				(13,300)	❸
Profit on ordinary activities before taxation ❶				240,260	
Taxation				(40,000)	❶
Profit after taxation				200,260	
Dividends paid		29,000	❷		
Dividends proposed		32,000	❷	(61,000)	
Profit retained for year				139,260	
Profit brought forward at 1/1/2005				78,000	❶
Profit carried forward at 31/12/2005				217,260	❸

Notes to the Accounts

1. Tangible Fixed Assets ❺

	Land	**Buildings**	**Vehicles**	**Total**
Cost or valuation 1/1/2005	150,000	530,000	140,000	820,000
Disposal	(100,000)	–	–	(100,000)
Revaluation surplus	110,000	170,000	–	280,000
Value at 31/12/2005	160,000	700,000	140,000	1,000,000
Depreciation at 1/1/2005	–	–	64,000	64,000
Depreciation charge for year	–	12,300	28,000	40,300
		12,300	92,000	104,300
Net book value 1/1/2005	150,000	530,000	76,000	756,000
Net book value 31/12/2005	160,000	687,700	48,000	895,700

2. Stock ❶
Stocks are valued on a first in first out basis at the lower of cost and net realisable value.

3. Dividends ❸

Ordinary dividends		
Interim paid 7.0c per share	21,000	
Final proposed 8.0c per share	24,000	45,000
Preference dividends		
Interim paid 5.0c per share	8,000	
Final proposed 5.0c per share	8,000	16,000

4. Operating Profit ❷

The operating profit is arrived at after charging:	
Depreciation on tangible fixed assets	40,300
Patent amortised	8,000
Directors' remuneration	89,000
Auditors' fees	8,400

5. Profit on Sale of Property ❷
The company sold land for €80,000 greater than it cost. Cost was €100,000.

(b) 🄸🄸

Audit ❹
An audit is the independent examination of and the expression of opinion on the financial statements of an enterprise by an appointed auditor.

The main objective of an audit is to enable the auditor, in keeping with the requirements of the Companies Acts, to report on the truth and fairness shown by:

- The balance sheet, the profit or loss shown by the profit and loss account; and
- Any other information required to be disclosed in the financial accounts.

The Companies Acts do not require the auditor to certify that the company records are correct or accurate but that the accounts give a *true and fair view* of the financial position of the business.

Qualified Auditor's Report ❽
A qualified auditor's report is when an auditor in his/her opinion is **not satisfied** or is unable to conclude that all or any of the following apply:

- The financial statements give a *true and fair view* of the state of affairs of the company at the end of the year and of its profit and loss account for the year.
- The financial statements are prepared in accordance with the Companies Acts.
- All the information necessary for the audit was available.
- The information given by the directors is consistent with the financial statements.
- The net assets are more than 50 per cent of the called up capital.

The report will state the elements of the accounts or of the directors' report that are unsatisfactory.

Workings

1 Cost of sales

Stock 1/1/2005	70,000	
Purchases	700,000	
Patents written off	8,000	
Stock 31/12/2005	(72,000)	706,000

2 Distribution costs

Advertising	23,000	
Depreciation – delivery vans	28,000	51,000

3 Administrative expenses

Directors' fees	89,000	
Salaries and general expenses	175,000	
Rent	30,000	
Auditors' fees	8,400	
Depreciation – buildings	12,300	314,700

Question 5 – Solution

(a) **45**

Interest cover

$$\frac{\text{Net profit before interest}}{\text{Interest}} = \frac{75,000}{20,000} = 3.75 \text{ times} \quad ⑨$$

Earnings per share

$$\frac{\text{Net profit after pref div}}{\text{Number of ordinary share}} = \frac{52,000}{300,000} = 17.33c \quad ⑨$$

Cash sales

$$\frac{\text{Debetors} \times 12}{\text{Credit sales}} = 2 \quad \text{Credit sales} = \frac{48,000 \times 12}{2}$$

Credit sales $= 288,000$

Cash sales $= 890,000 - 288,000 = €602,000 \quad ⑨$

Period to recoup price

$$\frac{\text{Market price}}{\text{Dividend per share}} = \frac{200}{15} = 13.34 \text{ years} \quad ⑨$$

Dividend yield for 2004

$$\frac{\text{Dividend per share} \times 100}{\text{Market price}} = \frac{18 \times 100}{210} = 8.57\% \quad ⑨$$

(b) **40**

The debenture holders would be dissatisfied with the following:

Dividend Policy ⑦

Based on this year's earnings, the dividends proposed (€48,000) are excessive. The dividend cover is 1.15 times. More of the profits should be retained or put aside for the repayment of the debentures.

Security – Real Value of Fixed Assets ❼

The debentures are secured on the fixed assets. The debenture holders would be interested in the size of the assets to make sure that there is enough security for the loan. There are fixed assets of €575,000, of which intangible assets are €150,000, leaving net assets excluding intangibles of €425,000. It would be prudent to ascertain the real value of fixed assets. However, the debenture holders would feel secure because of the excess in value of fixed assets over loan, particularly because of the investments of €90,000.

Profitability ❼

The return on capital employed for 2005 is 12.56 per cent. Last year the return was 14.2 per cent. This fall indicates an unhealthy trend. The company is in a profitable position as the return of 12.56 per cent is better than the return from risk-free investments of less than 5 per cent and is above the debenture interest rate of 10 per cent. If the downward trend continues, there is a risk of having to sell the fixed assets in order to repay debentures.

Liquidity ❼

The company has a serious liquidity problem. Last year, the quick ratio was 1.2 : 1. This year the quick ratio has fallen to 0.7 : 1. The company now has only 70c available for every €1 owed in the short term. The worsening of the ratio indicates a difficulty paying debts, including future interest. If this trend continues, ability to pay interest would come under pressure and funds would not be available to invest for the purpose of repaying loans.

Gearing – Interest Cover ❼

The company is lowly geared. In 2005, the gearing was at 41.8 per cent. The gearing has slipped from 35 per cent of total capital in 2004. Interest cover was five times but is now down to 3.75 times. This worsening trend could jeopardise interest payments.

Sector ❺

The long-term prospects are not encouraging in the dairy industry. There is a risk of overproduction and low-cost competition.

Market Value

The market value of one share in 2004 was €2.10, while in 2005 it dropped to €2. The earnings per share have dropped from 19c to 17.33c. The share may be overpriced, as it takes 11.54 years to recover its market price. These would indicate a lack of public confidence in the company and may discourage investment.

(c)   15

Raise cash and improve liquidity by:

1. Paying out lower dividends.
2. Selling investments rather than issuing debentures.
3. Issuing more shares.
4. Improving gross profit percentage of 21.9 per cent by reducing cost of sales or by passing on the increased costs.
5. Diversifying into other areas.
6. Collection of debts more quickly.
7. Sale and lease back.

Question 6 – Solution

	1/1/2005	Jan	Feb	Mar	Apr	May	Jun	Jul	Aug	Oct	Nov	Dec	31/12/2005
Land and buildings	260,000	120,000 ②	170,000 ③									③	550,000 ①
Depreciation	(25,000)							(900) ③				(8,000) ③	(8,000) ①
Equipment	50,000 ②		25,000 ③									②	49,100 ①
Depreciation	(20,000)											(9,700) ②	(29,200) ①
Goodwill		4,000 ②											4,000 ①
Stock	70,000				640 ③								70,640 ①
Debtors	90,000	10,000 ②			(720) ③		270 ③				(270) ②		99,280 ①
Bad debts provision	(4,500)			(1,500) ③		2,000 ②						(1,500) ②	(6,000) ①
Insurance								500 ③					500 ①
	420,500	**134,000**	**195,000**	**(1,500)**	**(80)**	**2,000**	**270**	**(400)**	**–**	**–**	**(270)**	**(19,200)**	**730,320**
Ord. shares	290,000 ②	80,000 ②								30,000 ③			400,000 ①
Share premium	14,000	16,000 ②								10,000 ③			40,000
P&L balance	29,000 ②			(1,500) ②	(80) ②		900 ②	100 ②	(18,500) ②			(17,700) ② (1,500) ① 3,840 ①	(5,440) ②
Creditors	61,000												98,500
Bank	23,000 ②	38,000				2,800 ③	630 ③	(500) ③	18,500 ③	40,000 ③	270		2,200 ①
Expense due	3,500												3,500 ①
Revaluation reserve			195,000 ③										195,000 ②
Rent rec.						4,800 ②						(3,840) ②	960 ①
	420,500	**134,000**	**195,000**	**(1,500)**	**(80)**	**2,000**	**270**	**(400)**	**–**	**–**	**(270)**	**(19,200)**	**730,320**

Question 7 – Solution

(a) `50`

		Dr	Cr
(i)	Purchases account	13,000 ❸	
	Equipment account	3,100 ❸	
	Suspense account		1,800 ❷
	Creditors account		14,300 ❷
	Being correction of incorrect recording of the purchase of a motor car on credit.		
(ii)	Purchases returns account	2,300 ❸	
	Creditors account	11,800 ❸	
	Suspense account		14,100 ❸
	Being recording of return of motor car and credit note incorporating a restocking charge.		
(iii)	Debtor account	850 ❸	
	Bank account		800 ❸
	Discount account		50 ❸
	Bad debts account	850 ❸	
	Debtor account		850 ❸
	Being recording of a dishonoured cheque and a bad debt.		
(iv)	Drawings account	770 ❸	
	Discount account	50 ❸	
	Debtors account		820 ❸
	Being recording of owner's private debt offset against a business debt for repairs owed to firm.		
(v)	Rent/profit and loss account	1,800 ❷	
	Rent/balance sheet	450 ❷	
	Capital account		2,250 ❸
	Being private funds used to pay twelve months' rent for the current year and three months' rent for the following year.		

(b) `6`

Suspense Account

	€			€
Original difference	15,900	Equipment	(i)	1,800 ❸
		Creditors	(ii)	14,100 ❸
	15,900			15,900

(c) **14**

Statement of Corrected Net Profit

			€	
Original net profit as per books			64,100	❶
Add discount allowed disallowed	(iii)		50	❷
			64,150	
Less Purchases	(i)	13,000 ❷		
Purchases returns	(ii)	2,300 ❷		
Bad debts	(iii)	850 ❶		
Discount	(iv)	50 ❶		
Rent	(v)	1,800 ❷	(18,000)	
Correct net profit			46,150	❸

(d) **20**

Balance Sheet as at 31/12/2005

		€	€	€	
Fixed assets					
Premises				700,000	½
Equipment	(60,000 + 3,100)			63,100	❷
Furniture				20,000	½
				783,100	
Current assets					
Stock	(91,400 – 15,900)	75,500 ❷			
Debtors	(35,200 + 850 – 850 – 820)	34,380 ❹			
Cash		500 ½			
Rent prepaid		450 ½	110,830		
Less creditors: amounts falling due within one year					
Creditors	(54,000 + 14,300 – 11,800)	56,500 ❸			
Bank	(28,000 + 800)	28,800 ❷	85,300	25,530	
				808,630	
Financed by					
Capital	(790,000 + 2,250)		792,250 ❷		
Add net profit			46,150		
			838,400		
Less drawings	(29,000 + 770)		29,770 ❷	(808,630)	
				808,630	❶

(e) 10

An error of commission occurs when the correct amount is posted to the correct side of the incorrect account, e.g. goods sold on credit to Pat O'Brien debited in error to John O'Brien's account.

An error of principle arises when an item is posted to the incorrect class of account, e.g. an electrical shop owner purchased a vehicle and entered it in the purchases account instead of the vehicles account.

Question 8 – Solution

80

		€	€ per unit
(A) Sales		720,000	12.00
Less variable costs			
Direct materials	288,000		
Direct labour	144,000		
Factory overheads (40%)	20,400		
Sales commission (5% × 720,000)	36,000	(488,400)	8.14
Contribution		231,600	**3.86**
Less fixed costs			
Factory overheads (60%)	30,600		
Administration expenses	96,000		
Selling expenses (excluding commission)	32,000	158,600	
Net profit		73,000	

(a) Breakeven point $= \dfrac{\text{Fixed costs}}{\text{CPU}} = \dfrac{158,600 \;\text{③}}{3.86 \;\text{④}}$ $=$ ③ 41,089 units

Margin of safety $=$ Sales – breakeven point

$=$ ④ 60,000 – 41,089 ③ $=$ ③ 18,911 units

(b) $\dfrac{\text{Fixed costs}}{\text{Contribution} - 10\% \text{ of S.P.}}$ $\dfrac{158,600 \;\text{④}}{⑥ \; 4.81 - 1.3 \;\text{⑥}}$ $=$ ④ 45,186 units

(c) Profit if selling price dropped to €11

		€	
Sales	(80,000 × 11)	880,000	④
Less variable costs	(80,000 × 8.09)	647,200	⑥
Contribution		232,800	
Less fixed costs	(158,600 + 10,000)	168,600	⑥
Profit		41,200	②

(B)

(a) **Absorption Costing**	€	€
Sales (6,000 × €6)		36,000 ❶
Less production cost of 8,000 units		
Direct materials (8,000 × 0.50)	4,000 ❶	
Direct labour (8,000 × 0.80)	6,400 ❶	
Variable overhead (8,000 × 0.50)	4,000 ❶	
Fixed overhead	3,000 ❶	
	17,400	
Less closing stock (1/4 of 17,400)	(4,350) ❶	(13,050)
Profit		22,950
Marginal Costing		
	€	€
Sales		36,000 ❶
Less production costs		
Direct materials	4,000 ❶	
Direct labour	6,400 ❶	
Variable overhead	4,000 ❶	
	14,400	
Less closing stock (1/4 of 14,400)	(3,600)	(10,800)
Contribution ❶		25,200
Less fixed cost		(3,000) ❶
Profit		22,200

(b) `5`

There is a different profit figure because closing stock is valued differently. Marginal costing does not include fixed costs when costing a product, whereas absorption costing does include the fixed costs.

Therefore, closing stock under marginal costing is valued lower than under absorption costing because a share of fixed costs is included in the value of stock under absorption costing but not included under marginal costing.

Under absorption costing, closing stock is valued at one-quarter of the production cost of 17,400.

Under marginal costing, closing stock is valued at one-quarter of the production cost of 14,400.

Closing stock – absorption costing	4,350
Closing stock – marginal costing	(3,600)

Difference 750
The profit difference is 22,950 – 22,200   =   750

Absorption costing should be used, as it agrees with standard accounting practice and concepts and matches costs with revenues. ❺

Question 9 – Solution

(a) 80

(i)			
Direct materials	❷ Variable		
Direct wages	❷ Variable		
Production overheads	❷ Mixed		
Other overhead costs	❷ Mixed		
Administration expenses	❷ Fixed		

(ii) **Production Overheads**		**Units** €	**Total Cost**
High		17,000	122,000
Low		10,000	73,000
Difference		7,000	49,000
The variable cost of 7,000 units is 49,000			
Therefore the variable cost per unit is			€7 ❻
Total production overhead costs	73,000	108,000	122,000
Less variable costs	70,000	105,000	119,000
Therefore, fixed cost	3,000	3,000	3,000 ❻

(iii) **Other Overhead Costs**		**Units** €	**Total Cost**
High		17,000	60,000
Low		10,000	39,000
Difference		7,000	21,000
The variable cost of 7,000 units is 21,000			
Therefore, the variable cost per unit is			€3 ❻
Total other overhead costs	39,000	54,000	60,000
Less variable costs	30,000	45,000	51,000
Therefore, fixed cost	9,000	9,000	9,000 ❻

(iv) **Production Overheads at the Required Flexible Budgeted Level of 95% – (19,000 Units)**

		€
Variable cost	(19,000 × 7)	133,000
Fixed cost		3,000
Total cost		136,000

Other Overhead Costs at the Required Flexible Budgeted Level of 95% – (19,000 Units)

		€
Variable cost	(19,000 × 3)	57,000
Fixed cost		9,000
Total cost		66,000

Construction of a Flexible Budget for a 95% Activity Level

		Flexible Budget
Activity Level		**95%**
Units		**19,000**
		€
Direct materials	(19,000 × 14)	266,000 ❸
Direct wages	(19,000 × 11)	209,000 ❸
Production overheads		136,000 ❻
Other overheads		66,000 ❻
Administration overheads (fixed)		28,000 ❹
Total cost (76% of sales)		705,000

(v) Flexible Budget in Marginal Costing Format

	€	€
Sales		927,632 ❶
Less variable costs		
Direct materials	266,000 ❶	
Direct wages	209,000 ❶	
Variable production overhead	133,000 ❶	
Other overhead costs	57,000 ❶	665,000
Contribution ❶		262,632
Less fixed cost		
Production overheads	3,000 ❶	
Other overheads	9,000 ❶	
Administration	28,000 ❶	40,000
Profit		222,632 ❸

(b) An adverse variance is where actual costs exceed budgeted costs. ❸

An adverse variance in direct material costs may arise if the purchase price of materials is higher than expected or if the quantities of material used are higher than expected. ❸

(c) **Controllable costs** are costs that can be controlled by the manager of a cost centre. She/he will make the decision about the amount of the cost or if the cost should be incurred and can be held responsible for variances in these costs, e.g. all variable costs are controllable. ❸

Uncontrollable costs are costs over which the manager of a cost centre has no control and therefore cannot be held responsible for variances in these costs, e.g. rates to the local authority are uncontrollable. ❸

Accounting Revision
for Leaving Certificate
Higher Level

Michael McLoughlin

Fourth Edition

Gill & Macmillan

Gill & Macmillan Ltd
Hume Avenue
Park West
Dublin 12
with associated companies throughout the world
www.gillmacmillan.ie

© Michael McLoughlin 1997, 2000, 2001, 2007

978 0 7171 4134 0

Print Origination by Replika Press Pvt Ltd, India

The paper used in this book is made from the wood pulp of managed forests. For every tree felled, at least one tree is planted, thereby renewing natural resources.

Contents

Chapter **1**
Company Final Accounts

Question 1

Question 1 is always a set of final accounts. This question carries 120 marks, which is 30 per cent of the total.

The question involves a set of company, sole trader, manufacturing or departmental final accounts, each including a lot of adjustments. It is essential to practise these questions thoroughly.

The fastest method is to lay out the questions in blank form. Enter the figures as they appear in the question beside the correct space in the blank form. Enter the figures in the first column and adjust them as required. The adjustments are included in the solutions to the questions. Sample marking schemes are included to some questions.

The basic rule is practise, practise, practise.

Remember, if you are not going to answer question 1, then you must answer two questions from numbers 2, 3 and 4. Each of these questions carries 60 marks.

Question 1.1
Ballindine Ltd has an authorised share capital of €960,000 divided into 560,000 ordinary shares of €1 each and 400,000 11 per cent preference shares of €1 each. The following trial balance was extracted from its books at 31 December 2007.

Entry	Debit (€)	Credit (€)
Issued Capital: Ordinary Shares		450,000
Preference Shares		200,000
Profit and Loss		18,000
Stocks (including heating oil €1,500)	48,500	
Debtors and Creditors	55,400	63,200
Buildings at Cost	495,000	
Delivery Vans (cost €160,000)	105,000	
12% Debentures		125,000
Provision for Bad Debts		2,000
Bank		34,000
Light and Heat	5,000	
Purchases and Sales	590,000	830,000
9% Investments (1/1/2007)	150,000	
Salaries and General Expenditure	86,700	
Audit Fees	14,000	

Question 1.1 Table *continued*

Entry	Debit (€)	Credit (€)
Insurance of Vans (including suspense)	5,800	
Advertising (incorporating 4 months' investment income)	18,000	
Interim Dividends for 6 Months	28,000	
Debenture Interest Paid for First 4 Months	5,500	
Directors' Fees	35,300	
Goodwill	80,000	
	1,722,200	1,722,200

You are also given the following information.

1. Stock at 31 December 2007 was valued at €52,300. This includes heating oil of €900 and stocks that cost €4,000 and have a net realisable value of €2,500.
2. The suspense figure arises because an incorrect figure was entered for debenture interest (although the correct figure has been entered in the bank account) and purchases returns of €800 were entered only in the creditors account.
3. Goods sent to a customer on approval on 31 December 2007 had been entered in error as a credit sale. The selling price of these goods was €4,500, which represents cost plus 50 per cent mark-up.
4. Repairs to delivery vans costing €3,000 were carried out by the firm's own workforce. €500 of this represented parts taken from the firm's own stocks, and the remainder represented salary paid.
5. Provide for depreciation at the rate of 20 per cent of cost per annum from date of purchase to date of sale. On 31 July 2007 a van that had cost €15,000 on 1 April 2004 was traded against a new van costing €20,000. An allowance of €6,000 was received for the old van. The cheque for the net amount was treated in error as a purchase of trading stock, and this was the only entry made in the books.
6. The directors recommend:
   (a) The preference dividend due be paid.
   (b) A final dividend of 10 per cent be paid on the ordinary shares.
   (c) Provision be made for debenture interest due.
   (d) A bad debt of €400 be written off and the provision for bad debts be adjusted to 4 per cent of the remaining debtors.

You are required to prepare the:
(a) Trading and profit and loss accounts for the year ended 31 December 2007.
(b) Balance sheet at 31 December 2007.

Solution to Q 1.1

Ballindine Ltd
Trading and Profit and Loss Accounts for the Year Ended 31 December 2007

	Workings	(€)	(€)	(€)
Sales			825,500	
Less Costs				
Opening Stock		47,000		
Purchases		574,700		
		621,700		
Closing Stock		52,900		
			568,800	
Gross Profit			256,700	
Investment Income	W5		13,500	
Profit on Disposal			1,000	
				271,200
Less Expenses				
Establishment and Administration				
Light and Heat	W2	5,600		
Salaries and General		84,200		
Directors' Fees		35,300		
			125,100	
Financial				
Audit Fees		14,000		
Bad Debt		400		
Increase in Provision		20		
			14,420	
Selling and Distribution				
Van Insurance	W3	7,100		
Delivery Van Repairs		3,000		
Depreciation for Year		32,417		
Advertising	W4	22,500	65,017	204,537
Operating Profit				66,633
Less interest	W6			15,000
Net Profit				51,633
Less Appropriations				
Ordinary Dividend	Paid		17,000	
	Proposed		45,000	(62,000)
Preference Dividend	Paid		11,000	
	Proposed		11,000	(22,000)
				(32,337)
Add P & L Balance 1/1/2007				18,000
P & L Balance 31/12/2007				(14,337)

Balance Sheet at 31 December 2007

	Workings	Cost (€)	Depreciation (€)	Net Book Value (€)
Fixed Assets				
Buildings		495,000		495,000
Vans	W1	165,000	77,417	87,583
		660,000	77,417	582,583
9% Investment				150,000
Goodwill				80,000
				812,583
Current Assets				
Stock			52,900	
Debtors		50,500		
Less Provision for Bad Debts		(2,020)	48,480	
Stock of Heating Oil	W2		900	
Investment Income Due	W5		9,000	
			111,280	
Current Liabilities				
Creditors		63,200		
Bank		34,000		
Debenture Interest Due	W6	10,000		
Ordinary Dividend Due		45,000		
Preference Dividend Due		11,000		
Working Capital/Net Current Assets			163,200	(51,920)
				760,663
Financed by		Authorised	Issued	
OSC		560,000	450,000	
11% Preference Shares		400,000	200,000	
		960,000		650,000
Reserves				
Profit and Loss				(14,337)
Long-Term Liabilities				
12% Debentures				125,000
				760,663

4

Workings

W1

	Cost (€)	Depreciation (€)	Net Book Value (€)
Vans	160,000	(55,000)	105,000
	(15,000)	10,000	(5,000)
	20,000		
Depreciation on Old Van			
2004 $15,000 \times 20\% \times \frac{3}{4} =$	2,250		
2005–2006 $15,000 \times 20\% \times 2 =$	6,000		
2007 $15,000 \times 20\% \times \frac{7}{12} =$	1,750		
	10,000		
Depreciation for Year			
$145,000 \times 20\% =$	29,000		
$15,000 \times 20\% \times \frac{7}{12} =$	1,750		
$20,000 \times 20\% \times \frac{5}{12} =$	1,667		
	32,417		

W2

Light and Heat

(€)		(€)
1,500	Profit & Loss	5,600
5,000	Balance	900
6,500		6,500
Balance 900		

W4

Advertising

	(€)		(€)
	18,000	Profit & Loss	22,500
Investment	4,500		
	22,500		22,500

W3

Van Insurance (including suspense)

(€)		(€)
5,800	Profit & Loss	7,100
500		
800		
7,100		7,100

W5

Investment Income

	(€)		(€)
Profit & Loss	13,500	Advertising	4,500
		Balance	9,000
	13,500		13,500
Balance	9,000		

NOTE: In this book, the solutions shown follow the official marking scheme for accounting in the Leaving Certificate Examinations.

The solutions are printed and the marks allocated to each line/figure are highlighted and shown in a circle like this **6** alongside. These marks are then totalled for each section/page and shown in a square like this **40**.

From 2005 exam, Question 1, page 185.
Solution to Q 1.1   **35**

Manufacturing Account of James Ltd for the Year Ended 31/12/2007

		€	€
Opening Stock of Raw Materials			48,000 **1**
Purchases of Raw Materials	W 1		432,280 **3**
Carriage In			5,510 **2**
			485,790
Less Closing Stock of Raw Materials			51,000 **1**
Cost of Raw Materials Consumed			434,790
Direct Costs:			
Factory Wages	W 2	158,220 **4**	
Hire of Special Equipment		12,000 **2**	170,220
Prime Costs		**605,010**	
Factory Overheads:			
General Factory Overheads		50,300 **2**	
Depreciation on Plant and Machinery	W 3	49,800 **3**	
Depreciation on Buildings		10,160 **3**	
Loss on Sale of Machine	W 4	1,500 **4**	
Factory Cost			111,760
			716,770
Work in Progress 1/1/2007			24,150 **2**
			740,920
Less Work in Progress 31/12/2007			(28,550) **2**
			712,370
Less Sale of Scrap Materials	W 5		(3,700) **4**
Cost of Manufacture			708,670 **1**
Gross Profit on Manufacturer			91,330
Goods Transferred from Factory at CMV			800,000 **1**

Trading and Profit and Loss Account for Year Ended 31/12/2007 **40**

		€	€
Sales	W 6		925,400 ⑤
Opening Stock of Finished Goods		85,500 ②	
Goods Transferred @ CMV		800,000 ②	
		885,500	
Less Closing Stock of Finished Goods	W 7	97,500 ⑥	
Cost of Goods Sold		788,000	(788,000)
Gross Profit on Trading			137,400
Gross Profit on Manufacture			91,330
			228,730
Less Expenses:			
Administration Expenses			
Administration Expenses	W 8	22,900 ⑥	
Selling and Distribution Expenses:			
Selling Expenses		68,420 ②	(91,320)
			137,410
Discount (Net)	W 9		3,000 ③
Operating Profit			140,410
Less Debenture Interest	W 10		(8,325) ④
Net Profit before Taxation			132,085
Less Taxation			(10,000) ②
Profit after Tax			122,085
Less Preference Dividend Paid		8,000 ①	
Preference Dividend Due		8,000 ①	
Ordinary Dividend Paid		9,000 ①	
Ordinary Dividend Due		18,000 ①	
			(43,000)
Retained Profit			79,085
Profit and Loss Balance 1/1/2007			82,300 ②
Profit and Loss Balance 31/12/2007			161,385 ②

Balance Sheet of James Ltd as at 31/12/2007 **45**

Intangible Assets					€
Patents					70,000 ②

		Cost	Accumulated Depreciation	Net	
Tangible Assets:		€	€	€	
Factory Buildings	W 11	508,000 ②	55,160 ②	452,840	
Plant and Machinery	W 3,12	238,000 ②	135,100 ③	102,900	
		746,000	190,260	555,740	555,740
					625,740

Current Assets:

Stocks Raw Materials		51,000 ②	
Work in Progress		28,550 ②	
Finished Goods		97,500 ②	177,050
Debtors	**W 13**		84,800 ⑤
			261,850

Creditors: Amounts Falling Due within One Year:

Trade Creditors	57,700 ②	
Bank	11,450 ②	
VAT	12,730 ②	
Dividends Due	26,000 ④	
Taxation	10,000 ②	
Debenture Interest Due	8,325 ③	126,205
Net Current Assets		135,645
		761,385

Financed By:
Creditors: Amounts Falling Due after More than One Year

9% Debentures	100,000 ②

Capital and Reserves:

	Authorised	Issued	
Ordinary Shares at €1 Each	550,000 ①	300,000 ②	
8% Preference Shares at €1 Each	250,000 ①	200,000 ②	
	800,000	500,000	
Profit and Loss Balance 31/12/2007		161,385	
			661,385
			761,385

Question 1.1 Workings

1	Purchases of Raw Materials	450,280 − 18,000	=	432,280
2	Factory Wages	198,220 − 40,000	=	158,220
3	Depreciation on Plant and Machinery	26,000 + 23,800	=	49,800
		47,600 + 2,200	=	49,800
	Accumulated Depreciation on Plant	104,000 − 18,700 + 49,800	=	135,100
4	Loss on Disposal of Machine	22,000 − 18,700 − 1,800	=	(1,500)
5	Sale of Scrap Materials	5,500 − 1,800	=	3,700
6	Sales	935,000 − 9,600	=	925,400
7	Closing Stock of Finished Goods	92,000 − 2,500 + 8,000	=	97,500
8	Administration Expenses	23,900 − 1,000	=	22,900
9	Discount	4,000 − 1,000	=	3,000
10	Debenture Interest	6,300 + 2,025	=	8,325
	Debenture Interest	1,575 + 6,750	=	8,325
11	Cost of Factory Buildings	450,000 + 18,000 + 40,000	=	508,000
12	Cost of Plant and Machinery	260,000 − 22,000	=	238,000
13	Debtors	94,400 − 9,600	=	84,800

Question 1.2

Carey Ltd has an authorised capital of €990,000, divided into 690,000 ordinary shares at €1 each and 300,000 7 per cent preference shares at €1 each. The following trial balance was extracted from its books on 31/12/2009.

	€	€
Land and buildings at cost	780,000	
Accumulated depreciation – land and buildings		39,000
Patents (incorporating 2 months' investment income received)	58,200	
6% investments 1/5/2009	180,000	
Delivery vans at cost	172,000	
Accumulated depreciation – delivery vans		78,000
Stocks 1/1/2009	76,600	
Purchases and sales	620,000	990,000
Directors' fees	80,000	
Salaries and general expenses	176,000	
Debenture interest paid	4,500	
Profit and loss balance 1/1/2009		67,600
Debtors and creditors	73,900	81,000
Provision for bad debts		3,600
Interim dividends for first 6 months	40,000	
9% debentures (including €80,000 9% debentures issued at par on 31/3/2009)		230,000
VAT		16,500
Bank		5,500
Issued capital		
550,000 ordinry shares at €1 each		550,000
200,000 7% preference shares €1 each		200,000
	2,261,200	2,261,200

The following information and instructions are to be taken into account:

1. Stock at 31/12/2009 at cost was €85,000 – this figure includes old stock which cost €8,000 but has a net realisable value of 60 per cent of cost.

2. Patents which incorporated two months' investment income are to be written off over a five-year period commencing in 2009.

3. Provide for depreciation on delivery vans at the annual rate of 20 per cent of cost from the date of purchase to the date of sale.
   NOTE: On 31/9/2009 a delivery van which had cost €60,000 on 1/6/2007 was traded in against a new van which cost €84,000. An allowance of €22,000 was given on the old van. The cheque for the net amount of this transaction was incorrectly treated as a purchase of trading stock. This was the only entry made in the books in respect of this transaction.

4. Buildings are to be depreciated at the rate of 2 per cent of cost per annum (land at cost was €130,000). At the end of 2009 the company revalued the land and buildings at €880,000.

5. The figure for bank in the trial balance has been taken from the firm's bank account. However, a bank statement dated 31/12/2009 has arrived showing a credit balance of

€4,040. A comparison of the bank account and the bank statement has revealed the following discrepancies:

(i) Investment income €2,700 had been paid direct to the firm's bank account.

(ii) A cheque for €780, issued to a supplier, had been entered in the books (cash book and ledger) as €870.

(iii) A credit transfer of €750 had been paid direct to the firm's bank account on behalf of a debtor who has recently been declared bankrupt. This represents a first and final payment of 30c in the €1.

(iv) A cheque for fees €6,000 issued to a director had not yet been presented for payment.

6. The directors recommend that:

(i) The preference dividend due be paid.

(ii) A final dividend on ordinary shares be provided, bringing the total dividend up to 9c per share.

(iii) Provision be made for both investment income and debenture interest due.

(iv) Provision for bad debts be adjusted to 4 per cent of debtors.

You are required to prepare a:

(a) Trading and profit and loss account for the year ended 31/12/2009. **(75)**

(b) Balance sheet as at 31/12/2009. **(45)**

(120 marks)

Solution to Q. 1.2

(a) Trading, Profit and Loss Account for the Year Ended 31/12/2007 **75**

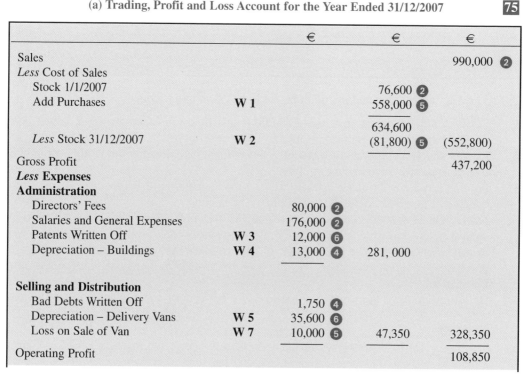

		€	€	€
Sales				990,000 ❷
Less Cost of Sales				
Stock 1/1/2007			76,600 ❷	
Add Purchases	W 1		558,000 ❺	
			634,600	
Less Stock 31/12/2007	W 2		(81,800) ❺	(552,800)
Gross Profit				437,200
Less **Expenses**				
Administration				
Directors' Fees		80,000 ❷		
Salaries and General Expenses		176,000 ❷		
Patents Written Off	W 3	12,000 ❻		
Depreciation – Buildings	W 4	13,000 ❹	281, 000	
Selling and Distribution				
Bad Debts Written Off		1,750 ❹		
Depreciation – Delivery Vans	W 5	35,600 ❻		
Loss on Sale of Van	W 7	10,000 ❺	47,350	328,350
Operating Profit				108,850

Decrease in Provision for Bad Debts	W 6	744 ⑤	
Investment Income	W 8	7,200 ④	7,944
			116,794
Debenture Interest			(18,900) ⑤
Net Profit for Year before Taxation			97,894
Less Appropriation			
Preference Dividend Paid		7,000 ②	
Ordinary Dividend Paid		33,000 ③	
Preference Dividend Proposed		7,000 ②	
Ordinary Dividend Proposed		16,500 ③	(63,500)
Retained Profit			34,394
Profit and Loss Balance 1/1/2007			67,600 ②
Profit and Loss Balance 31/12/2007			101,994 ⑥

(b) Balance Sheet at 31 December 2007   **45**

		Cost €	Accumulated Depreciation €	Net €	Total €
Intangible Fixed Assets					
Patents (60,000 – 12,000)					48,000 ③
Tangible Fixed Assets					
Land and Buildings	W 9	880,000 ①		880,000	
Delivery Vans	W 10	196,000 ②	85,600 ③	110,400	
		1,076,000	85,600	990,400	990,400
Financial Assets					
8% Investments					180,000 ②
					1,218,400
Current Assets					
Stock				81,800 ②	
Investment Income Due				2,700 ③	
Debtors	W 11		71,400 ③		
Less Provision			2,856 ①	68,544	
				153,044	
Creditors: Amounts Falling Due within One Year					
Creditors	W 12		81,090 ③		
Preference Dividend Due			7,000 ②		
Ordinary Dividend Due			16,500 ③		
Debenture Interest Due			14,400 ③		
VAT			16,500 ②		
Bank	W 13		1,960 ⑤	(137,450)	
					15,594
					1,233,994

Financed by

Creditors: Amounts Falling Due after More than One Year

	Authorised	Issued	
8% Debentures			230,000 ❷
Capital and Reserves	Authorised	Issued	
Ordinary Shares at €1 Each	690,000	550,000 ❶	
6% Preference Shares at €1 Each	300,000	200,000 ❶	
	990,000	750,000	
Revaluation Reserve **W 14**		152,000 ❸	
Profit and Loss Balance		101,994	
Shareholders' Funds			1,003,994
Capital Employed			1,233,994

Workings

1. **Purchases**	620,000 – 62,000	= 558,000
2. **Closing Stock**	85,000 – 3,200	= 81,800
3. **Patents Written Off**	(€58,200 + €1,800) × 20%	= 12,000
4. **Depreciation – Buildings**	2% of (780,000 – 130,000)	= 13,000
5. **Depreciation – Delivery Vans**	25,800 + 9,800	= 35,600
	34,400 + 1,200	= 35,600
	22,400 + 9,000 + 4,200	= 35,600
6. **Decrease in Provision for Bad Debts**	3,600 – 2,856	= 744
7. **Loss on Sale of Van**	60,000 – 22,000 – 28,000	= 10,000
8. **Investment Income**	1,800 + 2,700 + 2,700	= 7,200
9. **Land and Buildings at Cost**	780,000 + 100,000	= 880,000
10. **Delivery Vans at Cost**	172,000 + 84,000 – 60,000	= 196,000
Accumulated Depreciation D. Vans	78,000 + 35,600 – 28,000	= 85,600
11. **Debtors**	73,900 – 750 – 1,750	= 71,400
12. **Creditors**	81,000 + 90	= 81,090
13. **Bank Overdraft as per Trial Balance**	5,500	
Less Investment Income	(2,700)	
Less Credit Transfer Received	(750)	
Less Bank under Credited	(90)	= (1,960)
Alternative	(4,040 – 6,000)	= (1,960)
14. **Revaluation Reserve**	100,000 + 39,000 + 13,000	= 152,000

Question 1.3

The following trial balance was extracted from the books of M. O'Brien on 31/12/2006.

	€	€
9% Investments 1/6/2006	200,000	
Buildings (cost €980,000)	933,000	
Delivery Vans (cost €150,000)	80,500	
5% Fixed Mortgage (including increase of €200,000 5% mortgage received on 1/4/2006)		500,000
Patents (incorporating 3 months' investment income)	55,500	
Debtors and Creditors	77,600	86,500
Purchases and Sales	668,000	982,000
Stocks 1/1/2006	67,700	
Commission	24,000	
Provision for Bad Debts		3,800
Salaries and General Expenses	194,100	
Discount (Net)		4,600
Rent		15,000
Mortgage Interest Paid for First 3 Months	4,000	
Insurance (incorporating suspense)	8,700	
VAT		5,500
PRSI		2,300
Bank		70,900
Drawings	37,500	
Capital		680,000
	2,350,600	2,350,600

The following information and instructions are to be taken into account:

1. Stock at 31/12/2006 at cost was €74,500. This figure includes damaged stock which cost €6,600 but which now has a net realisable value of €1,900.
2. Provide for depreciation on vans at the annual rate of 15 per cent of cost from the date of purchae to the date of sale.
   NOTE: On 31/3/2006 a delivery van which had cost €42,000 on 31/5/2003 was traded against a new van which cost €48,000. An allowance of €20,000 was made on the old van. The cheque for the net amount of this transaction was entered in the bank account but was incorrectly treated as a purchase of trading stock. These were the only entries made in the books in respect of this transaction.
3. Patents, which incorporate three months' investment income, are to be written off over a five-year period commencing in 2006.
4. The suspense figure arises as a result of the posting of an inccorrect figure for mortgage interest to the mortgage interest account and discount received €700 entered only in the creditors account. The correct interest was entered in the bank account.
5. Provision to be made for mortgage interest due.
6. A new warehouse was purchased during the year for €240,000 plus VAT of 12.5 per cent. The amount paid to the vendor was entered in the buildings account. No entry was made in the VAT account.
7. Provide for depreciation on buildings at the rate of 2 per cent of cost per annum. It was decided to revalue the buildings at €1,100,000 on 31/12/2006.
8. Provision for bad debts to be adjusted to 4% of debtors.

You are required to prepare a:
(a) Trading and profit and loss account for the year ended 31/12/2006. **(75)**
(b) Balance sheet as at 31/12/2006. **(45)**

(120 marks)

Solution to Q 1.3

(a) Trading, Profit and Loss Account for the Year Ended 31/12/2006

		€	€	€
Sales				982,000 ❷
Less Cost of Sales				
Stock 1/1/2006			67,700 ❷	
Add Purchases	W 1		640,000 ❻	
			707,700	
Less Stock 31/12/2006	W 2		(69,800) ❻	(637,900)
Gross Profit				344,100
Less **Expenses**				
Administration				
Salaries and General Expenses		194,100 ❷		
Patents Written Off	W 3	12,000 ❻		
Insurance	W 4	9,650 ❽		
Depreciation – Buildings	W 5	19,000 ❸	234,750	
Selling and Distribution				
Loss on Sale of Delivery Van	W 7	4,150 ❻		
Commission		24,000 ❷		
Depreciation – Delivery Vans	W 6	23,175 ❺	51,325	(286,075)
				58,025
Add Operating Income				
Reduction in Provision for Bad Debts	W 8			696 ❹
Rent				15,000 ❷
Discount	W 9			5,300 ❺
Operating Profit				79,021
Investment Income				10,500 ❸
				89,521
Mortgage Interest	W 10			(22,500) ❻
Net Profit for Year				**67,021** ❼

(b) Balance Sheet as at 31 December 2006   **45**

		Cost €	Accumulated Depreciation €	Net €	Total €
Intangible Fixed Assets					
Patents (€60,000 – €12,000)					48,400 ❹
Tangible Fixed Assets					
Buildings	W 11	1,100,000 ❷		1,100,000	
Delivery Vans		156,000 ❷	74,825 ❸	81,175	
		1,256,000	74,825	1,181,175	1,181,175
Financial Assets					
Investments					200,000 ❷
					1,429,175
Current Assets					
Stock				69,800 ❷	
VAT	W 12			24,500 ❺	
Investment Income Due				6,000 ❸	
Debtors			77,600 ❷		
Less Provision			3,104 ❶	74,496	
				174,796	
Creditors: Amounts Falling Due within One Year					
Creditors			86,500 ❷		
Mortgage Interest Due			18,750 ❸		
PRSI			2,300 ❷		
Bank			70,900 ❷	(178,450)	(3,654)
					1,425,521
Financed by:					
Creditors: Amounts Falling Due after More than One Year					
9% Fixed Mortgage					500,000 ❷
Capital and Reserves					
Capital 1/1/2006				680,000 ❶	
Add Net Profit				67,021 ❶	
				747,021	
Less Drawings				37,500 ❷	
				709,521	
Revaluation Reserve	W 13			216,000 ❹	925,521
Capital Employed					1,425,521

Question 1.3 – *Workings*

1. **Purchases** — 668,000
   Less Payment for Van — (28,000) — 640,000

2. **Closing Stock** — 74,500
   Less Valueless Stock — (4,700) — 69,800

3. **Patents**
   (€55,500 + €4,500) ÷ 5 — 12,000

4. **Insurance** — 8,700
   Add Mortgage Interest — 250
   Add Discount Received — 700 — 9,650

5. **Depreciation – Buildings**
   2% of €950,000 — 19,000

6. **Depreciation – Delivery Vans**
   (€22,500 + €675) or (€5,625 + €17,550) or (€16,200 + €1,575 + €5,400) — 23,175

7. **Loss on Sale of Van**
   (€42,000 – €17,850 – €20,000) — 4,150 loss

   Provision for Depreciaton – Vans
   (€69,500 – €17,850 + €23,175) — 74,825

8. **Provision for Bad Debts**
   (€3,800 – €3,104) — 696 CR

9. **Discount** — 4,600
   Add Unrecorded Discount — 700 — 5,300

10. **Mortgage Interest** — 4,000
    Less Suspense — (250)
    Add Interest Due — 18,750 — 22,500

11. **Buildings** — 98,000
    Less VAT — (30,000)
    Add Revaluation — 150,000 — 1,100,000

12. **Vat Account** — 5,500
    Less VAT on Buildings — (30,000) — 24,500

13. **Revaluation Reserve**
    Land and Buildings — 150,000
    Provision for Depreciation (47,000 + 19,000) — 66,000 — 216,000

Chapter **2**
Ratios and Analysis

Ratios

It is essential that all the ratios are known. Even more important is the ability to comment on the significance of the ratios.

1. Gross Profit Percentage/Margin
2. Mark-Up Percentage
3. Rate of Stock Turnover
4. Net Profit Percentage/Margin
5. Length of Credit Given to Debtors
6. Length of Credit Received from Creditors
7. Interest Cover
8. Working Capital Ratio
9. Liquid Asset Ratio
10. Capital Gearing Ratio
11. Return on Capital Employed
12. Return to Equity Shareholders
13. Earnings per Share
14. Price Earnings Ratio
15. Dividend per Share
16. Dividend Cover
17. Dividend Yield

Practise writing out the ratios until you are absolutely sure that you know them all.

Indicators of Bankruptcy

The indicators of bankruptcy have been developed in the US and are called 'Z scores'. The higher the score, the less likelihood of insolvency. The results show that almost every company that failed in a particular year showed warning signs in the previous year's results.

Five ratios are used:

1. $\dfrac{\text{Working Capital}}{\text{Total Assets}}$

2. $\dfrac{\text{Retained Earnings}}{\text{Total Assets}}$

3. $\dfrac{\text{Profit before Interest and Tax}}{\text{Total Assets}}$

4. $\dfrac{\text{Market Value}}{\text{Total Debt}}$

5. $\dfrac{\text{Sales}}{\text{Total Assets}}$

When you are asked for a particular ratio, do not just write down the answer. Write down the formula in words. Then write down the first line of the formula in figures. Finally, show all your calculations to the last line. For example,

Issued Ordinary Share @ €1 €500,000

10% Preference Shares @ €1 €300,000

Net Profit €150,000

(ignore tax)

You are asked for the earnings per share.

$$\text{Earnings per share} = \frac{\text{Net Profit} - \text{Preference Dividend} - \text{Tax}}{\text{Number of Ordinary Shares}}$$

$$= \frac{150,000 - 30,000}{500,000}$$

$$= \frac{120,000}{500,000} = 24 \text{ cent}$$

(Note: The cent designation is essential.)

When asked to comment on the performance of the company, i.e. whether the company is a good investment either on the part of a prospective shareholder or a lending institution, it is vital that you are able to comment properly and make proper comparisons.

The following are the key areas.

1 Profitability

Profitability – return on capital employed and return to equity shareholder and compare to present return on risk-free investment. Compare with previous year if possible.

2 Liquidity

Current ratio 1.5 to 2 : 1.
Quick ratio 1 : 1.

3 Gearing

A lowly geared company cannot get into financial difficulty. High gearing **may** be acceptable if the company is highly profitable.

4 Trends

If you are given figures for only one year, it is very difficult to do anything other than look at the reserve figures. If you are given results for more than one year, there are a lot of comparisons that can be made, and it is a matter of emphasising the most important.

5 Company Sector

Comment and compare to industry norm if given.

6 Company Name

Look at company title to see if it is a plc or a private company.

7 Fixed Assets

Look for full breakdown, giving composition and depreciation policy.

8 Debentures

Rate of interest and amount of interest and interest cover. Refer back to gearing, look at redemption date and effect on future liquidity.

9 Dividends

Dividend cover and yield are important to ensure that dividends are not paid out of reserves. Look at the market price of the shares. If the company is not a plc, note that there is not a ready market for the shares.

10 Purchase of Shares

If being asked to buy shares in the company, see if the number of shares being bought would give control of the company. Look at the cost of borrowing and the present dividend policy.

11 Loan

If being asked to lend to the company, state that you must know for what purpose the finance is required and how the future interest cover, capital gearing ratio and liquid asset ratio will be affected.

12 Investments

If the company has investments, compare cost and market value to see if selling these might help alleviate any liquidity problem the company might have.

13 Earnings

Look at earnings per share and price earnings ratio, and consider the industry norm if one is given.

14 Audit

State that in order to comment fully on a particular company, you would require a full set of unqualified audited accounts for a number of years.

If the company has liquidity/profitability and you are asked to suggest some type of corrective action, you might suggest some of the following: sale and leaseback, factoring of debtors, sale of investment, issue of shares (if possible), capital reduction scheme or even closedown.

Question 2.1

The following figures have been taken from the final account of Down 'n' Out Ltd at 31 December 2007. This is a business involved in the manufacture of furniture. The authorised share capital is €960,000 made up of 500,000 €1 ordinary shares and 230,000 €2, 9 per cent preference shares.

	€
Sales	780,000
Cost of Sales	600,000
Total Expenses	150,000
Profit and Loss (1/1/2007)	90,000
Profit and Loss (31/12/2007)	30,000
Proposed Dividends	48,000
Fixed Assets	700,000
Current Assets (including stock €90,000)	140,000
Trade Creditors	60,000
General Reserve (1/1/2007)	40,000
10% Debentures 2008 Secured	120,000
Issued Ordinary Shares 300,000 @ €1 each	
Issued Preference Shares 100,000 @ €2 each	

(a) Calculate the following:
  (1) Opening stock if the rate of stock turnover is ten times.
  (2) Price earnings ratio if the market price of one ordinary share is 80 cent.
  (3) Interest cover.
  (4) Dividend yield on one ordinary share.
  (5) Gearing ratio and its effect on the distribution of profits.
(b) Down 'n' Out Ltd has applied to your bank for a loan of €180,000. You are the assistant lending officer. Write a report to your manager outlining your reasons for giving/not giving the loan.

Solution to Q 2.1(a)

Down 'n' Out Ltd		**Balance Sheet at 31 December 2007**
Trading and Profit and Loss Accounts		

Trading and Profit and Loss Accounts

	(€'000)	(€'000)
Sales		780
Less Cost		600
Gross Profit		180
Less Expenses		150
Net Profit		30
+ Balance		90
		120
– Proposed Dividends		
Preference	18	
Ordinary	30	48
		72
Balance (31/2/2007)		30
To General Reserves		42
General Reserve (1/1/2007)		40
General (31/12/2007)		82

Balance Sheet at 31 December 2007

	(€'000)	(€'000)	(€'000)
Fixed Assets			700
Current Assets			
Stock	90		
Drs, etc.	50	140	
Current Liabilities			
Creditors	60		
Dividends	48	108	
NCA			32
			732
Financed by			
Ordinary Shares		300	
9% Preference		200	
		500	
Reserves			
General Reserve	82		
Profit and Loss	30	112	
10% Debentures		120	
			732

(1)   Rate of Stock Turnover $= \dfrac{\text{Cost of Sales}}{\text{Average Stock}} = 10$

$$= \frac{600}{x} = 10$$

Therefore

$$x = 60$$

and if

$$\text{closing stock} = 90$$

then

$$\text{opening stock} = 30$$

(note a 300 per cent increase)

(2)   Price Earnings Ratio $= \dfrac{\text{Market Price}}{\text{Earnings per Share}}$

Earnings per Share $= \dfrac{\text{Net Profit} - \text{Preference Dividend}}{\text{Number of Ordinary Shares}}$

$$= \frac{30 - 18}{300} = 4 \text{ cent}$$

Price Earnings Ratio $= \dfrac{80}{4} = 20$ times

(3)   Interest Cover $= \dfrac{\text{Net Profit + Interest}}{\text{Interest}}$

$$= \frac{30 + 12}{12} = 3.5 \text{ times}$$

(4)   Dividend Yield $= \dfrac{\text{Dividend per Share}}{\text{Market Price}} \times \dfrac{100}{1}$

Dividend per Share $= \dfrac{\text{Ordinary Dividends}}{\text{Number of Ordinary Shares}} = \dfrac{30}{300} = 10 \text{ cent}$

Dividend Yield $= \dfrac{10}{80} \times \dfrac{100}{1} = 12.5\%$

(5)   Gearing Ratio and Debt/Equity Ratio

Preferences Shares + Debentures : Ordinary Shares
200 + 120 : 300
320 : 300
1.07 : 1

The company is highly geared, and this burden must be met before there is anything available for the equity holders.

Solution to Q 2.1(b)
To:
From:
Date:
Re: Loan to Down 'n' Out of €180,000
Down 'n' Out are well named, and I would not advance the loan for the following reasons.

(i)   The return on capital employed is only 5.74 per cent. Even in times of low interest rates, this is not acceptable and is less than the return achievable on risk-free investments.
(ii)   The company has a liquidity problem. The current ratio is 1.3 : 1, which is well below the norm of 2 : 1. The liquid asset ratio is only 0.46 : 1, which is well below the desired figure of 1 : 1.
(iii) The company is in the furniture-manufacturing business, which is extremely competitive and cyclical. The stock during the year has increased by 300 per cent, indicating a high build-up of slow-moving stock.
(iv)   Dividends are being maintained but are being paid out of reserves, while the company is trying to borrow money to solve its liquidity problems.
(v)   The debentures are due for repayment within the next twelve months and there are no liquid assets for this purpose; this is probably, in part, why the loan is being requested.
(vi)   The interest cover at present is only 3.5 times. Further borrowing will only reduce this at least in the short term.
(vii) The actual value of any fixed assets offered as security must be doubtful, and the debenture holders at present have a prior security.
(viii) The firm's Z scores (predictors of bankruptcy) are generally poor.

$$\frac{\text{Working Capital}}{\text{Total Assets}} = \frac{32}{840}$$

$$\frac{\text{Retained Earnings}}{\text{Total Assets}} = \frac{112}{840}$$

$$\frac{\text{Operating Profit}}{\text{Total Assets}} = \frac{42}{840}$$

$$\frac{\text{Market Value}}{\text{Total Debt}} = \frac{240}{320}$$

$$\frac{\text{Sales}}{\text{Total Assets}} = \frac{780}{840}$$

Note: The actual value of the fixed assets and the stock must be questioned.

(ix)   The company is not a plc, and this makes it less attractive as a lending proposition.

(x)   The company is already highly geared, and further borrowing will, in the short term at least, only increase this high gearing and place an even bigger burden on the firm.

(xi)   To even consider lending to this company in future, a clear explanation of why the finance is required would have to be given, together with three to five years of unqualified audited accounts. Even then, it is doubtful if this company would be a good lending proposition.

Question 2.2

The following are the summarised final accounts of two manufacturing companies, Soda Ltd and Tonic Ltd, for the year ended 31 December 2007.

Summarised Profit and Loss Accounts for the Year Ended
31 December 2007

	Soda Ltd		Tonic Ltd	
	(€)	(€)	(€)	(€)
Sales		700		540
Cost of Goods Sold		310		230
Gross Profit		390		310
Debenture Interest	40		20	
Other Expenses	190	230	140	160
Net Profit		160		150

23

Balance Sheet at 31 December 2007

	(€)	(€)	(€)	(€)
Fixed Assets at Cost		820		370
Accumulated Depreciation		360		80
		460		290
Current Assets				
Trade Debtors	115		60	
Stocks	80		40	
Bank	10			
	205		100	
Current Liabilities				
Trade Creditors	80		55	
Net Current Assets		125		45
		585		335
Financed by				
Shareholders' Funds		345		220
Debentures		240		115
		585		335

The following information is also available:

1. Approximately 90 per cent of each company's sales are made on credit.
2. Each company's stock level remains approximately constant throughout the year.

Requirement: Write a report to the managing director of Soda Ltd comparing the performance of her company with that of Tonic Ltd. Your report should include reference to appropriate ratios and any other information that you consider relevant.

Solution to Q 2.2
Your answer should be put into report format with comments on the following.

	Soda Ltd	Tonic Ltd
Gross Profit (%)	55.71	57.41
Net Profit (%)	22.86	27.78
Return on Capital Employed	34.19	50.75
Expenses/Sales (%)	32.86	29.63
Interest Cover	5	8.5
Working Capital Ratio	2.56 : 1	1.82 : 1
Liquid Asset Ratio	1.56 : 1	1.09 : 1
Credit to Debtors (days)	66	45
Credit from Creditors (days)	94	87
Stock Turnover	3.88	5.75
Working Capital/Total Assets	0.19	0.12
Debt/Equity	0.7 : 1	0.52 : 1

Question 2.3

The following figures have been taken from the final accounts of Gill plc, a wholesaler in home computers and games software, whose authorised capital is €1,000,000, made up of 800,000 ordinary shares at €1 each and 100,000 8 per cent preference shares at €2 each. The firm has already issued 500,000 ordinary shares and 50,000 preference shares.

	(€)
Fixed Assets (cost €500,000)	490,000
Investments (market value €80,000)	160,000
Current Assets (stock €200,000, debtors €69,000)	269,000
Current Liabilities (bank €2,000, trade creditors €90,000)	92,000
General Reserve (1/1/2008)	25,000
9% Debentures 2010 secured	90,000
Sales	920,000
Opening Stock	58,000
Cost of Sales	730,000
Total Expenses for the Year	96,000
Profit and Loss Balance (1/1/2008)	18,000 CR
Profit and Loss Balance (31/12/2008)	12,000 CR
Proposed Dividends	32,000

(a) Calculate the following:
  (i) Dividend per ordinary share.
  (ii) Interest cover.
  (iii) Market value of one ordinary share whose dividend yield is 5 per cent.
  (iv) Cash sales if the average period of credit is 1.2 months.
  (v) Price earnings ratio.
(b) Would the shareholders be satisfied with the policies, performance and state of affairs of the above company? Use relevant ratios and information to support your answer.
(c) Comment on the liquidity of Gill plc and suggest appropriate action.

Solution to Q 2.3(a)

(i) Dividend per ordinary share

$$\frac{\text{Ordinary Dividend}}{\text{Number of Ordinary Shares}} = \frac{24,000}{500,000} = 4.8 \text{ cent}$$

(ii) Interest cover

$$\frac{\text{Net Profit + Interest}}{\text{Interest}} = \frac{94,000 + 8,100}{8,100} = 12.6 \text{ times}$$

(iii) Market value of one ordinary share

$$\frac{\text{Dividend per Share} \times 100}{\text{Market Price}} = \frac{4.8 \times 100}{5 \times \text{Market Price}} = 96 \text{ cent}$$

(iv) Cash sales

$$\frac{69,000 \times 12}{\text{Credit Sales}} = 1.2$$

Credit Sales = 690,000
Total Sales = 920,000
Cash Sales = 920,000 – 690,000 = €230,000

(v)   Price earnings ratio

$$\frac{\text{Market Price}}{\text{Earnings per Share}} = \frac{96}{18.8} = 5.1 : 1$$

Solution to Q 2.3(b)

Trends: Gill plc has increased its reserves from €43,000 at the beginning of the year to €105,000 at the end of the year. This has more than doubled its reserves even after providing for dividends amounting to €32,000. This would seem to suggest an improved performance over recent years.

Profitability: The firm's profitability is satisfactory. The return on capital employed and the return to equity shareholders of 12.8 and 15.9 per cent, respectively, are better than the return available at present from risk-free investments. The earnings per share is 18.8 cent, and it would take 5.6 years for a share to recoup its market price.

Dividend policies: The dividends are covered 2.9 times. Therefore the shareholders are receiving 34 per cent of available profits. The policy of paying out dividends is creating cash flow problems for the company. The dividend per share is 4.8 cent and the dividend yield is 5 per cent, whereas the preference shareholders receive 8 per cent.

Investment policy: The investments have dropped 50 per cent in value, from €160,000 to €80,000. This places a question mark over its investment policy.

Debentures: The debentures are due for repayment in 2009. This will put a great strain on the firm's liquidity. As the debentures are secured on the fixed assets, the repayments could place the future of Gill plc in jeopardy, as the 2 per cent depreciation indicates that these assets are buildings or they are totally under-depreciated, and therefore the depreciation policy must be questioned.

Sector: Gill plc is involved in the home computer and games software business. This is a very competitive sector.

Closing stock: The shareholders would be very concerned that the firm's huge closing stock is more than four times its opening stock.

Interest cover: The interest cover is 12.6 times. This is a very favourable situation and indicates that borrowings are being put to good use.

Gearing: The firm is low geared as the fixed interest capital is 24 per cent of total capital employed.

   The shareholders would not be satisfied with the policies and state of affairs but would be satisfied with the performance of Gill plc.

Solution to Q 2.3(c)

The working capital ratio and acid test ratio are 2.2 to 1 and 0.6 to 1, respectively. The working capital ratio is above the accepted norm of 2 : 1. This shows that working capital is sufficient to meet the day-to-day costs of running the firm. The firm should not let this go too high above 2 : 1, as this would indicate a build-up of stock or a poor use of resources.

The acid test ratio is below the accepted norm of 1 : 1. This shows more accurately the ability of the firm to pay its short-term debts. Gill plc would have difficulty paying its immediate debts:

1. Sell investments. Any surplus cash not required for working capital should be reinvested more profitably. Income from this would improve profitability.
2. Sell stock at an auction and raise at least €55,000.
3. Make a right issue of about 60,000 shares.
4. Sell some of the fixed assets and lease back.
5. Delay the payments of dividends.

Question 2.4
The balance sheets of J. Giles are as follows.

	31 March 2007		31 March 2008	
	(€)	(€)	(€)	(€)
Fixed Assets		260,000		205,000
Current Assets				
Stocks	86,000		84,000	
Debtors	94,000		58,000	
	180,000		142,000	
Current Liabilities	(174,000)	6,000	(59,000)	83,000
		266,000		288,000
Capital				
Opening Balance	262,900			266,000
Add Net Profit	15,600			36,000
Less Drawings	(12,500)			(14,000)
Closing Balance	266,000			288,000

The following information was extracted from the trading accounts for the years ended 31 March 2007 and 2008, respectively.

	2007 (€)	2008 (€)
Sales	505,000	385,000
Gross Profit	152,900	172,750
Opening Stock	82,000	86,000

Required: Calculate the following ratios for each year and comment on the position shown for the second year as compared with the first.

1. Gross profit ratio.
2. Stock turnover.
3. Working capital ratio.
4. Acid test ratio.
5. Period of credit given.

Solution to Q 2.4

1. Gross Profit Ratio

= (Gross Profit × 100)/Sales
Year Ended 31 March 2007: €152,900 × 100/€505,000 = 30.3%
Year Ended 31 March 2008: €172,750 × 100/€385,000 = 44.9%

The ratios have increased from 30.3 to 44.9 per cent. Possible explanations are:

(i)   Changes in the types of goods sold, where some lines carry different rates of gross profit than others.
(ii)   Increase in the selling price of goods without a proportionate increase in the cost price.
(iii) Elimination of inefficiencies and factors such as theft which would reduce the profit margin.

2. Stock Turnover

= Cost of Sales/Average Stock
where Cost of Sales = Sales Gross Profit.
Year Ended 31 March 2007: €352,100/€84,000 = 4.2 times
Year Ended 31 March 2008: €212,250/€85,000 = 2.5 times

In the first year the average stock was turned over 4.2 times. This has deteriorated to 2.5 times in the second year. This has happened because although sales and purchases have fallen considerably, stock levels have remained relatively constant. It may well be possible to reduce stock levels if this reduction is likely to be permanent.

3. Working Capital Ratio

= Current Assets : Current Liabilities
As at 31 March 2007: €180,000 : €174,000 = 1.04 : 1
As at 31 March 2008: €142,000 : €59,000 = 2.41 : 1

Current assets were roughly equal to current liabilities at 31 March 2007. However, Mr Giles might have difficulty paying his liabilities on time, depending on how quickly his current assets could be turned into cash. His position at 31 March 2008 appears comfortable, with current assets equal to 2.41 times current liabilities.

4. Acid Test Ratio

= Current Assets – Stock : Current Liabilities
As at 31 March 2007: €94,000 : €174,000 = 0.54 : 1
As at 31 March 2008: €58,000 : €59,000 = 0.98 : 1

At 31 March 2007, quick assets (those readily convertible into cash) amounted to only 54 per cent of current liabilities. If the current liabilities are required to be paid promptly, Mr Giles would not be able to meet these in full. At 31 March 2008, quick assets approximately equalled current liabilities, and he should then have been in a position to meet the total liabilities.

5. Period of Credit Given

= (Debtors × 365)/Sales
Year Ended 31 March 2007: (€94,000 × 365)/€505,000 = 68 days
Year Ended 31 March 2008: (€58,000 × 365)/€385,000 = 55 days